Relationship Marketing in Sports

Relationship Marketing in Sports

André Bühler & Gerd Nufer

ELSEVIER

AMSTERDAM • BOSTON • HEIDELBERG • LONDON • NEW YORK • OXFORD
PARIS • SAN DIEGO • SAN FRANCISCO • SINGAPORE • SYDNEY • TOKYO
Butterworth-Heinemann is an imprint of Elsevier

Butterworth-Heinemann is an imprint of Elsevier
Linacre House, Jordan Hill, Oxford OX2 8DP, UK
30 Corporate Drive, Suite 400, Burlington, MA 01803, USA

First edition 2010

British Library Cataloguing in Publication Data
A catalogue record for this book is available from the British Library

Library of Congress Cataloging-in-Publication Data
A catalog record for this book is available from the Library of Congress

ISBN: 978-0-7506-8495-8

For information on all Butterworth-Heinemann publications
visit our website at elsevierdirect.com

Printed and bound in Great Britain

09 10 11 12   10 9 8 7 6 5 4 3 2 1

Working together to grow
libraries in developing countries

www.elsevier.com | www.bookaid.org | www.sabre.org

ELSEVIER   BOOK AID   Sabre Foundation
             International

Contents

Preface

For more than ten years we have been engaged in the business of sports as academics and practitioners. We feel indeed privileged that our passion also became our profession. We have followed the development of sports marketing from an almost exclusive field of interest to a serious and independent form of marketing which nowadays fascinates a growing number of people from all over the world. In view of our experience we felt a strong need to write and publish a book on Relationship Marketing in Sports in order to contribute a new aspect to the field of sports marketing.

Writing this book was both hard work and fun. Similar to any relationship we had good times and tough times. But we always respected, trusted and appreciated each other – and that's what makes the difference between healthy relationships and unhealthy ones (as you will see in the course of this book). At the end of nearly two years of researching and writing we are confident to present a book which significantly contributes to the field of sports marketing. As a matter of fact, this book is the first one which solely and explicitly focuses on the relationship between professional sporting organisations and their various stakeholders. We hope that our book meets your – the reader's – expectations. And we hope that many fellow academics will use our publication as a base or inspiration for their future work about the relational aspects of sports marketing.

We would like to thank many people who proved to be important and valuable in the process of writing this book.

First, we want to thank all those who contributed a number of interesting case studies, namely Alexander Amiri, Alexander Berlin, Frank Daumann, Martin Lochmüller, Julia Lohrer, Linda Lupinacci, Marritt Posten, Anne Schall, Constantino Stavros and Hartmut Voss.

Secondly, we want to thank all those sporting organisations who were willing to provide us with data and information about their daily management of various relationships. Besides, thanks goes to all those authors and publishers who granted us permission to use their work and allowed us to incorporate their thoughts and artwork in this book.

Thirdly, we would like to thank some fellow academics who have inspired and encouraged us in writing this book, especially Simon Chadwick and Matthew D. Shank.

Finally, we want to thank you – the reader! You have taken the trouble to get hold of this book and to read it. Therefore, you have showed interest in a topic which definitely deserves closer attention. We hope that this book contributes to your knowledge and that it provides you with many new ideas.

In the true sense of relationship marketing we would like to engage in a mutually beneficial relationship with our readers. So if you want to tell us something about relationship marketing in sports or if you have a question or comment, please feel free to contact us any time. We are sincerely looking forward to your questions, feedback as well as criticism. You can reach us at andre.buehler@gmx.net or gerd.nufer@reutlingen-university.de.

Now we wish you a pleasant and interesting journey through this book.

With all best wishes,
André Bühler & Gerd Nufer

Last – but definitely not least:

André Bühler: I want to express my gratitude to the two most valuable relationships of my life. I therefore dedicate this book to my wife Nadja and my daughter Leonie.

Gerd Nufer: I want to thank my wife Karin and my daughter Gabriela for their support and consideration. I like to dedicate this book to my one-year-old daughter Isabel who – just as Leonie Bühler – was born at the time we were working on this book project.

CHAPTER 1

Introduction

Nowhere FC – The "real" Problems of a Fictional Club

Nowhere FC is a professional football club somewhere in Europe. It has a long tradition, a considerable and very loyal fan base, some longstanding sponsors and a team which regularly finishes mid-table. The club is run by a dedicated Board of Directors and the business is conducted by professional members of staff. However, the club finds it increasingly difficult to keep up with the advancing commercialisation of the game. Having been a pure football club over all these years, Nowhere FC now is a medium-sized company in terms of annual turnover and members of staff. That, in turn, brings about new tasks and challenges. Some sponsors, for example, have already claimed more value for their money, the local authorities are not willing to support the club anymore, the regional media are giving the club a hard time by being overcritical and if this wasn't enough the club has to deal with a significant number of trouble-makers from their own fan base. The reputation of Nowhere FC is on the line and the Board of Directors is under enormous pressure. They decided that something has to be done and that the club needs a coherent strategy in order to deal with all these problems. Gary Smith, the newly appointed Marketing Director of Nowhere FC, is in charge of designing such a strategy. Gary soon realised that most problems are caused by the club's inability to establish and maintain healthy relationships with its various stakeholders. As a consequence, Gary has decided to design and implement a sophisticated relationship marketing strategy. A full week of research revealed a number of books on relationship marketing as well as some good articles in magazines and papers in academic journals. However, Gary found out that most of them relate to ordinary businesses and cover the typical supplier – customer relationship. Books on sports marketing, on the other hand, dealt occasionally with relationship marketing in single chapters thereby focusing mainly on royalty schemes rather than strategies. Gary nearly accepted that he had to do the basic thinking himself. But suddenly a door opened where there was no door, when the local bookshop announced the publication of a book called *Relationship Marketing in Sports...*

Learning Outcomes

On completion of this chapter the reader should be able to:

- understand our motivation for publishing a book on *Relationship Marketing in Sports*
- differentiate between the potential readers of the book
- describe the main challenges which sporting organisations have to face today
- explain why relationship marketing seems to be so important for professional sporting organisations
- identify the main contents of this book

OVERVIEW OF CHAPTER

In order to take the reader on the journey this first chapter kicks off with a fictional story about a professional football club and its emerging need for a coherent relationship marketing strategy. On the following pages we will explain the reasons for writing this book, using empirical data from a current study to support our point of view. We will then introduce the main focus of the book and our general attitude towards relationship marketing in sports. We will also address the problem of the different target groups this book aims at and how we tried to meet the expectations of all readers. The next section then deals with the challenges and tasks professional sporting organisations face nowadays. As to that, the Qatar Stars League serves as a real-life example by providing insights from a modern and professional sports body. In this context, we once more emphasise the importance of relationship marketing in professional sports. Before providing some conclusions on Chapter 1, we explain the content of the book on a chapter-by-chapter basis and describe the overall structure of the book.

INTRODUCTION

Relationship marketing is nothing new in the context of sports. As long as there have been professional sports, there have been deep relationships on different levels. For example, sponsorship (or patronage as it was called in the early days) was mostly based on personal relations between the local bene-factors and their favourite sports club. Regarding media, clubs always maintained special relationships with selected journalists. Furthermore, the bond between fans and their clubs was always a close and mutually beneficial one. All these relationships existed from the start of the sports business. Many sporting organisations always knew the value of a deep and good relationship with their stakeholders and practised relationship marketing without being aware of it. Successful sports managers, however, take the old wisdom and turn it into a modern relationship marketing approach by structuring the different relationships in order to make them more effective and profitable for the own sporting organisation and the various stakeholders. This book shall therefore illustrate the many different facets of relationship marketing and the possibilities it offers in the context of (professional) sports.

RATIONALE FOR WRITING THIS BOOK

We have written this book for many different reasons. After an extensive literature review we came to the conclusion that research on relationship marketing in sports is limited. Only few studies have examined the relational aspects within the sports business so far (e.g. Chadwick, 2002; Farrelly and Quester, 2003; Bühler, Heffernan and Hewson, 2007). The topic is ignored in most books on sports marketing or touched superficially by few others. It is remarkable that until 2009 no book exclusively focused on relationship marketing in sports given the status relationship marketing enjoys in marketing literature on the one hand and the ever-growing commercialisation of sports on the other hand. We believe that relationship marketing still is a widely ignored concept in the world of professional sports and that only a few clubs and associations have implemented a coherent 'Customer

EMPIRICAL DATA 1.1. An Empirical Study on the Status Quo of Relationship Marketing in Professional Sports

Alexander Berlin and Frank Daumann

In times of highly competitive markets, professional sport clubs have to put their focus on the diverse needs of their customers. Customer orientation is a key to retain sport consumers (i.e. fans/spectators) in order to prevent defection, reduce dependence of financial success on performance on the pitch, and in consequence to maintain or improve a competitive position. The implementation of customer retention instruments being just one element of strategic customer relationship management is an important requirement for successfully handling customer relationships. In many industries the most common instruments including bonus programs, newsletter, customer clubs, and complaint management are by now an inherent part of the companies' business. But what role do these instruments play in the business of sports?

Continued

In order to answer this question, a quantitative survey was conducted in February 2008. The German Bundesliga served as the context of research in view of the fact that Germany's top football clubs are considered to be effectively driven businesses. A questionnaire was developed which allowed an assessment of the status quo of Customer Relationship Management (CRM) in German professional soccer and an evaluation of the prevalence of customer retention instruments. The questionnaire was sent by e-mail to 65 marketing managers of clubs being part of one of the first three divisions of German football. The number of usable questionnaires returned was 35 – this equates to a highly satisfying response rate of 54%. The following figure shows the mostly used customer retention instruments:

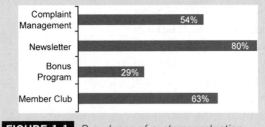

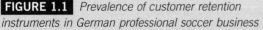

FIGURE 1.1   *Prevalence of customer retention instruments in German professional soccer business*

The findings make clear that *newsletters* are by far the most frequently used instrument of German professional soccer clubs. This is not a big surprise because the vast majority of the clubs (75%) have already implemented customer databases which are a crucial requirement for systematic mailings. Nevertheless, it seems to be arguable if, due to the small number of clubs recognizing the heterogeneity of their customers and segmenting them into discrete groups, the use of newsletter is effective at all.

Another instrument that is widely used and highly accepted by fans is the *member club* – a special form of customer club in the sport sector. More than 60% of German professional soccer clubs have already installed a member club to build up customer relations. Yet, the content and the organizational implementation vary between clubs. While some clubs still use member clubs in terms of

membership cooperation others have implemented some kind of membership which is similar to the way of British soccer clubs: Exclusive information, special services, and financial benefits thereby are supposed to retain not only (hardcore) fans but also ordinary spectators. In this context however, clubs have to consider the results of many empirical studies which revealed a higher adequacy of member clubs for already retained customers.

Real effects of retention could better be reached by bonus programs and complaint management. But these two are the least popular instruments in German professional soccer. In particular *bonus programs*, which directly influence repurchase decisions and commitment, are used by only 29% of the clubs. A reasonable argument for this constellation can be found in the evaluation of fans' acceptance of this instrument. Some marketing managers expected the bonus program to be the worst accepted instrument in relation to others.

Complaint management is another instrument that embodies an organizations' degree of customer orientation. But only slightly more than half of the clubs handle customer complaints systematically. This implicates that many clubs forgo the opportunity to increase customers' retention by increasing complaint satisfaction.

The findings point out that some instruments of customer retention do play a role in the marketing of soccer clubs, albeit not comprehensive. Nevertheless, most of the clubs are still far away from an integrated CRM approach. They rather waste potentials of CRM by not fully using the opportunities of a systematic proceeding. Only 14% have already implemented a state-of-the-art process by building a unique customer database, surveying customer and analyzing customer data regularly, defining customer segments, creating specific marketing-mix strategies, and controlling segment strategies systematically. Supplemented by structural deficiencies and a lack of CRM-competencies, the German professional soccer business lags behind other industries. However, there is no doubt about the necessity of CRM in this sector. In order to reduce the dependency of financial success from on-pitch performance professional sporting organisations should know their customers and must establish, maintain, and enhance long-term customer relationships. This enables stable income streams, contributes to business success, and helps to defend or improve the competitive position in the leisure market. The majority of marketing managers already recognize these potentials. Yet, only if they also recognize the need for an integrated CRM approach and therefore set up basic conditions they will profit from it.

Alexander Berlin is currently doing a PhD at the University of Jena. His supervisor, Dr. Frank Daumann, is Professor for sports economy at the University of Jena.

Relationship Management' (CRM) strategy so far. Our hypothesis is supported by some empirical data as the example of a study on the prevalence of customer retention instruments in German professional football shows.

Based on the above study and our experience as sports marketing academics we feel that a new paradigm is needed in sports marketing, to take relationships within sports to a new level which, in turn, leads to a better structured and more professional marketing approach at sports organisations. This book closes the existing gap and offers a detailed view on the matter and incorporates many aspects which have not been dealt with in previous publications. Therefore, the main reason to write this book was the strong belief that there is a need for such a book both in academia and in the business of sports.

THE MAIN FOCUS OF THIS BOOK

Building and maintaining healthy relationships with customers and stakeholders is a crucial success factor in today's sports business. Relationships, however, are nothing new to us. Everyone of us has different roles and therefore different relationships. For example, we relate to each other as sons or daughters, fathers or mothers, partners, colleagues, citizens or friends. And we didn't have to read a book in order to understand that good and positive relationships are based on very few basic principles. For instance, we need to trust each other, we need to communicate with each other and we need to value the relationship itself. All these principles can be applied to commercial relationships as well because interpersonal relations are at the heart of every business-to-business relationship. It is not the companies who work with each other, it is the people in the companies. That's why we argue throughout this book that trust, communication and commitment refer to relationships within the business of sports as well.

In the course of this book we will describe the basics of relationship marketing with regard to sports and we will present some relationship marketing techniques. *Relationship Marketing in Sports*, however, is more than just introducing general points-based loyalty programmes as considered by some marketers and sports managers. We will show that a **strategic relationship marketing approach** should truly focus on the relationship between sporting organisations and their various stakeholders. Our book therefore includes many different concepts and incorporates a number of different perspectives. We think that it is essential to understand the relationship between organisations and their customers as well as stakeholders before designing relationship marketing programmes. Thus we will describe in detail the various stakeholders of sporting organisations and the resulting relationships before dealing with the respective marketing aspects in detail.

POTENTIAL READERS OF THIS BOOK

This book is primarily aimed at readers who have a strong interest in sports, in marketing and the combination of both. To be more precise, we aim this book at:

- sports marketing students (undergraduate and postgraduate)
- sports marketing academics
- practitioners at professional, semi-professional and non-professional sporting organisations
- students of lower level sports, leisure and tourism qualifications
- students and academics of generic marketing with an interest in sports
- practitioners operating in the business of sports

Bearing in mind the different target groups and their individual interests, we did our best to provide a comprehensive book which fulfils the expectations of all readers. We therefore made sure that this book meets the requirements from an academic as well as a practical point of view, by providing the necessary references and offering new empirical data on the one hand and providing a lot of real life examples on the other hand in order to show how relationship marketing works in practice.

RELATIONSHIP MARKETING AS A NEW CHALLENGE FOR PROFESSIONAL SPORTING ORGANISATIONS

We already emphasised that relationships are at the core of any business. But what has that to do with sports? The answer is a simple one: professional sports has become a multi-billion business with many different stakeholders involved. Chapter 3 describes the commercialisation of sports and the nature of the sports business in more detail. For a start, we would like to bear in mind that a lot of sporting organisations (such as clubs or associations) have turned themselves into medium-sized companies over the last decades. The **commercialisation** of sports and the **professionalisation** of sporting organisations bear some interesting challenges. Because sports is nowadays characterised by a high degree of commercialisation, new trends are constantly emerging in the sports business. In order to stay competitive sports clubs have to explore new markets, take advantage of new media and technology developments, change their ownership structures, transform their arena into state of the art sports-leisure multiplex architecture and create value-added products and services for their fans. All these challenges will be described in the following.

Exploring new markets

More and more sporting organisations have to deal with saturated home markets or the inability to increase turnover in their national market. Therefore, they have to explore new markets in order to keep growing. Football clubs such as Manchester United, Real Madrid or AC Milan have tried to set foot in Asian or US-American markets, for example. The English Premier League established an Asian tour in order to establish its brand in China, Japan and Singapore; and the German clubs Bayern Munich and VfB Stuttgart regularly play pre-season friendlies in the United States and Mexico. The North-American Football League (NFL) takes the internationalisation of sports even a step further as case study 1.2 shows.

CASE STUDY 1.2. Exploring New Markets – The NFL in Europe

The National Football League (NFL) as the largest professional American football league in the world soon realised that they have to explore new markets outside their North-American home base in order to build their brand. Therefore, they established the *World League of American Football* in 1991. This American football league operated in Europe was mainly seen as a spring developmental league with players who were predominantly assigned by NFL teams who wanted these younger players to get additional game experience and coaching. Over the years the league not only saw several European team changes but also some name changes (NFL Europe League, NFL Europe, NFL Europa). In 2007, the NFL announced that NFL Europe would immediately cease operations after some financial troubles and decreasing attendances. At the time of disbanding the league consisted of five German teams and one team from the Netherlands.

The NFL, however, came up with a new strategy to target the European market. In 2007, the NFL decided to stage two regular season games a year outside of the United States for the following five years. After tough negotiations London beat competition from Toronto, Mexico City as well as the

Continued

German cities of Berlin, Frankfurt, Dusseldorf and Hamburg to be the location for the first ever National Football League game to be held outside the Americas. The game between the Miami Dolphins and the New York Giants held on 28 October 2007 at the Wembley stadium was considered to be the start of an international campaign to take American football to a global audience. Indeed, the game was a complete success. Hundreds of thousands of people were applying for the NFL London tickets weeks before the event took place, thousands of tourists were making their way to the English capital, a total of 81,176 spectators were following the match live inside the stadium and television recorded huge ratings. Even the players seemed to be impressed. Miami cornerback Will Allen said: 'I loved playing at Wembley Stadium. It made me feel a lot like I was a gladiator.' And Dolphins linebacker Joey Porter added: 'This really was like it is in the play-offs or even the Super Bowl. We usually play in front of 60,000 or 70,000 spectators, but playing in front of almost 90,000 people is great and something you are looking forward to.' The New York Giants eventually ran out with a 13-10 win. After the huge success of the game, the demand for another game couldn't be higher and therefore the NFL announced a second game to be played outside the United States. The 2008 London game took place on 26 October and saw the New Orleans Saints defeat the San Diego Chargers 37 to 32 at Wembley Stadium.

Chargers President Dean Spanos described the reasons for establishing a regular season game away from the home market: 'This is another positive step in the effort to globalize our great sport. It's an opportunity for the NFL to show off two of its marquee teams and some of its best players as well as a chance for the Chargers to expand our international fan base. In particular, it's going to be good exposure for the team, our players and our city and another opportunity for our team to grow together.'

However, the basic idea is nothing new in the world of sports business. During the 1990s the National Hockey League (NHL) staged three regular season games in Tokyo and clubs of the National Basketball Association (NBA) were attending friendlies in Europe and Asia on a regular basis and therefore attracting a lot of new fans outside their home market.

Taking advantage of new media and technology developments

The internet offers huge opportunities for sports clubs these days. For example, sporting organisations which never made it into the limelight of public interest now have the chance to broadcast their games and competition via their own internet channels or clubs' websites. Therefore, they can reach more people – on a local, regional, national and international level. In addition, by the means of new media and technology developments, sports clubs and associations are able to communicate with their fans more effectively. For example, supporters might be kept up-to-date with text messages or regular pod casts.

Changing ownership structures

Sports clubs used to belong to the people or to local benefactors and were mainly run as non-profit organisations. Nowadays, sporting organisations have to be companies aiming for profits. The commercialisation of sports and the clubs' ability to generate considerable income attracts more and more external investors. In addition, a growing number of prestigious sports clubs are taken over by billionaires. This is most evident in the English Premier League where Chelsea Football Club, Liverpool FC and Manchester United were bought by foreign businessmen. The change of ownership structure often leads to investments in strategic structures and therefore to a further professionalisation of the clubs, but also to a potentially dangerous dependence on a single individual.

Transforming stadiums into state-of-the-art sports-leisure multiplex arenas

A lot of clubs are known for their traditional home grounds and their fantastic atmosphere. However, despite their outstanding atmosphere most traditional stadia are too small or do not meet today's safety requirements. In order to generate more income from gate receipts and hospitality, clubs transform their stadiums into state of the art arenas. For example, the old-established Wankdorf-Stadion in Berne (the place were the German national team won its first World Cup in 1954) was transformed into the Stade de Suisse, an all-seater arena with modern office premises, a large shopping mall and the biggest discotheque in Switzerland. In order to modernise their home grounds, sporting organisations need to build project groups and take care of the financing. They have to negotiate with potential investors and with local authorities. Furthermore, they need to take on know-how and expertise in order to make the transformation of their arenas a success.

Engaging in various different relationships

One of the biggest challenges in today's sports business is the engagement with various stakeholders and the establishment of numerous relationships. Sporting organisations compete for people's attention, for fans' commitment, for sponsors' money, for media coverage, for high potential as new employees and for public subsidies. This tough competition leads to the survival of the fittest. Sporting organisations that are able to build and maintain healthy relationships with their various stakeholders and have the resources and the know-how to implement sophisticated relationship marketing strategies will gain a competitive advantage over their rivals on and off the pitch.

Case study 1.3 illustrates the various different tasks and challenges of a professional sporting organisation using the example of the Qatar Stars League. Once more the importance of healthy relationships in the context of professional sports is emphasised.

CASE STUDY 1.3. Challenges and Tasks of a Professional Sporting Organisation – The Case of the Qatar Stars League Management

Alexander Amiri

One of the key focuses for the Qatari government is the development of sport at the local, national and international levels. Therefore, a new professional football league – the Qatar Stars League – was established in 2008. As part of the overall re-modelling and re-structuring of Qatar's football league, a management team consisting of expats and locals was created – starting in January 2007 – with the clear purpose of professionalizing Qatar's National Football League in every single business sector. The Qatar Stars League Management (QSLM) is the new legal entity founded by the mother association – the Qatar Football Association (QFA) – and held under the rules and regulations of the AFC (Asian Football Confederation) in order to structure, manage and organize all matters with regards to the new 'Qatar Stars League', the top-tier professional football league in Qatar.

With this in mind, the overall primary targets to be achieved are as follows:

- developing the league and clubs into institutions of sporting excellence
- introducing a new and improved format to the game (such as a home & away system) that complies with FIFA and AFC rules & regulations
- building the league brand and increase its national and international recognition
- developing strong, professional and truly popular players and creating heroes
- maximising the commercial value of the league and clubs by fully exploiting commercial interests
- creating an entertaining, positive football event environment for everyone
- driving overall interest and awareness with the goal to significantly increase audience attendance and to develop a relevant and passionate fan-base.

The QSLM itself is made up of five different departments with each one having its own action plan and professionalising program which supports the overarching aims and strategic business plan of the QSLM. Each department has to face different challenges and has to deal with various stakeholders:

The Sports Department aims to build, develop and maintain strong and positive stakeholder relationships with relevant sporting organisations. Regarding the stakeholders of the Sports Department it is almost impossible to implement any kind of CRM measurement as this department is closely working together with government bodies, football associations/federations and other sporting committees on a day to day basis. Currently the only measure is the annual friendly federation tournament. At this event all stakeholders are invited to participate in the football tournament providing a social networking platform.

The Audience Marketing Department seeks to raise awareness, promote and market the league to specified target audiences and create and maintain a sense of loyalty to the league and clubs, within individuals and key social and demographic groups within the State of Qatar, the Golf Region and internationally. To do this the Audience Marketing Department has to identify potential target audiences both domestic and international, build, develop and maintain a fan-base for each club and for the league, create, develop and implement audience revenue strategies for the clubs and the league, enhance entertainment value of the stadium event, turning it into a 'must go' event, develop and promote fan appreciation instruments and incentives and create audience appreciation throughout a comprehensive community involvement. CRM measures within the Audience Marketing Department are closely related to fan activities (e.g. fan appreciation days and family days including meet & greet at an entertainment park, free transportation to away games for fans and special incentives for fans involved in several fan activation programs such as being invited to join the favourite club for the next training camp). Although the football fans form the foundation of the Audience Marketing Department's stakeholders, equally important are the Royal Family including Government Ministries and Government associated agencies; the Ministry of Sport as well as the Ministry of Education.

The Rights and Licenses Department aims to maximize the business and commercial value of the league and its clubs by fully exploiting the national and international market potentials. In order to achieve this, the Rights and Licenses Department has to develop and introduce a respective sponsorship rights structure, generate incremental revenue by selling sponsorship, merchandising, media and hospitality rights to national and international companies, execute implementation of contractual rights of the league and the clubs (delivery of rights), collaborate with media (broadcasting, print and online) in order to sell licensing contracts to gain exposure for the league, develop, install and maintain a CRM system. In order to establish good relations to the main stakeholders such as sponsors, product-partners and media-partners the Rights and Licenses Department introduced a range of activities (e.g. VIP invitations to football matches and the "final season reception", meet & greet with stars/officials, sponsor meetings in order to generate additional business for them, sponsors' friendly tournament as well as other social networking events).

The Communication Department aims to create, develop and implement a communication strategy for the Qatar Stars League in order to build, grow and implement the league brand. Furthermore, the Communication Department needs to develop and implement a strong, consistent and cohesive internal corporate communication strategy as well as building strong media stakeholder relationships specifically with local and international media. Therefore, media round tables and a media football tournament have been introduced for social networking.

The Administration Department aims to provide best practice financial and administrative management which supports the strategic level business plan. To achieve this, the Administration Department has to manage the allocated budget using best practice financial processes and procedures, develop and implement human resource management services and procedures for the league management, provide and maintain efficient and effective IT system to the league and league management, develop and implement both legal advice and technical expertise for the league.

The QSLM and its five main departments face various challenges as described above. It also needs to deal with a wide range of different tasks which are typical for most sporting organisations. However, the cultural situation is an important issue which has to be considered very thoroughly. In general, the Arab culture works in a different way than the Western culture. Strong and "good" relations – in terms of "high value relations" with regard to the Sheikhs and the Royal families are essential for any kind of business. Without the gate keeping relations no business will be successful in the Arab world or especially in Qatar. The more "high value" relations exist, the better the chance to get a successful business started. Relationship marketing is therefore not a nice thing to have but the basic foundation in order to make the Qatar Stars League a successful project. The aims and objectives of the QSLM are very challenging, but everyone involved in the project is confident that the Qatar Stars League will become a successful element of the international sports business.

Alexander Amiri serves as the Manager for Rights and Licences at QSLM.

THE CONTENT AND STRUCTURE OF THIS BOOK

Key content on a chapter-by-chapter basis

In **Chapter 2** we will describe the principles of relationship marketing. We will provide a brief overview of relationship marketing history and introduce the main concepts of relationship marketing. Based upon a comprehensive discussion on various relationship marketing definitions we will eventually develop and present the first definition of relationship marketing in the context of sports.

Chapter 3 introduces the business of sports and its various stakeholders with special emphasis on the relationship between sporting organisations and their customers, e.g. fans, media, sponsors. We will also talk about the involved complexities and differences compared to non-sports sector organisations. Amongst other examples from the world of sports, Chapter 3 includes an extensive case study about Bayern Munich and the club's stakeholders.

Chapter 4 describes the role of the fans in the sports business and the importance of fans for sporting organisations. We will also discuss how sporting organisations can build an effective relationship with their fans. A number of examples coming from different sports and various leagues all over the world are used in order to show the variety of relationship marketing offers in relationships with fans.

In **Chapter 5** we will deal with the relationships emerging from sports sponsorship and thereby address the importance of sponsors for clubs, teams and associations. In order to provide a bigger picture we will refer to current empirical studies as well as practical examples (e.g. the NBA team Los Angeles Lakers, FC Barcelona from the Spanish football league Primera Divisón or famous sports sponsors such as McDonalds or Carlsberg).

Chapter 6 comments on the role of the media in the sports business and addresses the question of how sporting organisations can build an effective relationship with the media. Some of the examples used in Chapter 6 refer to the European TV station Eurosport, the famous Australian-American global media tycoon Rupert Murdoch and his media network as well as a number of professional sports teams from different sports and countries.

In **Chapter 7** we will describe the extended marketing mix with regard to relationship marketing in sports. In order to show how sports teams and sports event can apply marketing techniques regarding the 7 Ps (product, price, place, promotion, people, process and physical evidence) we have used many real-life examples as well as a comprehensive case study on the Formula 1 Grand Prix 2009 in Melbourne.

In **Chapter 8** we will first summarise the previous chapters and provide an overview of the key issues. A detailed case study will then present a strategic relationship marketing approach which already has been implemented at some professional sporting organisations. Finally we will name and describe the general trends of relationship marketing as well as specific

Introduction

When you read, you have to do many things. Your eyes have to recognize (see and understand) letters and words on the page. The information about the letters and words goes to your brain. Your brain tries to connect the new information to things you already know:

- about the sentence
- about other sentences in the passage
- about the topic and the writer
- about language and the world

If you are a good reader, this happens automatically—very, very quickly. You don't have to think about the letters, the words, and the sentences. You can think about the ideas in the text.

To become a better reader, you need to learn the skills that good readers use:

- Word and sentence skills: Recognizing words and understanding the grammar of sentences. In Part 2, you learned and practiced some of these skills. In Part 3, you will get more practice.

- Higher-level skills: Ways that readers think about the ideas in a text.

The units in Part 3 of *Reading Power 2* will give you practice in these skills.

challenges for professional sporting organisations in the future. The final chapter will then end with the continuation of the fictional story we have introduced at the beginning of this book.

The structure of chapters

Although each chapter has a different focus, the same structure applies to all of them. Every chapter starts with the statement of the respective learning outcomes. This is mostly a service for students who can get an idea of what they should know after completion of the chapter. The brief overview of the chapter takes the reader onto the journey through the respective chapter, before the introduction sets the scene for the topic in question. For the main body of the chapters we will use a funnel approach, which means that we first describe the general issues of the topic before narrowing it down. Thus we are able to introduce both the basic principles as well as very specific aspects of each topic. Whenever appropriate we provide the latest empirical data to support our arguments. In addition, we have incorporated a lot of actual case studies and real-life examples in order to emphasise the practicability of relationship marketing in sports. At the end of the main body of the chapters we have put our thoughts together by providing some conclusions. In order to test the learning outcomes readers have the option to answer the discussion questions. At the end of each chapter we recommend some publications which we think are most appropriate for readers who wish to learn more on specific subjects. All references that have been used throughout the chapters are listed at the end of the book. For the sake of linguistic simplicity we have mainly used the male version ('he') rather than the female version ('she') when referring to people in general because sports still is a male-dominated area. However, as we will see in the course of this book, professional sports attracts more and more female fans which we do not intend to neglect, of course.

CONCLUSIONS

In view of the ongoing commercialisation of sports, new challenges emerge for professional sporting organisations. One of these challenges is the need to build and maintain healthy relationships with the organisation's stakeholders. Establishing a coherent relationship marketing strategy is not an easy task for clubs and associations, but a crucial one. However, the existing literature on relationship marketing is far too general for the specific context of sports on the one hand. Books on sports marketing, on the other hand, have touched relationship marketing only slightly to date. We therefore not only saw an opportunity, but also a strong need to publish a book which solely focuses on relationship marketing in sports and which provides academics as well as practitioners with a compilation of relationship marketing concepts and practical examples. Thereby we hope to increase the importance of the topic and generate a broad understanding of the possibilities and opportunities relationship marketing might offer in the context of professional sports.

DISCUSSION QUESTIONS

(1) How would you describe the development of professional sports in recent years?

(2) What are the main challenges of professional sporting organisations these days?

(3) What have professional sports entities to do in order to meet these challenges?

(4) Why can relationship marketing be seen as a necessity for professional sporting organisations?

(5) Do you think that your favourite sports club has implemented a coherent relationship marketing programme?

(6) Imagine you are the Marketing Director of your favourite sports club. How would you implement a coherent relationship marketing programme?

(7) What do you personally expect from this book?

GUIDED READING

We would recommend a book by Matthew D. Shank called *Sports Marketing: A Strategic Perspective* for further reading. Shank provides a framework and conceptual model of the strategic marketing process that can be applied to the sports industry.

WEBSITES

Australian National Rugby League
http://www.nrl.com.au

The National Basketball Association (NBA)
http://www.nba.com

The National Hockey League (NHL)
http://www.nhl.com

The National Football League (NFL)
http://www.nfl.com

The Qatar Stars League (English version)
http://en.qfa.com.qa

CHAPTER 2

The Principles of Relationship Marketing

Learning Outcomes

On completion of this chapter the reader should be able to:

- explain the 'paradigm shift' from transactional marketing to relationship marketing
- define relationship marketing in general as well as related to the sports sector
- list the goals and name the key variables for relationship success
- give an overview of the main instruments of relationship marketing
- discuss the advantages and possible trade-offs of relationship marketing

CONTENTS

OVERVIEW OF CHAPTER

First we will explain what is often called a 'paradigm shift' in marketing: the changing focus from transactional marketing to relationship marketing. Next we will present different characterizations of relationship marketing and propose a definition of relationship marketing in the context of sports. Then we will show how to create value for the organisation with relationship marketing. Further the main instruments of relationship marketing will be introduced in general and transferred to the sports context. Finally we will discuss the advantages and limitations of relationship marketing both from the organisation's and the customer's perspectives. Various real life case studies will be used to illustrate the principles of relationship marketing.

INTRODUCTION

More than a decade ago, Buttle (1996, p. 1) came to the following conclusion when talking about the evolution of marketing:

> *'Marketing is no longer simply about developing, selling, and delivering products. It is progressively more concerned with the development and maintenance of mutually satisfying long-term relationships.'*

Indeed, managing relationships with customers and other interest groups has become the core of marketing. In the age of globalisation competition is increasing. With product and service quality becoming a common standard in many industries and being no longer a major source of competitive advantage, organisations are especially adopting a 'Customer Relationship Marketing' (CRM) approach as a means of differentiating themselves. CRM is a strategic orientation assuming that the customer prefers to have an ongoing relationship with one single organisation rather than changing organisations. Based on this assumption and on the fact that it is less expensive to retain satisfied customers than to attract new ones, marketers focus on building and keeping groups of profitable, loyal customers by moving them into long-term, mutually beneficial relationships (Sandhusen, 2008).

In recent years relationship marketing has also become a key topic in the sports sector. While the concept of managing relationships with customers is well established in the sporting goods industry, sporting organisations have just started to adopt the concept of relationship marketing. The fact that many sporting organisations are nowadays acting like commercial enterprises has strongly influenced the adoption of relationship marketing, above all on the professional level. The shift to relationship marketing requires fundamental changes in a sporting organisation's structure, a powerful customer database, a newly oriented marketing focus that understands stakeholder's needs and expectations and markets the idea of relationship marketing inside an organisation.

FROM A TRANSACTIONAL MARKETING APPROACH TO RELATIONSHIP MARKETING

Berry (1995, p. 236) concluded that relationship marketing is an 'old new' idea but with a new focus. In fact the concept of relationship marketing can be traced back to as early as the Middle Ages when merchants were already aware of how important it was to keep a relationship with the customer. One only has to think of the ancient Middle Eastern proverb: 'As a merchant you'd better have a friend in every town' (Grönroos, 1994, p. 347). However, with the beginning of the industrialisation and its resulting mass production as well as the constant growth of business organisations the level of personal contact between buyer and seller has considerably decreased and the customer often was turned from a relationship partner into a market share statistic (Harwood, Garry and Broderick, 2008).

The paradigm shift

Figure 2.1 illustrates the development of central marketing foci over the last hundred years, emphasising the long-time dominance of the product, the subsequent market focus, and in the 1990s, the adoption of relationship marketing, which has been practised most widely in the service area.

Academic and practitioner interest in relationship marketing took off to the extent that many marketers viewed it as the new key marketing issue. Indeed many marketing experts propose that there has been a 'paradigm shift' away from the traditional transaction marketing approach towards a more relationship-oriented one during the last few years. An initial starting point for relationship marketing was the notion that in order to retain customers in the long term, marketing exchanges need to be seen not just as transactions between the seller and the buyer, but as a set of activities in which relationships are developing. Another factor influencing the development of relationship marketing was above all, the maturing of service

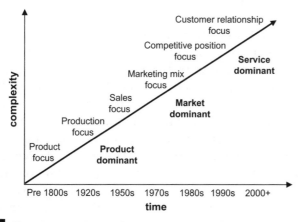

FIGURE 2.1 *The changing focus of marketing.*
(*Source:* Harwood, Garry and Broderick, 2008, p. 9; Christopher, Payne and Ballantyne, 2008, p. xiv)

FIGURE 2.2 *The relationship marketing orientation.*
(*Source:* Christopher, Payne and Ballantyne, 2008, p. 9; Harwood, Garry and Broderick, 2008, p. 11)

marketing in the service industry: The dimensions of customer care and quality arose and overlapped traditional marketing philosophy. Advances in information and communication technology further facilitated the effectiveness of relationship marketing (Nufer, 2006). So the relationship marketing orientation is bringing together service, quality and marketing philosophies (Figure 2.2).

Differences between relationship marketing and transaction marketing

To provide a deeper understanding of the development from transactional to relationship marketing, Hennig-Thurau and Hansen (2000) collected and summarized the main differences between these two marketing concepts (Table 2.1).

Transaction marketing considers the satisfying of customer needs as an exchange of goods and services for money. With its short-term goal of making the sale through single transactions and minimal communication or interaction, it contrasts sharply with the relational-based approach. Relationship marketing puts major emphasis on close, personal and long-term provider-customer relations as well as on high interaction, and focuses on the maintenance of existing customers rather than on the acquisition of new ones (Nufer, 2006; Hennig-Thurau and Hansen, 2000). Depending on the products sold and customers served, both relationship and transactional marketing can coexist in a company's strategic marketing plan. Conditions under which transactional marketing is most likely to apply include generic commodities or low-value consumer products and services. As there are usually no or low costs associated with switching suppliers, customers have

| Table 2.1 | Key Differences between the Concepts of Relationship Marketing and Transaction Marketing |

Criterion	Relationship Marketing	Transactional marketing
Primary object	Relationship	Single transaction
General approach	Interaction-related	Action-related
Perspective	Evolutionary-dynamic	Static
Basic orientation	Implementation-oriented	Decision-oriented
Long-term vs. short-term	Generally takes a long-term perspective	Generally takes a short-term perspective
Fundamental strategy	Maintenance of existing customers	Acquisition of new customers
Focus in decision process	All phases focus on post-sales decisions and action	Pre-sales activities
Intensity of contact	High	Low
Degree of mutual dependence	Generally high	Generally low
Measurement of Customer satisfaction	Managing customer base (direct approach)	Monitoring market share (indirect approach)
Dominant quality dimension	Quality of interaction	Quality of output
Production of quality	The concern of all	Primary concern of production
Role of internal marketing	Substantial strategic importance	No or limited importance
Importance of employees for business success	High	Low
Production focus	Mass customisation	Mass production

Source: Hennig-Thurau and Hansen, 2000, p. 5

little interest in building a particular relationship with the provider, but prefer transactions. Relationship marketing is most appropriate in competitive, saturated markets with few key providers of supplies, where switching costs are high and when there is a consumer's ongoing need and desire for a certain product or service (Sandhusen, 2008; Harwood, Garry and Broderick, 2008).

DEFINING RELATIONSHIP MARKETING

Relationship marketing has arisen from a number of different academic disciplines like economics, psychology and sociology. The expression 'relationship marketing' has been used since the early 1990s only, but there is still no consensus about an agreed definition of relationship marketing. Even the meaning of the two-letter acronym 'RM' is contested: some understand it as 'relationship marketing', others use the acronym for 'relationship management'. There have also been several substitute terms for relationship marketing: from 'loyalty marketing', 'personalised marketing', 'database marketing' to 'interactive marketing' – all looking at the same concept, 'relationship marketing' from different points of view (Buttle, 1996).

As a result of its various roots, theorists developed a range of **conceptual models** to represent the nature of relationship marketing, as for example:

- Berry (1983, p. 25) from a **services perspective**:
  'Relationship marketing is attracting, maintaining, and – in multi-service organizations – enhancing customer relationships.'
- Jackson (1985, p. 120) from an **industrial marketing perspective**:
  'Marketing concentrated towards strong, lasting relationships with individual accounts.'
- Grönroos (1995) from a **network perspective**:
  'To identify and establish, maintain and enhance relationships with customers and other stakeholders at a profit, so that the objectives of the partners' interests are met; and is achieved by mutual exchange and fulfilment of promises.'

All these definitions include statements about attracting, maintaining and enhancing mutually beneficial relationships characterized by interactions (Harwood, Garry and Broderick, 2008).

Figure 2.3 demonstrates a hierarchy. Customer management means tactical, proactive management of the customer's interactions with the organisation and serves as the basis for both customer relationship management and relationship marketing. The goal of customer relationship management is the identification and selection of target customers. Relationship marketing is the peak of the pyramid. It is a philosophy oriented towards stakeholders – this means that relationship marketing is not limited to an organisation's relationship with its customers (Hennig-Thurau and Hansen, 2000).

A broader definition considers relationship marketing within a much wider **network of stakeholders**. This relationship of networks is illustrated by the 'Six markets' model from Christopher, Payne and Ballantyne (2008). Relationship marketing, as an integrated overall marketing activity focuses on the retention of existing relationships in six defined core markets (Figure 2.4).

This broader view of relationship marketing is based on the idea of stakeholders and has a number of core markets to which it needs to direct marketing activities and establish positive relationships in order to achieve long-term loyalty. While these market domains are interdependent, they vary

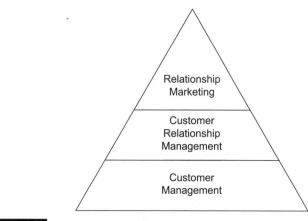

FIGURE 2.3 *The relationship hierarchy.*
(*Source:* adopted from Christopher, Payne and Ballantyne, 2008, p. 17)

in importance. Every (sporting) organisation needs to determine its most relevant market domains.

As customers are normally the main target group of marketing activities, the **customer markets** are in the centre of the model. Within customer markets, the focus of relationship marketing is to keep existing customers and build up a long-term relationship with them. We will have a detailed look at one customer group of a sporting organisation – 'the fans' – in the next paragraph.

Internal markets refer to marketing activities within the organisation itself. It aims at producing customer-oriented staff and optimising the organisational process inside the organisation. The idea is that every employee and department of an organisation is treated as an internal customer and as an internal supplier. An effective internal relationship

FIGURE 2.4 *The 'Six Markets' model.*
(*Source:* Christopher, Payne and Ballantyne, 2008, p. 80.)

marketing programme is reached when every employee of the organisation both provides and receives an excellent level of service from the other employees. There are two main effects of internal relationship marketing. First it helps the employees to understand the importance of their roles and encourages them to work in accordance with the organisation's strategic mission, goals and values. Second a well-implemented internal marketing plan is a precondition for effective external marketing efforts (Hennig-Thurau and Hansen, 2000). For example, the German Football Bundesliga Club VfB Stuttgart started its relationship marketing programme by sending its employees to workshops where each department was trained on its tasks concerning relationship marketing activities.

Referral marketing means a relationship marketing plan that stimulates referrals and advocates on the principle that 'the best form of marketing is to get the customer to do the marketing for you'. However, referral and advocate sources not only include existing customers, but intermediaries and other third parties who may recommend the organisation or its products to potential customers (Harwood, Garry and Broderick, 2008). So, for instance, a fan who is a member of a specific sports club could inspire and convince another fan to join the club, too. In the same manner a sponsor may tell other potential sponsors about his positive experiences with the club and in this way encourage them to start sponsorships as well. Marketing activities in referral markets usually take more time before the effects can be seen, but it is one of the most effective marketing methods and one of the most reliable resources.

Influencer markets refer to a wide range of sub-markets including financial and regulatory organisations as well as the government. They vary depending on the branch and market in which the organisation operates. Publicly traded companies, for example, face the financial market such as stockbrokers, analysts, shareholders as their influencer market, and comply with the guidelines of consumers' associations and the government. A sporting organisation setting up a sports event, may address as its influencer markets governmental regulators, environmental associations, transport infrastructure, communication system organisations, and energy-related projects as well as catering and advertising agencies. Marketing activities within influencer markets are typically carried out by the organisation's public relations department.

Supplier relationship marketing aims at ensuring a long-term, conflict-free collaboration between the organisation and its suppliers in which all parties both recognise each other's needs and exceed each other's expectations. This may result in improved quality and higher flexibility as well as time and cost savings in the supply chain. In this way a sporting goods supplier and a merchandise shop are increasingly regarded as partners in the value chain rather than as adversaries from whom the best price must be extracted.

One of the rarest resources of many enterprises and especially of sporting organisations, is its qualified personnel who are a key element in the area of customer service (see internal markets). Since highly qualified staff is so important for attracting and retaining customers and employees, relationship marketing has developed several marketing plans for **recruiting** – for instance sponsoring prizes at universities, assigning scholarships or offering trainee programmes.

As we can see, although the customer is the centre of attention in relational marketing activities, relationship marketing includes many parties other than the buyer and seller or the sports fan and the sporting organisation. Therefore we propose the following definition of relationship marketing in sports:

DEFINITION

Relationship marketing in sports refers to the establishment and maintenance of positive, enduring and mutually beneficial relations between professional sporting organisations and their stakeholders.

The different kinds of stakeholders of professional sporting organisations are fans, sponsors, media, employees as well as further internal and external stakeholders.

CREATING VALUE FOR THE ORGANISATION

The customer's value for the organisation is the outcome of providing superior value to all stakeholders– and thus must be considered when looking at the goals of relationship marketing. In this section we will discuss the goals and key variables for relationship success before describing the measures and tools which can help an organisation to reach it's goals.

General goals of relationship marketing

Figure 2.5 demonstrates the generally assumed correlation between profit-potential and the consumer-supplier relationship over time.

With the increasing duration of relationships with customers, and thus customer loyalty, the profitability of a consumer as part of the business' general profit increases. At the beginning of relationships, investments have to be made (**acquisition costs**). However, due to the newly won consumer's demand for the company's products and services a **basic profit** is assumed to

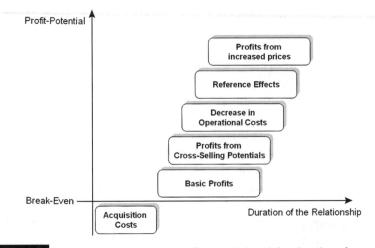

FIGURE 2.5 *Correlation between the profit potential and the duration of consumer-supplier relationships.*
(*Source:* Friedrichs, 2005, p. 7)

be made shortly afterwards. If the company manages to establish a long-term relationship with the consumer and if the customer is loyal to the company, a further increase in profit can be expected due to a more efficient saturation of customer related turnover and revenue potentials (**profits from cross selling**). The basis for this assumption is that growing trust in the company will lead to an increase in the customer's purchase frequency and intensity. Moreover, a long-term customer relationship leads to better knowledge about consumers as well as better informed consumers, which in turn leads to **decreased operational costs** for each consumer over time. Another important effect resulting from consumer relationships are **reference effects** provided by satisfied customers through positive word-of-mouth communication. Non-consumers usually rate the opinion or judgement of other customers above the communication messages of companies. So for a company, satisfied long-term customers are the best advertisers and a great potential of free advertisement. A further effect of relationship marketing implementation is seen in the possibility of charging **increased prices**. Within long-term relationships customers begin to appreciate the value of the product or service at such a rate that the price elasticity of demand increases (Friedrichs, 2005; Diller, 2000; Morgan, Crutchfield and Lacey, 2000).

Basis of relationships: bonds

According to Chiu, Hsieh, Li and Lee (2005), bonds are the basis of relationships. The process of bonding can be defined as the component of a business relationship that results in two parties acting in a unified manner towards a desired goal. The most common bonds in the context of relationship marketing are financial, social and structural bonds.

Financial bonds are a type of business practice, which aims at enhancing customer loyalty through pricing incentives. The idea behind this strategy is based on the fact that consumers are highly motivated to engage in relational exchanges if they can save money as a result. Financial bonding works especially well within the service industry. This is due to the specific characteristics of services: The actual value of a service is often very subjective and largely dependent on a consumers' perception. Many companies from the sports sector offering service related products can benefit from this fact and use the strategy of financial bonds frequently. Seasonal tickets for football games including several free games, family pricing of sports clubs memberships with the offer of 'one family member for free' when engaging in an annual family contract, or the sporting goods manufacturers' customer cards offering financial incentives in the form of rebates tagged onto the purchase price serve as examples within the sports industry. Despite many advantages, the big challenge concerning financial bonds is that they do not generally provide long-term benefits to a company. Due to financial incentives customers may feel attached to a company for a short time but the incentives do not create long-term commitment. Moreover, financial bonds alone are not enough to differentiate an organisation from its competitors in the long run and therefore should always be used in combination with other bonding strategies (Berry, 1995; Chiu, Hsieh, Li and Lee, 2005).

Social bonds consist of investments of time and energy which produce positive, interpersonal relationships between the partners. The ultimate goal is to get customers personally involved in the relationship. Companies try to give each of their customers the feeling of being something special and of being important to the company as an individual, by constantly keeping in touch with them and by increasing their knowledge about consumers' individual needs and desires. Multilevel contacts are the basis of these social bonding strategies. The more 'positive' contacts a company manages to make with the customer, the closer the social bond will be. However, a company should always be aware of the fact that too much contact can be perceived by consumers as intrusion, and the intensity of contacts therefore should stay on an agreeable level for the consumer. Only if the contact provides benefit to the consumer will it be perceived as 'positive' by him or her. The most important benefits that social bonds provide for consumers are of a psychological nature. Social bonds not only improve the mutual understanding between consumer and company, but also create positive emotions in the consumer towards the organisation and its products. More than any other industry the sports sector is predisposed for the creation of social bonds. In general, sports is a philosophy for life, an attitude or tenure, and not on any account a short-term decision. Emotional bonding with the sports element is already established in a majority of customers from the very beginning – an ideal starting position for any sporting organisation (Chiu, Hsieh, Li and Lee, 2005).

A **structural bond** is a business' attempt to tie a customer to a company's products or services by providing value-added benefits. These benefits are often valuable services that are not available or only with difficulty available from other sources. The offer of integrated services through a company's business partners as well as long-term contracts between the consumer and the supplier serve as examples of structural bonds. Another important aspect of structural bonds is their effect of increasing the difficulties of ending a relationship due to the complexity and cost of any change. For the consumer the existence of structural bonds raises the cost of switching to a competitor (Barnes, 1994;Chiu, Hsieh, Li and Lee, 2005). Sporting organisations can establish co-operation with partners in order to provide value-added benefits. An example is the partnership of the German football club Bayern Munich with the bank HypoVereinsbank: owners of a bank account at Hypo get higher interest rates with every tenth goal of the club in home matches.

Key variables for relationship success

A crucial issue from a practical point of view concerns the constructs determining customer retention or loyalty. Here relationship marketing research has reached a relatively advanced state. While different variables have been proposed, the discussion clearly focuses on the three constructs of satisfaction, trust and commitment – the key variables for relationship success (Hennig-Thurau and Hansen, 2000; Christopher, Payne and Ballantyne, 2008).

Satisfaction is the result of a psychological process of evaluation. Consumers unconsciously compare the subjectively perceived benefits offered by the supplier with their own expectations concerning the offered benefits. Generally speaking, if the perceived benefit exceeds the expectations of the consumer he is satisfied; whereas the other way round, if the expectations are higher than the perceived benefit, the customer will be dissatisfied. However, the evaluation process actually is more complex. This is especially due to the fact that customers ex post correct their expectations as well as the perceived benefit. For instance, if a customer realises that his dissatisfaction is due to too high expectations, he might correct his expectations to a lower level in order to reach satisfaction (Figure 2.6). From a supplier's point of view satisfied customers have various advantages. For

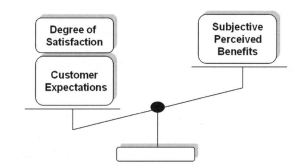

FIGURE 2.6 *Determining the degree of satisfaction.*
(*Source:* Dittrich, 2002, p. 75)

instance, an increase in customers' purchase quantity and frequency, a reduction of acquisition costs due to positive word-of-mouth propaganda and consequently an increase in image and reputation. From a customer's point of view, a high level of satisfaction in many cases increases the customer's willingness to maintain the relationship (Dittrich, 2002).

In general, the concept of **trust** refers to the degree of confidence one has in a relationship. Trust provides a key element not only for human relationships, but also plays a major role within buyer-seller relationships. If the customer believes the company to be reliable and to have a high degree of integrity, he trusts. This belief in the trustworthiness of a company is the result of personal experience with the seller's past performances and expresses itself in specific expectations concerning the seller's future behaviour. Only if the customer has been satisfied with past transactions will he begin to feel trust in future transactions with the same company, and thus the consumer's perceived risk in a transaction will decrease. Consequently, trust is a concept that needs to be built on a long-term and overall basis, because every negative interaction between consumer and seller results in a loss of trustworthiness (Hennig-Thurau and Hansen, 2000; Grossman, 1998).

Commitment refers to the consumer's tendency to feel attached to a relationship and his conviction that remaining in the relationship will yield higher net benefits than terminating it. It further includes the willingness of the relationship partners to provide short-term sacrifices. The concept of commitment can be divided into two different aspects of commitment: Calculative commitment is based on a cognitive evaluation of the value of the relationship. Affective commitment is based on a sense of liking and emotional attachment to the relationship. Research has found out that from a consumer's point of view, the perception of future rewards, a high degree in relationship identification, limited desire to seek out alternatives, a high amount of effort extended in a relationship, investments made in a relationship, and the individual's willingness to assume responsibility are the effects of a high level of commitment (Grossman, 1998). Furthermore, commitment is believed to be a predictor of whether the relationship will last during the absence of direct rewards. Therefore, commitment can be seen as a psychosocial barrier to switching over to competitors, which results from the perception of attractiveness or value of the relationship or from emotional attachment (Grossman, 1998, Hennig-Thurau and Hansen, 2000; Dittrich, 2002).

As already mentioned, the collaboration of satisfaction, trust and commitment leads to retention or loyalty – which we will analyse in detail in the next section.

The ladder of loyalty

The relationship marketing ladder of customer loyalty as illustrated in Figure 2.7 identifies different stages of relationship development.

The first three steps of the ladder focus on the acquisition of customers just as in the traditional transactional marketing approach, while the three upper steps concentrate on further development of the customer's relationship to the organisation. The ladder's first rung consists of **suspects** including people who come across the organisation's promotions. This is followed by **prospects** who have not purchased yet but are likely to do so in the future since they are interested in the organisation's promotions. Once they have purchased a product or utilised a service they convert into **first time customers** – and the relationship with the organisation begins. The ladder is continued by the

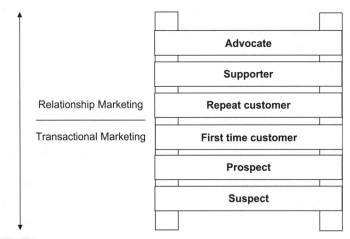

FIGURE 2.7 *The ladder of loyalty.*
(*Sources:* adopted from Christopher, Payne and Ballantyne, 2008, p. 48; Harwood, Garry and Broderick, 2008, p. 13)

successive rungs of **repeat customers** who buy regularly. **Supporters** obviously like the organisation and serve the organisation at least passively. **Advocates** represent the highest level of loyalty: An advocate purchases regularly and as he is so satisfied with the product or service he wants to encourage others to buy from the particular organisation (Harwood, Garry and Broderick, 2008; Christopher, Payne and Ballantyne, 2008).

The objective of relationship marketing is to turn new customers into vocal advocates of the company, thus playing an important role as a referral source. This normally involves providing more personalised service and service quality that not only meets the customer's expectations but exceeds them.

OVERVIEW OF THE MAIN INSTRUMENTS OF RELATIONSHIP MARKETING

The instrumental dimension of relationship marketing refers to the traditional 4 P classification of marketing instruments (product, promotion, price, place) but with a more relational orientation. Irwin, Sutton and McCarthy (2008, p. 125), even speak of 'rethinking the four 4 Ps' (Figure 2.8). In this section we will introduce the main instruments of relationship marketing and present examples of how these can be related to the sports sector.

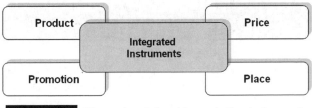

FIGURE 2.8   *The main relationship marketing instruments.*

Product

Product quality is the basis for sustainable customer relationships. The provision of reliable products with a constant level of high quality is especially an instrument of creating trust in consumers. Based on positive past experiences this trust leads to sustainable social bonds between customer and product or rather company. Therefore many companies intensively use the implementation of particular quality standards to establish and enhance customer relationships. However, the recent developments of an ongoing equalisation of high level quality standards require a differentiation from competitors via other attributes necessary (Bühler and Nufer, 2006; Bruhn, 2002; Grossman, 1998).

The integration of **customised elements** instead of standardised products for the mass market is a key aspect of a company's product policy nowadays. The fast evolution of the internet makes product differentiation not only much easier than in the past, but also makes it a core instrument in building customer relationships. Innovative information technology with data procurement methods give companies the opportunity to procure individual customer data with the goal of a mass customisation of products (Hennig-Thurau and Hansen, 2000).

The offer of **value-added services** is another important instrument of product differentiation. Basically, sellers can choose between four different methods of value-added services: material or immaterial services, both with or without surcharge (Bruhn, 2002). Product differentiation appeals to consumer's emotional feelings for a company. Consumers who feel that the company is actually caring for their individual needs and desires, are highly likely to have a feeling of trust and commitment. This can become the basis for a sustainable social bond between the customer and the company.

In order to serve individual customer needs a company can **integrate the customer into its product development process**. The Adidas group, for instance, initiated in 2001 a project of collaboration in product development

CASE STUDY 2.1. Collaboration in Product Development – The Example of 'mi adidas'

Linda Lupinacci

Within a co-design process the customer has the opportunity of participating in the composition of individualised sports shoes. He can decide about the individual fit, performance, colour and design of his shoes. The final product can be of the customer's favourite sports club's colour, can have his name or player number stitched onto it – even two different sizes of the right and the left shoe are possible. This makes the 'mi adidas' a thoroughly customised product. The communication slogan of mi adidas is 'CREATE YOUR OWN' and brings it to the point: mi adidas aims to retain customers by offering them more than just a product.

The adidas customisation process of fit and performance works with the aid of a computerised measurement apparatus. Basically, the mi adidas customisation programme is a three-step process:

Step 1: mi fit

The shop expert measures via the computerised machine the customer's feet – exact width and lengths of the feet are found out.

Step 2: mi performance

By walking on the treadmill, the machine also measures the pressure distribution and physical attributes of the customer's feet. The customer tells the expert how he plans to use the shoes, e.g. on trial or track or in the summer or winter. In this way, the shoes can be personalised according to the expected performance. Based on the results of steps 1 and 2, the shop expert is then able to make suggestions as to what form and kind of shoes best fit the customer's feet.

Step 3: mi design

On a computer screen in the shop, clients may choose colour, material and even own imprints or logos for their individual shoes. For instance, a client may select white strips with green seams and his or her own name on the shoes.

When the shoes are finished, the customer receives mail informing him that his shoes are on the way. After three to four weeks the client may pick up the shoes at the retail store. On average, a pair of customised shoes costs about 250 €, depending on the complexity of form and design. The 'originals line' targets people who want to distinguish themselves by the latest design. Their motto is: Being the first and unique. The main target group of the 'performance line' are people who regularly exercise and professional athletes. This target group expects high performance and wants the latest technology. Some of the most famous clients

of mi adidas shoes are professional football players like Lukas Podolski and Bastian Schweinsteiger from the German national team or other famous internationals like David Beckham and the former captain of the French national team Zinédine Zidane.

In the next step, adidas plans to not only offer customised shoes but also customised sports clothing. The company also aims at allowing customers to configure their individual shoes online and setting up a mi adidas e-commerce.

Linda Lupinacci graduated at ESB Business School of Reutlingen University and wrote her bachelor thesis on relationship marketing under the supervision of Prof. Dr. Gerd Nufer.

Source: Interview with Pradip Lal, Global e-CRM Manager, adidas AG (11/14/2008).

between the consumer and the company called 'mi adidas'. Case study 2.1 introduces this programme.

Price

Pricing instruments particularly influence consumers' costs of changing to another supplier. Through the use of pricing policy, companies create monetary stimulations providing reasons for customers to maintain the existing relationship with the company.

One successful proven pricing instrument is **price differentiation**. Marketers charge different prices for one and the same product/service. The ultimate goal is to increase the overall result by dividing the general market into smaller submarkets, according to specific characteristics like temporal aspects, spatial aspects, personnel aspects, quantitative aspects, or casual aspects.

Price bundling means the offer of two or more products or services in a package at a combined price. This relationship marketing approach usually enhances the customers' costs in changing the provider (Teles, 2007).

Other relationship marketing practices rely heavily on pricing strategies promising customers obvious **discounts**. The offered discount could be either monetary in the form of rebates or non-monetary such as additional free products. Through the use of rebates or bonus programmes companies often try to increase customers' consumption and try to tie them to their company with the goal of establishing long-term relationships (Hennig-Thurau and

CASE STUDY 2.2. Bonus Programmes – The Example of the Feldberg-Schwarzwald Customer Card

Julia Lohrer

Bonus programmes reward loyal customer behaviour and repeated purchases, additional purchases, or recommendations. The rewards are highly connected to temporal or economical factors with the goal of developing a system of rewards that motivates the customer to reach for more rewards. While bonus programmes in general are no new phenomenon it is particularly important for a company or organisation to integrate new and innovative value-added features for the customer in order to differentiate from competitors.

The popular German winter sports area Feldberg-Schwarzwald has initiated a bonus programme with customer cards in addition to its price strategy of direct quantity rebates. A daily adult passport for the usage of the ski lifts was sold at a price of 25 € in season 2007/08, whereas a 7-day passport was sold at a price of only 130 €. This quantity rebate of 45 € is an incentive for consumers to buy the weekly passport rather than several daily passports and may even lead to the outcome that

consumers who intend to stay only six days at the winter sports area due to the rebate may extend their stay. Moreover, this rebate may be the reason that consumers decide to spend their holidays at Feldberg-Schwarzwald instead of travelling to another winter sports area.

Additionally, with the purchase of any ski lift passport a specific number of bonus points is credited onto the consumers chip card. When a consumer has collected 180 points he gets a daily ski lift passport for free. Furthermore, the card stores information about the individual skiing performance of the consumer. So, for instance, he can recall the number of altitude difference he or she has overcome during the day or get other individual performance information.

Julia Lohrer graduated at ESB Business School of Reutlingen University and wrote her bachelor thesis on relationship marketing under the supervision of Prof. Dr. Gerd Nufer.

Hansen, 2000; Bruhn, 2002). Case study 2.2 provides an example of such a bonus programme.

Promotion

Promotion is a highly important tool in relationship marketing used in order to establish a consistent interaction with customers with the goal of maintaining or enhancing trust in the company or product (Nufer, 2007).

A classical part of customer loyalty strategies are **direct mailings**. Birthdays or other special occasions or events are used to communicate directly and personally to customers in order to capture their attention and to convey to the individual customer that he is special and highly valuable for the company. Thus the social bonds with him are strengthened. Product samples can also be included in direct mailings. For example, it is quite common that a fitness-club with the upcoming of the expiration date of a customer's annual contract, contacts the customer directly to call his attention onto a possible extension of the contract and simultaneously attracts him with a voucher for a massage or a stay at the spa area of the club (Bruhn, 2002).

With the aim of informing customers and strengthening the emotional bonds **customer journals** or **newsletters** are an equally popular means of communication in relationship marketing. In general they appear free of charge and are issued at a specified periodic cycle. They can appear in any formal or informal shape. Particularly with complex products, for instance fitness equipment or services, customer journals or newsletters offer advice for a more effective use of the product. Moreover the entertainment value should not be neglected (Bruhn, 2002). The McFit Corporation, for example, Germany's biggest chain of fitness clubs (with more than 600,000 members and 92 locations), launches a monthly fitness and lifestyle journal which consumers can get free of charge within the locations. The journal provides reportages, interviews and tests around fitness and lifestyle as well as tips for effective and healthy nutrition and fitness training.

Telephone and online marketing are other important means of communication in relationship marketing – mostly within findings of customer satisfaction surveys or follow-up action in response to written mailings. During recent years the use of telephone marketing has been increasingly replaced by the use of online marketing. The advantage of online marketing is the possibility of a more direct and more individualised contact with the customer (Bruhn, 2002). Further relevant and related communication instruments are customer forums, chat rooms and of course service hotlines.

Place

The main focus of distribution within relationship marketing should be to contribute to a transition into a flexible distribution system according to customers' individual needs.

Direct sales and catalogue sales can be seen as traditional distribution channels of relationship marketing.

However, the evolution of the world wide web plays an increasingly important role in the choice of distribution channels and is the major source of the emergence of new channels such as **online shops**. The distribution via a company's homepage offers the advantage to the customer that he or she does not depend on strict rules concerning shop opening hours. The customer can make his desired purchases directly from home, conveniently and fast, and can control the status of his order and the estimated delivery date via product tracking systems (Bruhn, 2002).

Beyond mere distribution functions the web offers the provider the advantage of an invaluable source of **information procurement** (Hennig-Thurau and Hansen, 2000). The growing information management needs of organisations regarding individual customer data is of great importance especially in relationship marketing. Therefore online shops offer companies the chance of a precise purchasing analysis of consumer goods which enables a targeted communication with the customer.

Within the field of sports marketing the **media** are another important distribution channel (Freyer, 2003). For example, sports results can be disseminated worldwide within the shortest possible time via satellite to keep customers up to date. Further, live broadcasts on television allow the sports audience to watch the event directly on the national television without the need to take long and maybe inconvenient trips to sports event locations.

BENEFITS AND LIMITATIONS OF RELATIONSHIP MARKETING

The relationship marketing theory has always tended to focus on the organisation's perspective rather than on the customer's. Little attention has been paid to the customers' willingness to become or remain a relational partner, even though there has been wide agreement that relationships have to be mutually perceived and mutually beneficial (Berry, 1995). With the implementation of relationship marketing programmes both organisations and customers have increasingly become aware of the benefits not only of relationship marketing but also of some trade-offs. We will discuss these points in the following section.

The organisation's perspective

Benefits

Increased profitability

From an organisation's perspective the overall benefit of relationship marketing is without doubt the economic effect of increased, long-term profit. An often cited study by Reichheld and Sasser (1990), claims that a 5% improvement in customer retention rates can increase Net Present Value (NPV) profitability by between 25 and 85%, depending on the industry. The increased profitability is a result of cost reductions, sales increases, positive word of mouth, brand loyalty, competitive advantage and employee satisfaction.

Cost reduction

Recent studies have shown that in markets with increasing competition it may cost five times more to attract new customers than it would cost to retain current customers, because it requires much more extensive resources to acquire a new customer than to retain an existing customer (Sandhusen, 2008). One of the reasons is that the costs of acquisition (e.g. publicity) occur at the beginning of a relationship. So the longer the relationship lasts, the lower the amortised costs are. Other cost reduction effects include a decrease in service costs as a result of the customer's growing expertise over time. This means that customers are getting familiar with the procurement procedures and are consistent in their order placement, so that service providers have fewer costs in serving customers (Hennig-Thurau and Hansen, 2000).

Increased sales

Relationship marketing also contributes to growth in sales and stable unit sales. The fact that loyal customers are less likely to switch over to other brands and providers, make it difficult for competitors to enter the market or gain market share. Furthermore, long-term customers tend to be less price-sensitive and are more likely to purchase high margin and ancillary products as they get to know an organisation better and are satisfied with the quality of its services or products. Loyal customers are even more willing to increase their expenditure over time and to pay a price premium (Sandhusen, 2008).

Positive word of mouth

Loyal and satisfied customers may generate a strong word-of-mouth promotion and referrals to prospective customers. This is one of the most efficient promotional methods for an organisation since most consumers who are looking for providers, first ask advocates for advice. Thus positive word of mouth may not only enhance the organisation's image but also reduce acquisition costs, and therefore impact favourably on profit (Sandhusen, 2008).

Brand loyalty

As relationship marketing encourages customers to build up long-term relationships with the organisation and its products, it may lead to a permanent preferential treatment for all the organisation's products which results in brand-loyal customers (Nwakanma, Singleton, Jackson and Burkhalter, 2007).

Competitive advantage

The concept of product differentiation and competitive advantage is closely related to brand loyalty. By placing greater emphasis on listening to the customers' desires, marketers can adapt the product to the customers' individual needs. This ability to better serve a customer may help marketers to better differentiate the organisation's products and consequently gain competitive advantage over non-responsive organisations (Nwakanma, Singleton, Jackson and Burkhalter, 2007).

Employee retention

The concept of employee retention implies an indirect benefit of customer retention and loyalty. Employees prefer working for organisations whose customers are satisfied and loyal as it makes their job easier and more satisfying. In return, happy employees bring about better customer satisfaction and thus contribute to efficient relationship marketing. Fan cards as described in Case study 2.3 combine many of the benefits of relationship marketing.

CASE STUDY 2.3. Loyalty Cards – The Example of the VfB Stuttgart Fan Card

Linda Lupinacci

Most professional sports clubs offer the opportunity to become a member of the club. An official fan club serves as an integrative instrument. It integrates communication (e.g. fan magazines, club events), distribution (e.g. fan catalogues) as well as product-related (e.g. merchandising articles) and price-related activities (e.g. discounts for members). A special integral part of a fan club is represented by a club card which allows sports fans to demonstrate their membership and thus enhances their emotional commitment to and personal identification with the sporting organisation. If a club card is also combined with a payment function or even with a rebate system, customers are more likely to purchase more. This may thereby contribute positively to customer commitment, trust and satisfaction and thus leads to a long-term relationship with the respective sporting organisation.

A new challenge in this context is the brandnew 'VfB Stuttgart Fan Card' which is planned to be implemented in the season of 2009/10. This club card, which also provides the function of a credit card in cooperation with the bank Landesbank Baden-Württemberg, has a very special function: it is used to enter the stadium as well as its parking facilities, and to purchase drinks, food and merchandising articles in and around the stadium. Additionally, the included credit card is applicable worldwide. In the 2008/09 season the VfB fan card was being tested by pre-selected loyal customers. The club is already considering enlarging the functions of the card, for example, providing discounts for card holders.

Source: Interview with Christian Ruf, Event and CRM Manager, VfB Stuttgart (12/16/2008).

Limitations

Costs of technological systems

One major limitation in implementing relationship marketing strategies is the failure of an organisation to implement and maintain relationship marketing software, above all for financial reasons. The average costs of CRM software ranges from 500,000 to 800,000 € or more for a system-wide application. Many vendors lure organisations with promises of CRM systems that are omnipotently applicable. However, in practice almost 55% of relationship marketing programmes fail due to a lack of infrastructure inside the company (Ramkumar and Saravanan, 2007).

'Cold' Loyalty

A relationship marketing price strategy promising customers 'immediate' benefits e.g. by offering discounts, could cause the contrary effect. 'Cold' loyalty rather than true customer commitment may emerge. Customers may take received benefits for granted and even develop a 'what have you done for me lately?' attitude, which makes them even more sensitive to costs and benefits. So long-term customers may be just as price sensitive as short-term customers and may not necessarily be cheaper to serve as their level of expectations is likely to rise. This may work against an organisation's relationship-oriented effort and create additional costs (Hennig-Thurau and Hansen, 2000; Gruen, Summers and Acito, 2000).

Change in organisation's culture

When implementing relationship marketing programmes significant changes are necessary in an organisation's culture. Organisations should adopt a company wide, customer-centric culture characterised by consistent customer service and strong customer orientation. The modifications of an organisation's value base, strategies and structures in accordance with the basic axioms of relationship marketing imply high expenditures of time and costs (Harwood, Garry and Broderick, 2008; Hennig-Thurau and Hansen, 2000).

Relationship Marketing is not applicable everywhere

Another problem is the fact that relationship marketing is less appropriate for relatively low-value consumer products and services or generic commodities, and is more likely to develop in a concentrated market structure with few suppliers (Harwood, Garry and Broderick, 2008).

The customer's perspective

Benefits

Confidence

The main benefit customers derive from relationship marketing is the feeling of confidence generated by trust in the provider. Relationship marketing allows providers to know more about customer's requirements and needs. Thus having a long-term, ongoing and stable relationship with a provider may reduce risk, uncertainty and discomfort in knowing what to expect in buyer-seller relations. As a result, special needs are accommodated and the expectation level is set to the extent that in some cases customers may even be aware of competitors who might provide the same or better service, but yet choose to stay in the relationship due to its predictability and comfort (Harwood, Garry and Broderick, 2008; Sandhusen, 2008).

Social benefits

In some long-term relationships the provider and its products or services may become part of the consumer's social support system (Sandhusen, 2008). For instance, a fan may interpret his or her relationship with the salesperson in the fan shop similar to friendship, or a member of a sports club may consider the other members to be his 'family'. An extreme example represents a dysfunctional fan who identifies so strongly with the sporting organisation, team or athlete that he dedicates his entire social life to it.

Economic benefits

From a customer's perspective, economic benefits contain monetary advantages like special price offers, discounts and cost savings as well as non-monetary advantages like time saving resulting from a long-time relationship with the organisation (Hennig-Thurau and Hansen, 2000). Members of a sports club, for example, may receive rebates for fan articles, or permanent season ticket holders may save money compared to those who purchase single tickets only.

Special treatment

Another relational advantage for customers is receiving individualised treatment including, for instance, being given a special deal or price, getting a special information policy (e.g. fan newsletter) etc. Permanent ticket holders own guaranteed pre-sales rights for ticketing, so that they do not need to worry about not getting tickets in times of high demand.

Interactive communication

Effective relationship marketing provides interactive communication with customers allowing them to tell the organisation what their special needs and wants are. Consequently, organisations can match their offerings according to the individual customers' wishes. For example, Nike uses a 'product and recommendation system' to help meet customer's needs. In this system prospective customers intending to buy Nike shoes answer questions about themselves and how they plan to use the shoes. The system then reveals which shoes are suitable for the customer so that the customer may go into a local store and directly ask for the desired shoes (Nwakanma, Singleton, Jackson and Burkhalter, 2007).

Case study 2.4 describes an unusual approach used in Germany by a sports club to involve fans called 'Dein Fussball Club' Fortuna Köln (in England, Ebbsfleet United used a similar approach).

CASE STUDY 2.4. The Direct Involvement of Fans – The Example of 'Dein Fussball Club' Fortuna Köln

Julia Lohrer

Special emotional benefits are created by communicating the 'we-sentiment', a feeling of belonging together, and the appreciation of the customer as an individual. In the sports sector, fan clubs and related programmes serve as examples.

In April 2008, the German amateur football club SC Fortuna Köln, which has a considerable history and tradition, has created a programme called 'Dein Fussball Club'. Under the patronage of the reputed film director, Sönke Wortman, the club offers fans the opportunity of owning a part of their favourite sports club. By becoming a member of the club the fan gets the chance to actively participate in managerial decisions conjointly with the club's chairman, Klaus Ulonska. Fans can decide upon the assortment of the seeded players, the signing of new players or the creation of a new sports club hymn. However, the premise is that 30,000 fans register as members and pay the membership fees. This innovative and integrated marketing strategy aims at creating social bonds between the fan and the sports club. If consumers are actually taking part in decisions concerning the future of the club, their level of commitment and loyalty is assumed to rise, and a solid base for a long-term relationship between consumer and sports club is being created.

Limitations

Intrusion into privacy

In many organisations the offering of special treatment benefits requires that the customer provides personal information (e.g. date of birth, buying habits) that he or she would not normally share with a provider. Many customers consider this to be an intrusion into their privacy and fear that their data will be used for other purposes or even passed on (Hennig-Thurau and Hansen, 2000).

Dependence

A close relationship with an organisation may be perceived as a limitation to the customer's desire for independence and freedom of choice. Customers are often bound for several months or years to membership contracts preventing them from discontinuing the relationship with the current organisation and thus reducing their option to switch to alternative providers. Some customers also worry about a company behaving coercively, by altering certain conditions e.g. increasing the price (Hennig-Thurau and Hansen, 2000).

Additional costs

Entering a long-term relationship and receiving its benefits is often associated with a membership which in turn requires the payment of a fee. Although a membership is supposed to compensate the costs by certain benefits of the organisation, the costs of·obtaining the benefits may sometimes outweigh their perceived value. For example, students who are members of a gym and have a one-year contract but will not use the gym during the summer vacation, still have to pay the membership fee during that time.

Different treatment of customers

Long-term relationships often lead to the fact that organisations give preferential treatment to their most profitable customers. This may arouse a discontent among other customers as they might feel hurt and consider that they are treated unfairly because the organisation does not regard them to be of the same value (Ramkumar and Saravanan, 2007).

CONCLUSIONS

Relationship marketing has been one of the key developments of modern marketing and has generated enormous interest both in theory and practise. The emphasis on relationships –as opposed to transaction-based exchanges-continues to redefine the marketing domain. Relationship marketing challenges organisations externally to support a shift to long-term relationships with a broad range of stakeholders, among which the customer is of central but not exclusive importance. Internally cross-functional change in management is required to implement the ideas of relationship marketing. In this chapter we explained the shift from transactional to relationship marketing, described the key variables for relationship success, introduced the main instruments of relationship marketing and analysed the benefits (as well as limitations) of this concept in general.

For sporting organisations it seems at a first glance that fans remain loyal to their favourite club anyway and therefore do not really need to be retained by relationship marketing. Would a football fan abandon his club only because ticket prices elsewhere are cheaper? Of course not. At a closer look even fan loyalty is not unlimited. Definitely fewer people would attend a football game if there was no customer service provided or if the ticket prices were too high. It is also less likely that a fan becomes a member of a sports club if he does not receive any extra information or get rewarded for his membership in any form. So even within the sports market the implementation of sophisticated marketing strategies is an absolute precondition for competing with the large variety of leisure time activity offers. No professional sporting organisation can do without a long-term orientation towards its customers and stakeholders in order to gain competitive advantage. Therefore sporting organisations, too, have identified the necessity of relationship marketing and are increasingly focusing on this approach. Relationship marketing in sports refers to the establishment and maintenance of positive, enduring and mutually beneficial relations between professional sporting organisations and their stakeholders.

DISCUSSION QUESTIONS

(1) How can the 'paradigm shift' from transactional to relationship marketing be explained?

(2) How would you characterise relationship marketing in general?

(3) Describe the 'six markets' model!

(4) Explain the ladder of loyalty!

(5) What are the main instruments of relationship marketing in sports?

(6) Which are the advantages of relationship marketing?

(7) Which limitations compromise the success of relationship marketing?

GUIDED READING

We would recommend two up-to-date books for further reading: The first one is from Harwood, Garry and Broderick and titled *Relationship Marketing. Perspectives, Dimensions and Contexts*. The authors provide the principles of relationship marketing both in theory (8 chapters) and practice (8 case studies). The second book comes from Christopher, Payne and Ballantyne and is titled *Relationship Marketing. Creating Stakeholder Value*. It approaches relationship marketing from different perspectives and also covers the management of relationships in networks.

WEBSITES

Adidas
http://www.adidas-group.com

Bayer 04 Leverkusen
http://www.bayer04.de

Ebbsfleet United
http://www.myfootballclub.co.uk

FC Bayern Munich
http://www.fcbayern.de

McFit
http://www.mcfit.de

Nike
http://www.nike.com

SC Fortuna Köln (Cologne)
http://www.deinfussballclub.de

VfB Stuttgart
http://www.vfb.de

Winter sport area Feldberg-Schwarzwald
http://www.liftverbund-feldberg.de

CHAPTER 3

Professional Sporting Organisations and their Relationships

Learning Outcomes

On completion of this chapter the reader should be able to:

- explain the characteristics of the sports business
- list the main market players of the sports business
- define professional sporting organisations
- name the main customers of professional sports entities
- illustrate the various relationships a sporting organisation is involved in

OVERVIEW OF CHAPTER

First, we will introduce the context in which professional sporting organisations operate – the business of sports. We will show that sports has become a serious business on the one hand. On the other hand we will explain why the sports business is unlike any other business. Consequently, we will deal with the sports product itself. We will then focus on the characteristics of the sports business and its main stakeholders, followed by a definition of what we think a professional sporting organisation is. Finally, we will look at the various customers of professional sports entities and the resulting relationships. Bayern Munich as one of Europe's top football clubs will serve as a real life example at the end of this chapter.

INTRODUCTION

Relationship marketing is aimed at customers as we have seen in the previous chapter. But who are the customers of professional sporting organisations? What types of relationships are they involved in? And what exactly do we mean by professional sporting organisations? This chapter is going to answer all these questions and will also take a look behind the scenes of the sports business.

THE BUSINESS OF SPORTS AND ITS UNIQUE CHARACTERISTICS

Sports is without any doubt a serious business nowadays. The US-American National Football League (NFL) generated more than 6 billion (that is six thousand million) US Dollars in 2008. The European football market (involving the top football leagues in England, Spain, Italy, Germany and France) is a business worth more than €13 billion. In addition, individual sportsmen/women such as golfer Tiger Woods or tennis player Serena Williams earn millions of dollars year after year.

Sports has established itself as a sound and independent business sector, often described as part of the entertainment industry. Indeed, certain similarities cannot be denied. People watch sports in order to be entertained. However, sports might be entertainment, but it also differs in the following aspects from other entertainment sectors or ordinary businesses.

The organisation of professional sports

Sporting organisations often operate in a cartellike competition. National competitions (such as the NBA, the English Premier League or the Australian National Rugby League) and international competitions (such as the UEFA Champions League in football or the EHF Cup in team handball) are organised in the form of leagues. The governing bodies of the leagues set the rules of the game and the competition in order to guarantee a certain level of **competitive balance**. Ehrke and Witte (2002) note, for example, that professional sports leagues are determined by agreements regarding the rules of the competition. They make the assertion that these agreements would bring the Monopolies and Merger Commission or some similar organisation on the scene in any other industry. Szymanski and Kuypers (1999, p. 248) support this view by stating that it would be deemed illegal if an industry body in any other business were to set the numbers of producers and allocate the resources between them. They claim, however, that the competition authorities have 'to recognize the unique nature of sports and allow leagues to carry out their functions as co-ordinators'.

The principle of associative competition

Sporting organisations compete on and off the pitch but need each other in order to produce the sporting competition. This phenomenon, where economic and sporting competitions are linked in exactly the opposite way, is known as 'associative competition' (Heinemann, 2001). Whereas companies in traditional industry sectors seek to gain a monopoly situation in order to determine the market, sporting organisations are concerned to retain some level of parity between them; otherwise sports as a product would be in danger of losing much of its appeal and value (Sloane, 1997; Szymanski and Kuypers, 1999; Greenfield and Osborn, 2001).

The attitude towards profits

The sports industry in general and some sporting organisations in particular, sometimes have an 'unhealthy' relationship to the principle of profitability. The overall aim of each and every company in ordinary business sectors is to make as much profit as possible. Football clubs, for example, were intended to act as sporting clubs in the first place and therefore have never been run as pure profit maximisers (Sir Norman Chester Centre for Football Research, 2002). Shilbury, Quick and Westerbeek (1998, p. 21) add that 'viability and winning games are important outcomes and become the primary measure of attractiveness for sporting organisations.' In addition, financial profits in sports depend heavily on sporting performance and the sporting performance, in turn, is not predictable.

The public perception

The public perception of some sports (i.e. main sports such as soccer, rugby, Formula 1) is extraordinary and beyond any comparison with other business sectors. Shilbury et al. (1998, p. 6) note that 'very few businesses in the world are viewed with such simplicity and such personal identification by the consumer.' But it's not only the personal involvement of consumers (as we will see in Chapter 4) but also the extensive media coverage of sports (as shown in Chapter 6). Morrow (1999), for example, claims that the extent and the type of coverage football receives would be greatly diminished if it were only an ordinary business. The problem of sports' extraordinary public perception occurs when people interfere in sporting organisations' decisions. Indeed, numerous decisions taken by a club are discussed in public (i.e. through the media or in pubs). This, in turn, makes it difficult for sporting organisations to decide independently and without pressure from outside.

All these aspects make the business of sports extraordinary. However, the main difference between the sports business and other business sectors is the sports product itself as explained in the following section.

THE SPORTS PRODUCT

If sport is a business and if every business needs something to sell, the question arises what exactly the product of the sports business is. This section will first explain the main characteristics of the sports product and then describe its peculiarities in comparison with products from other industry sectors.

Shank (1999, p. 16) defines a sports product as 'a good, a service, or any combination of the two that is designed to provide benefits to a sports spectator, participant, or sponsor.' Sports products as provided by sporting organisations can be divided into the core product and product extensions (Figure 3.1).

The **core product** is the initial game, the sporting event or competition, whereas **product extensions** are all goods or services which relate to the core product or are based on it. The core product combines all the characteristics of a service (intangibility, inseparability of production and consumption, heterogeneity, perishability), whereas the product extensions can be goods (e.g. merchandising) or services (e.g. hospitality; information provided on a club's website).

The core product can be differentiated between **participant sports** and **spectator sports**. The differentiation makes sense as both forms target

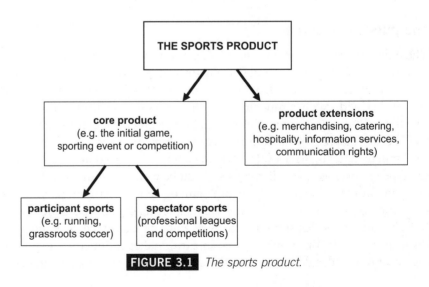

FIGURE 3.1 *The sports product.*

different consumer groups. Besides, the message differs. In case of participant sports, sporting organisations try to stimulate as many people as possible to become active in the specific sport. In the case of spectator sports, however, sporting organisations are trying to attract people to attend the event/game. Therefore, attendance at sporting events could be classified as a **people-based service** directed at people's minds following Lovelock's (1991) classification regarding the nature of the service act. The motives to actively engage in a sport or just passively watch it are very different and therefore sporting organisations need different techniques to promote their products (Nufer, 2002, 2007). Although the importance of participant sports increases in view of the fitness wave, spectator sports is the bigger part of the sports industry with billions of people watching sports events either live or on television. For example, the sixty-four games of the FIFA World Cup 2006 in Germany were watched by more than 3.5 million fans inside the stadiums and around twenty-six billion people on television.

Let us have a closer look at the game itself. The core sports product shows some unique characteristics which makes it different from products of other business sectors. As mentioned earlier, the core product (i.e. the match/competition) is a **joint product**. Teams (e.g. soccer teams, rugby teams, basketball teams) or individuals (e.g. boxer, tennis player) need each other to create the core sports product. For example, if there is just Manchester United, there will be no football game. If there is just Arsenal London, there will be no football game. But if Manchester United plays Arsenal London they create a joint product: the football game. In addition to this peculiarity, sports marketers have no control over the quality of the core product because every game and/or competition is highly spontaneous and unpredictable (Shilbury et al., 1998). The **uncertainty of outcome** is the lifeblood of every competition as one cannot be certain how the competition will end. But it is not only the final result which is unpredictable; it is also the game itself which cannot be planned. Shank (1999, p. 3) explains:

> 'One important way in which sport differs from common entertainment forms is that sport is spontaneous. A play has a script, and a concert has a program, but the action that entertains us in sport is spontaneous and uncontrolled by those who participate in the event. When we go to a comedic movie, we expect to laugh, and when we go to a horror movie we expect to be scared even before we pay our money. But the emotions we may feel when watching a sporting event are hard to determine. If it is a close contest and our team wins, we may feel excitement and joy. But if it is a boring event and our team loses, the entertainment benefit we receive is quite different. Because of its

spontaneous nature, sport producers face a host of challenges that are different than those faced by most entertainment providers.'

In summary, the business of sports is not only an extraordinary industry but also provides an extraordinary product. These unique characteristics have to be considered and appreciated when marketing the sports product. In addition, these unique features play a crucial role when it comes to relationship marketing in sports as the following chapters will show. But let us now focus on professional sporting organisations first. On the following pages we will explain the role sports entities play in the sports business, before we focus on the main customers of professional sporting organisations and the resulting relationships.

THE MAIN MARKET PLAYERS OF THE SPORTS BUSINESS

The sports business – as nearly every other business – has many different market players. Figure 3.2 illustrates the key market players of the sports business.

Some market players might be more important than others but it is difficult to tell which market player is the most important. Certainly, there would be no competition without any players or clubs. There would be no

- THE BUSINESS OF SPORTS -

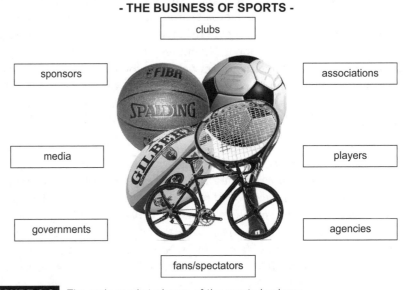

clubs

sponsors

associations

media

players

governments

agencies

fans/spectators

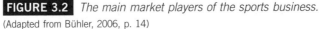

FIGURE 3.2   *The main market players of the sports business.*
(Adapted from Bühler, 2006, p. 14)

rules without the governing bodies, i.e. the associations. If there were no media, games and competitions would lack publicity. And if there was no public interest, companies would hardly sponsor sports entities. In fact, the various market players more or less depend on each other. Furthermore, they interrelate with each other. For example, **clubs**, **associations** and **players** are responsible for creating the core product which is then transferred by the **media**. **Sponsors** and **governments** both support sport (through sponsorship fees and subsidies) and both benefit from sports (through image improvements and tax income). **Agencies** may act as an intermediate between sporting organisations and media/sponsors when negotiating broadcasting rights or sponsorships on the one hand. On the other hand, agents and managers may advice players when it comes to contract negotiations. Thus, the business of sports is a net of relationships.

Despite the many different groups involved in the business of sports, the focus in this book is on professional sporting organisations, which we define as follows:

> *Professional sporting organisations* are clubs, associations or teams which are involved in spectator sports on a professional level.

We therefore look at the various relationships a professional sports club, association or team is involved in and how professional sporting organisations can apply the principles of relationship marketing to their various customers. The next section identifies the various customers of a professional sporting organisation and briefly explains the relationship between the sports entity and the respective customer.

PROFESSIONAL SPORTING ORGANISATIONS AND THEIR MAIN CUSTOMERS/STAKEHOLDERS

Some decades ago, many sports clubs and associations operated on a non-professional level with voluntary staff. In the early days, gate receipts were the only source of income. Nowadays, sporting organisations can be compared with medium-sized companies in terms of annual turnover and number of employees (as will be shown in the case study at the end of this chapter). Gate receipts are only one of many revenue sources of professional sporting organisations and one which becomes less important in comparison to the other revenue streams.

The biggest share of a sports entities' annual turnover normally comes from **television income** (see Chapter 6) and **sponsorship revenues** (see Chapter 5) these days. **Merchandising** and other commercial revenues (e.g. **hospitality** and **licensing**) is another important source of income, at least at the top level. Further money might come from shareholders or external investors. This is well illustrated in the case of some English football clubs which were taken over by foreign businessmen. For example, Chelsea FC was bought by the Russian oil tycoon Roman Abramovich in 2003, the American businessman Malcolm Glazer took control over Manchester United in 2005, and in 2007 the American businessmen Tom Hicks and George Gillett became the owners of Liverpool Football Club. Foreign billionaires are therefore an important source of income for professional sporting organisations.

Another revenue stream could be the fees paid by the members of the sports organisation. Clubs such as FC Barcelona or FC Bayern Munich have more than one hundred thousand members. In addition, some associations such as the German Football Association (DFB) count more members (6.5 million in 2009) than the national political parties. The money generated from the membership fees might therefore amount to a significant income stream for some sports entities.

Another important aspect which reflects the development of sports towards serious business is the quality of the people working in the business. The key decision makers of sporting organisations are mostly professionals who know their business. For example, Erwin Staudt, the latest president of the German Bundesliga club VfB Stuttgart, once was the Chief Executive Officer of IBM Germany. When he came to power, he soon applied various management techniques and instruments (e.g. the Balanced Scorecard) in order to run his football club more effectively. Indeed, the club became profitable again and eventually improved its image as a serious national brand. Some other teams (e.g. Manchester United, Real Madrid, the New York Yankees, or the Australian rugby national team All Blacks) have established themselves even as global brands with considerable fan bases all around the planet.

Not all sports entities are the same, of course. Thus, we should not make any generalisations. Professional sporting organisations differ not only in the sport involved but also in their size and importance. English football clubs are bigger and attract more people than a Swedish handball team, for example. However, it is also true that the basics are nearly the same for each and every sporting organisation. They have to deal with the unique characteristics of the business and the sports product as well as with the various market players. Therefore, it is just fair to conclude that all professional sports entities have the same type of stakeholders. Figure 3.3 therefore provides a general overview of the various stakeholders of a professional sporting organisation.

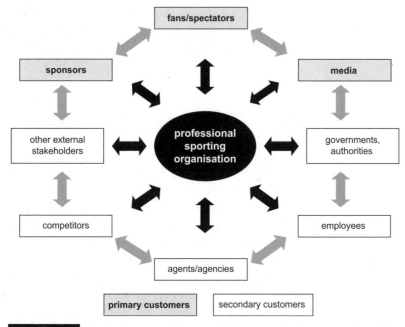

FIGURE 3.3 *Professional sporting organisations and their main stakeholders.*

A **customer** is generally defined as someone who purchases a product and/or a service. According to this simple definition we can identify three groups of **primary customers**: fans, sponsors and the media. All three groups pay the sporting organisation in order to get something in return. Fans purchase tickets, sponsors buy communication rights and television channels pay a lot of money for the broadcasting rights.

All other stakeholders usually do not pay the sporting organisations. Employees and suppliers, for example, even get paid. However, from a modern marketing point of view, companies have to treat their stakeholders like customers in order to engage in a positive relationship which benefits both parties. We therefore propose to view all internal and external stakeholders as **secondary customers** of professional sporting organisations.

In the following, we will briefly introduce the primary and secondary customers of a professional sporting organisation and explain the nature of their relationships. Case study 3.1 will then use Bayern Munich as an example to demonstrate the variety of stakeholders of a professional sporting organisation.

Fans/spectators

The whole sports business is based on people who are prepared to pay money for the various sports products. Fans, supporters and spectators are the main customers of professional sporting organisations and their relationship can be described as a customer-supplier relationship. Chapter 4 will explain the nature of fans as well as the relationship between supporters and sports entities in detail.

Sponsors

In the early days, local businessmen supported their favourite sports club for patronising reasons. Over the years, patronage became commercial sponsorship with companies realising that sports is a perfect communication tool. Nowadays, professional sports would not be possible without revenues generated from sponsorship. But not only have the sponsorship fees increased in the last few years, but also the number of sponsors of each and every sports entity. Clubs have multiple sponsors nowadays and therefore they have to deal with various relationships. Basically, the relationship between professional sporting organisations and their sponsors can be described as a business-to-business relationship, in view of the fact that both sponsor and sponsee are enterprises. Chapter 5 will focus on the relationship between sports entities and sponsors.

The media

The business-to-business relationship between professional sporting organisations and the media is a two-way-process because both need each other and both benefit from each other. Television channels, newspapers, radio stations, websites, publishers and all other types of media need content for their customers. And sports deliver not only games or competitions but also good stories. Sports entities, on the other hand, need publicity in order to develop their brand and make them more known. The relationship between sporting organisations and the media is an interesting one because there are a number of factors which can benefit as well as damage the relationship as Chapter 6 will explain in detail.

Competitors

Professional sporting organisations have a number of different competitors. First, there are the direct national competitors (clubs of the same national leagues) and direct international competitors (clubs competing in the same international competition). Then there are competitors of different national and international leagues within the same sport (e.g. clubs in lower leagues or other international competitions). Here, sporting organisations not only compete on the field but also off the field for sponsorship revenues, players and fans. Then there are competitors of different sports (e.g. cricket is competing with rugby for attention and and the customers' money). Last, but not least, sporting organisations compete with the entertainment industry (cinemas, theatres, television) as a whole. Here, the sports entity competes for people's time and money. For example, a customer might have the option to spend the evening watching a movie in the local cinema or attending a game of the local football club. However, competitors don't necessarily have to compete with each other, but could also seek collaboration. After all, the relationship between sporting organisations and their various competitors can be seen as a very special business-to-business relationship.

Agents/agencies

Some agencies have specialised on selling marketing rights on behalf of a particular sports entity. For example, Sportfive (a daughter company of the French media group Lagardère) markets individual rights for the Pan American Games, the Men's Handball Champions League, the Argentine Rugby Union, the World Rally Championship, the Rugby Six Nations Tournament, the Swedish ice hockey league and many more. Sportfive therefore engages in many different relationships with various sporting organisations. In order to make the relationship with agencies a successful one, sporting organisations have to apply relationship marketing techniques in this context as well.

Employees

As described earlier, a lot of sporting organisations can be viewed as medium-sized companies in terms of people working for the company full time. In this respect, Human Resource Management becomes more and more important. Furthermore, sporting organisations are increasingly looking for high-potentials on a top management level. In order to attract and subsequently keep professionals, sports entities have to seek a positive relationship with their employees.

Governments/authorities

Governments and communities have an interest in professional sports in view of the fact that major sport events (such as the Football World Cup or the Olympic Games) not only put the respective country or city in the global limelight, but also attract millions of tourists to visit the country and/or city. In addition, sports entities are huge tax payers and employers. On the other side, sporting organisations have to collaborate with national/local authorities (such as the police) in order to secure their home games. Furthermore, professional sporting organisations benefit from governments as well, in view of the fact that public money has been spent tremendously in order to subsidise the building or modernisation of sport venues. It is therefore essential for sporting organisations to establish and maintain a good relationship with the government and/or local authorities.

Other external stakeholders

Professional sporting organisations have a number of other external stakeholders, e.g. investors and shareholders. Some sport clubs (especially in British football) have gone public in order to attract more money. In the early days, the main shareholders of football clubs were fans who wished to call at least a small part of their favourite club their own. But as soon as commercialisation of sports began, professional investors realised that shares of sport clubs can be a profitable investment. Professional sporting organisations which are noted on the stock exchange, have to establish and maintain a positive relationship with their shareholders for the sake of their company.

Furthermore, a sporting organisation is involved in many relationships with various suppliers, such as companies supplying copy paper for the back office or a service provider taking care of the sports club's IT system. Here as well, a positive relationship approach is needed in view of the fact that a long and healthy relationship between buyer and supplier benefits both.

Besides suppliers and sponsors, sporting organisations maintain various relationships with other business associates, e.g. companies with which the sporting organisation collaborates on a non-sponsorship level such as producers of merchandising. Furthermore, retailers selling and distributing the sports entities' merchandising is another example of a business associate.

Finally, the hometown or the local community can be another important external stakeholder of a professional sport club. A lot of those are not-for-profit organisations (e.g. the local retirement home) which collaborate with the local sporting organisation. This relationship is determined more by social issues than by commercial ones.

PROFESSIONAL SPORTING ORGANISATIONS AND THEIR MAIN RELATIONSHIPS

As we have seen above, professional sporting organisations have to deal with different stakeholders. All these stakeholders have to be viewed as (primary and secondary) customers from a modern marketing perspective. Various types of customers lead to various types of relationships, in which a sports entity might be engaged. Figure 3.4 illustrates the different customers of

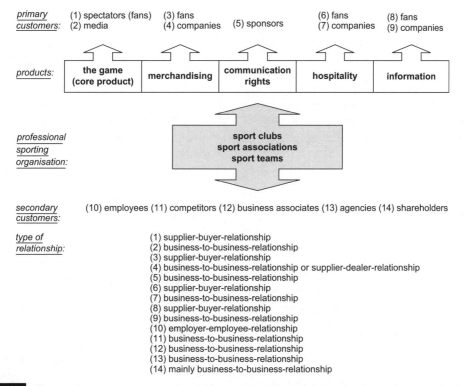

FIGURE 3.4 *The products, customers and resulting relationships of professional sporting organisations.*
Adapted from Bühler (2006, p. 16)

professional sporting organisations and the resulting relationships. Case study 3.1 then describes them in detail by using the example of Bayern Munich.

CASE STUDY 3.1. Professional Sporting Organisations and their Various Stakeholders – The Example of Bayern Munich

Bayern Munich is the showpiece of German football. It is not only the most famous football club in Germany but also the most successful one with more than fifty national and international titles. And it is one of the most professionally run sporting organisations in Europe. Bayern Munich is therefore predestined to serve as a case study in order to show the variety of stakeholders a professional sporting organisation has.

The different stakeholders of FC Bayern Munich:

Competitors

Bayern Munich has to compete with all 17 clubs of the German Bundesliga on a national level. Furthermore, 35 other professional football clubs are competing for German football fans' attention. On an international level 31 other

Continued

clubs are trying to win the UEFA Champions League, let alone the 80 clubs playing in the UEFA-Cup. In addition, other sports teams (e.g. handball, basketball, ice hockey clubs) are trying to get a piece of the cake. Finally, the entertainment industry (e.g. cinemas, theatres and other leisure activities) in and around Munich and the television programme across Germany is competing for people's time and money.

Sponsors

Bayern Munich has a number of different sponsors. The main sponsor is Deutsche Telekom, the largest German tele-communication company, which pays up to 20 million Euros each season. In addition, Adidas serves as the kit supplier for more than four decades. Furthermore, a number of other companies pay significant fees in order to be associated with Bayern Munich. For example, 15 companies have obtained the status of a 'Premium Partner' and seven companies are allowed to call themselves 'Classic Partner' of FC Bayern Munich.

Fans

Bayern Munich has developed a huge fan base over the years. In 2009, the club has registered nearly 2500 official fan clubs with nearly 177,000 members from all over the world.

Members

The club is a registered society which means that it is indi-rectly run by the club's members who elect the club's board. FC Bayern has currently more than a hundred thousands members which makes them the second largest club world-wide (after FC Barcelona) in number of members.

Shareholders

In order to become more competitive and to implement modern structures, the football division of the club was transformed into an incorporated company. Ninety percent of the shares remained in possession of the club itself. Ten percent were sold to Adidas which paid around 77 million Euros for their 10% stake. Although it seems very unlikely that Bayern Munich goes public, the club has the option to sell more shares to other strategic partners.

Media

Bayern Munich has to deal with various media on different levels such as the main local newspapers (e.g. the local paper Abendzeitung) as well as a large number of radio stations in and around Munich. Furthermore, national media such as the public free-to-air TV stations ARD and ZDF, the privately owned TV stations SAT1, RTL or ProSieben, sports channels such as the Deutsches Sport Fernsehen, the pay-TV-channel Premiere, national newspapers (e.g. Süddeutsche, Frankfurter Allgemeine Zeitung) as well as a number of German tabloids (e.g. BILD-Zeitung) are covering Bayern Munich from different angles. Finally, international media is interested in Bayern Munich as well, especially when it comes to European club competition. All theses different types of media have to be satisfied and therefore Bayern Munich has to establish and maintain good relationships with the media.

Authorities

Bayern Munich deals with different types of authorities. In the context of football, the club has to maintain relationships to governing bodies such as the German Football Associa-tion (DFB), the European Football Association (UEFA) and the world governing body of football (FIFA). In a general context, collaboration has to take place with official authori-ties such as the government (e.g. the tax office) or local authorities (the City of Munich and the police).

Local community

Although Bayern Munich is an international brand nowa-days, it does not forget its local community. The club there-fore collaborates with different local and regional football clubs in order to improve the skills of young players in and around Munich. Furthermore, Bayern engages in charity matches therefore contributing to local projects and events.

Employees

In 2009, Bayern Munich employed around 200 people full time, including players, coaching staff and managing staff. The number of staff and the variety of employees is a challenge for the Human Resource Department at Bayern Munich as they have to ensure good and efficient working relationships with their staff.

Agents/agencies

Bayern Munich has to deal with different agents and agencies on different levels. Some agents/agencies represent signed or potential players, some others (e.g. advertising agencies, sports properties agencies) act as an intermediate between the club and other stakeholders (e.g. sponsors, media).

Other external stakeholders

Despite the different stakeholders mentioned above, Bayern Munich has to deal with other interest groups (e.g. suppliers) as well in order to keep the business running.

As the case of Bayern Munich shows, professional sporting organisations have to deal with various stakeholders and interest groups, implying a multitude of different relationships. Understanding the significance of relationships and how to make use of them is a competitive advantage which becomes more and more important in today's business of sports.

CONCLUSIONS

The development of the sports business towards an independent and very serious business, in terms of income, number of employees as well as people and companies depending on each other is a fascinating one. Although sports nowadays incorporates many issues of a serious business, it also provides some very unique features which makes it the most extraordinary business in the world, as we have seen on the previous pages. Business and marketing people have to take these specific characteristics into consideration when dealing with sports. The business of sports generally incorporates various different market players who are all interrelated with each other. All links between the various market players begin with and end at the sports entity. It is therefore at the centre of the sports business. Consequently, professional sporting organisations have to serve various stakeholders and therefore have to deal with many different relationships. Thus, sports clubs, associations and teams need to apply the principles of relationship marketing in order to make and keep their primary and secondary customers happy.

DISCUSSION QUESTIONS

(1) Why can the sports business be seen as extraordinary?
(2) How would you describe the sports product?
(3) Who are the main stakeholders of the sports business?
(4) How do these stakeholders interrelate with each other?
(5) Who are the main customers of professional sporting organisations?

(6) Why is it appropriate to view stakeholders such as employees or suppliers as customers?

(7) How would you describe the relationships between sports entities and their customers?

GUIDED READING

We would recommend two books for further reading:

The first one comes from Beech and Chadwick and is titled *The Business of Sport Management*. The authors provide the basic management theories as well as real-life examples within the functional areas of sports management (e.g. human resource management, finance and marketing). Furthermore, contemporary issues such as risk management, sponsorship and the media are presented.

The second book comes from Parks, Quarterman and Thiebault and is titled *Contemporary Sport Management*. The book offers a global perspective, current research and developments in the field, and personalised contributions from more than thirty stellar scholars and professionals in sports management.

WEBSITES

Australian National Rugby League
http://www.nrl.com.au/

Chelsea FC
http://www.chelseafc.com

FC Barcelona
http://www.fcbarcelona.com

FC Bayern Munich
http://www.fcbayern.de

Liverpool FC
http://www.liverpoolfc.tv/

Manchester United
http://www.manutd.com

National Basketball Association (NBA)
http://www.nba.com/

Real Madrid
http://www.realmadrid.es

The English Football Association
http://www.thefa.com

The English Premier League
http://www.premierleague.com

The Sports Business Group at Deloitte
http://www.deloitte.com

Sportfive
www.sportfive.com

The All Blacks
http://www.allblacks.com/

The New York Yankees
http://newyork.yankees.mlb.com

VfB Stuttgart
http://www.vfb.de/

CHAPTER 4

Relationship Marketing in Sports – The Fan Perspective

Learning Outcomes

On completion of this chapter the reader should be able to:

- describe the nature of supporters
- explain why fans are so important for professional sporting organisations
- provide examples of special offers to fans
- discuss the various opportunities for sporting organisations to obtain information about their fans
- describe how sporting organisations can react to fans' complaints
- illustrate how sports entities can build good relationships with their fans

OVERVIEW OF CHAPTER

This chapter starts off with a brief section on the importance of fans for professional sporting organisations, followed by a detailed description of the nature of sports fans. Then the relationship between sports entities and their fans will be analysed and specific examples of relationship marketing instruments provided. The chapter includes various case studies, involving the English Football Association as well as clubs from the NHL, the NBA and different football leagues around the world.

INTRODUCTION

Imagine the business of sports without fans. No spectators at sports matches, no buyers of merchandising, no potential customers for sponsoring companies, no recipients for the sports media. Such a scenario would be unthinkable. The sports business in general (and professional sporting organisations in particular) need fans who are willing to spend their time, their emotions and their money for their favourite sports team. Supporters are the primary – and arguably most important – customers of a sports entity. Therefore, it is essential for every professional sporting organisation to establish and maintain a healthy relationship with their fans. This chapter focuses on the relationship between sports entities and their supporters and explains how professional sporting organisations can apply the principles of relationship marketing with regard to fans.

THE IMPORTANCE OF FANS FOR PROFESSIONAL SPORTING ORGANISATIONS

As mentioned in Chapter 3, the whole sports business depends on fans. Companies engage in sports sponsorship because they want to reach their target group (i.e. the fans) through their association with the respective sporting organisation. Furthermore, fans buy newspapers and sports magazines, they watch sports programmes and buy all manner of merchandising. Therefore, fans can be seen as the lifeblood of the sports business and the most important customer group for sporting organisations. Sports entities need fans in order to generate money and keep their business running because a sports club without a considerable fan base is not very attractive for sponsors and the media. That's why professional sporting organisations should have the greatest interest to maintain old fans as well as win new ones in order to grow their fan base. Relationship marketing offers a variety of techniques and instruments to successfully achieve this rather difficult task. In order to understand the relationship between sporting organisations and their fans we first have to understand the fans themselves. The next section will therefore describe the nature of fans in more detail.

THE NATURE OF FANS

The term 'the fan' is rather misleading because opinions differ widely when it comes to defining 'a fan'. For example, the Collins English Dictionary defines a fan as 'an ardent admirer of a sports team'. The Cambridge International Dictionary of English, however, notes that a fan is 'a person who has a great interest in and admiration for a sports team'. For the Sir Norman Chester

Centre for Football Research (2003) a fan is simply anybody who follows a club. Lenhard (2002, p. 38) in his work discusses the most relevant definitions and develops a more sophisticated one:

> '*A fan or supporter respectively is a human being who identifies with a particular sports club on a cognitive, affective and behaviour-specific level.*'

He adds that neither an empirical system of measure nor an identifiable threshold value between 'fan' and 'not-fan' exists because each and every sports supporter shows different levels of identification.

In the context of business and marketing, it is important to note that 'typical' sports supporters differ in numerous ways from ordinary consumers of ordinary companies. First, they are usually more passionate about their favourite sports club than consumers are about their preferred brand. Have you ever seen someone in a supermarket adoring and celebrating a pack of cornflakes? Second, fans show a high level of loyalty to their sports team. Whereas some people might switch from one car brand to another, sports fans stick to their favourite team forever. Dempsey and Reilly (1998) explain this loyalty with the fact that supporters find something in sports that they cannot find anywhere else, e.g. the escape from the ordinary workaday world, the adrenalin rush and thrill of a match or the feeling of being part of a community. Therefore, fans pledge allegiance to their clubs. Hornby (1996, p. 35), in his bestseller *Fever Pitch*, illustrates fan loyalty from a football supporter's point of view:

> '*I had discovered after the Swindon game that loyalty, at least in football terms, was not a moral choice like bravery or kindness; it was more like a wart or a hump, something you were stuck with. Marriages are nowhere near as rigid – you won't catch any Arsenal fans slipping off to Tottenham for a bit of extra-marital slap and tickle; and though divorce is a possibility (you can just stop going if things get too bad), getting hitched again is out of the question. There have been many times over the last 23 years when I have pored over the small print of my contract looking for a way out, but there isn't one.*'

Passion and **loyalty** leads to the third difference: **irrationality**. Sports fans are often irrational in their consumer behaviour. Purchase decisions are seldom taken on commercial grounds, or as Cashmore (2003, p.23) puts it: 'Part of being a fan involves buying all manner of products related to the object of adulation' regardless of price or quality. A related consequence of loyalty is the fact that supporters don't have a real choice when it comes to purchase decisions. While ordinary consumers may have their preferences, they normally have a choice between several products. Sports fans, however, would rarely change to another club only because the ticket price of the competitor is more reasonable.

Apart from that, football supporters are just as important when it comes to the product itself. Morrow (1999) notes the important role of the fans in creating the product which they actually consume. The atmosphere is a crucial part of the attractiveness of the game and is created by the supporters. In this respect the fans can be seen as co-producers of an event they pay for in order to attend.

Another approach to describe the personality of sports fans comes from social psychologists. Elements of the social identity theory have been used in order to analyse the behaviour of dedicated supporters. Posten (1998) explains the concept of **BIRG-ing** and **CORF-ing** in a vivid way.

BACKGROUND INFORMATION 4.1. Basking in Glory and Cutting off Failure

Marritt Posten

Why is it that the day after a 'big win' everyone pulls out their old sweatshirts and tee shirts, that haven't been worn since the team last won a game two years ago, and proudly displays their school colours or team logos? Or right after a team wins a championship the sales of their products sky rocket until another team wins the next year? This phenomenon has been labeled by social psychologists as BIRGing and CORFing. BIRGing is an arconym for Basking in Reflected Glory and CORFing means Cutting Off Reflected Failure.

The concept of BIRGing is rooted in the social identity theory which explains how one's self esteem and evaluation can be enhanced by the identification with another person's success. One of the keys to BIRGing is that the person trying to receive this glory has done nothing tangible to bring the team's success (Hirt and Zillmann, 1992). They are truly basking in reflected glory not earned. When a person's public image is threatened the tendency to BIRG is even stronger, and BIRGing becomes an important impression management technique to counter any threats to self-esteem (Lee, 1985).

The different levels of commitment that a fan might have towards a team dictate the degree to which he or she can distance him or herself from that team when failure occurs. If a fan is strongly allied, the social identity theory states that it will be hard for them to distance themselves, and therefore, to not threaten their self-esteem, the fans must attribute the loss to external cues of the situation but not the team itself. If a person is not so closely linked they then engage in the phenomena of CORFing, which means cutting off reflected failure, done by distancing themselves as far as possible from the losing team (Cialdini and Richardson, 1980). These fans want to avoid any negative evaluations by others in relation to the team that was unsuccessful. The closer the identification to the team and the degree of commitment by the fan, the greater the risk the fan has of suffering a loss in self-esteem if their team has lost.

Fans CORF in a variety of different ways. For example one might change the language they use to describe the game after a defeat or after a win. For example a Knicks basketball fan might not even know the psychological defenses he or she is using when they say, 'We won' when the Knicks won and 'They lost' or 'the Knicks lost' when the team suffered a defeat.

Fans might also distance themselves from the team by not wearing any team-affiliated clothing after a loss and not supporting the team until they win again. But as soon as the team is victorious, the individual will waste no time in associating with the team once again (Hirt and Zillmann, 1992).

(*Source: Posten, M. (1998) obtained from http://www.units.muohio. edu/psybersite/fans/bc.shtml*)

The differences mentioned above are one of the main reasons why the relationship between sports clubs and their supporters cannot be adequately captured in purely economic terms. Morrow (1999) claims that the customer concept is incomplete because it fails to consider the idea of a **fan's identity** with a club. Support for this interpretation comes from Lenhard (2002, p. 19), who states that 'identity and identification are significant themes' in professional sports.

The whole issue of fan loyalty, irrational consumer behaviour, passion, identity and identification lead economic analysts and professional investors to the conclusion that sports fans are **'captive consumers'** within a **'captive market'** (Pierpoint, 2000; Conn, 2001; Banks, 2002). A captive market is defined in general marketing literature as a group of consumers who have limited choice in terms of the products they can select/purchase or no other alternative but to buy a product from a specific source respectively.

However, some authors suggest that the relationship between clubs and supporters is changing and that the new generation of fans will not be as passionate and loyal as the traditional supporters (Morrow, 1999). Grünitz and von Arndt (2002) speak about a trend towards the alienation of fans and players. Lenhard (2002) supports this view by discussing the relationship between fans, players and clubs through the ages. He concludes, for example, that the sports stars of today are becoming remote from the game's supporters with regard to daily routine and future perspective on life. He identifies an increasing distance between clubs, players and fans which is leading to a decrease in identification. Dempsey and Reilly (1999) blame the commercial exploitation of supporters by clubs for the fact that more and more traditional fans have been priced out over the years, especially in professional football. Indeed, the social structure of game-attending supporters has changed. Middle-income fans are being attracted to the game and low-income fans are being driven away. Malcolm et al. (2000) mention the shift from the **'traditional fan'** to the **'affluent customer'** in this context. One of the reasons for this shift, particularly in professional football, is the transformation of traditional stadiums with standing-only stands into all-seater stadiums or multifunctional arenas with shopping centres and amusement parks which attract more and more non-traditional supporters (e.g. families). On the other hand traditional supporters are dwindling away because they cannot afford the increased ticket prices anymore (Conn, 1999; Morrow, 1999; Greenfield and Osborn, 2001). The change in supporter is reflected also in the fact that the geographical bond between English football clubs and their supporters was much stronger in the early years than it became later, according to Dobson and Goddard (2001). Their argument is supported by the example of the 54 million people who proudly call themselves fans of Manchester United of whom the majority never has been to a single game.

It is important not to overlook the fact that the people who follow a club nowadays are not necessarily the loyal, irrational and passionate supporters mentioned above. Greenfield and Osborn (2001) have observed the development of a new generation of **sedentary armchair fans** resulting from the new sports broadcasting coverage. These fans have a different relationship to the clubs in comparison to those who attend live games. Hermanns and Riedmüller (2008) also distinguish between the television audience and spectators in the stadium in the first place. Lenhard (2002) examines the latter group in greater detail and identifies the spectators in the stadium as a heterogeneous group. He then presents various classifications of the overall term 'fan' and finally ranks the interpretation scheme of Heitmeyer and Peter (1988) as the most common one. Figure 4.1 illustrates the classification of sports supporters.

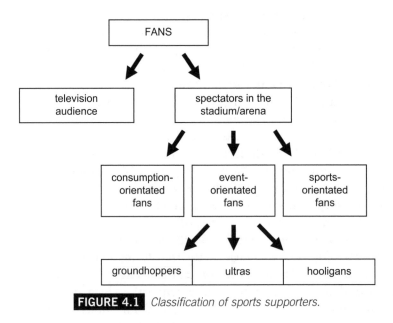

FIGURE 4.1 *Classification of sports supporters.*

People who attend live games can be divided into three main categories: Firstly the **consumption-orientated fan** who wants to have a certain level of entertainment value for his money. In this case, the emotional bond to the club is not very well-developed and sports games are more or less an exchangeable leisure activity. The exact opposite is the **sports-oriented fan** who shows the same characteristics as the irrational, loyal and passionate traditional supporter mentioned earlier. The third category is the **event-orientated fan** who seeks to have fun in and around the stadium regardless of the match itself, i.e. Hooligans, Ultras or Groundhoppers. Ultras are specific fan movements who have their origins in Italy. Ultras consider themselves as being responsible for the atmosphere in the stadiums and therefore organise extensive choreographies or flags for example. Groundhoppers, however, are truly football fans who make it their business to visit as many football games and stadiums as possible whether their own club is involved or not. Lenhard (2002) notes that the line cannot be drawn clearly as the example of Ultras and Groundhoppers shows. Both groups are indeed sports-orientated but want to experience more than a pure sporting competition.

In the end, it has to be summarized that a lot of sports fans show a loyal and passionate attitude towards their clubs and therefore tend to make less rational purchase decisions than consumers of other products and services. Furthermore, the heterogeneity of sports fans means that professional sporting organisations have to deal with different kinds of consumers and therefore different relationships. How sporting organisations might define and address the different groups of fans will be discussed later in this chapter. First we will have a closer look at the relationship between sports entities and their fans.

THE RELATIONSHIP BETWEEN SPORTING ORGANISATIONS AND THEIR FANS

The association between professional sporting organisations and their fans can be described as a two-way relationship. Alan Edge (1998, p. 18), in his bestseller *Faith of our Fathers*, describes the fans' perspective as follows:

> '*Being a fan goes far beyond the bounds of simply regular or even spasmodic match attendance; fandom is not just limited to literally following your team. There are evidently deeper bonds at work; stronger unseen ties, linking fan to club and club, in turn, to the local community.*'

Fans need their clubs as an integral part of their lives; and sports entities need their fans in order to survive – both in financial terms and as organisations. It is difficult to characterise the relationship between sporting organisations and their fans in view of the different levels of **emotional attachment**. Sometimes the relationship is one of love and hate. Fans love their team when it gets promoted and they hate it if it gets relegated. Sport stars and teams can be heroes one day and losers on the other. In sports, there is often only black or white because not all supporters have the intellectual ability (or the emotional distance) to differentiate. Therefore, the relationship quality between sporting organisations and their fans often depends on the performance on the pitch. If a team is doing well, the relationship is likely to be a good one. If the team is not doing so well the relationship is likely to suffer. There are various examples (especially in Italian football) where fans have abused and attacked players of their teams because of poor performance on the pitch. Nearly every sports club has some troublemakers in their fan base. Sporting organisations are well-advised not to ignore these troublemakers, but to address them appropriately. Case study 4.1 uses the example of a German football club in order to describe how to deal with a problematic fan base.

CASE STUDY 4.1. Dealing with Troublemakers – The Example of Hertha BSC Berlin

Hertha BSC Berlin, a German Bundesliga club, is a good example of how to deal with fans in order to prevent trouble and solve potential conflicts. The club has a long history in terms of fans with a bad reputation. In order to organise the fan base more effectively and to deal with supporters' problems, Hertha appointed three full-time employees to look after their fans. Organised supporter clubs who wish to be granted official recognition have to sign a contract where they commit themselves to behave in a positive manner. In turn, they are awarded with the status 'OFC' (Official Fan Club of Hertha BSC Berlin) and receive some benefits such as ticket discounts. The club organises regulars' tables with their OFCs where players of the first team appear on a regular basis. Furthermore, special events and actions of OFCs are subsidised by the club. To date, more than 350 supporters clubs of Berlin have been granted the status of an OFC.

However, it has to be noted that the majority of sports fans seek a positive relationship with their favourite club. The next section shows what a professional sporting organisation can do in order to establish and maintain a healthy relationship with their fans.

ESTABLISHING AND MAINTAINING HEALTHY RELATIONSHIPS WITH FANS

Although most sports fans are very committed to their favourite team, more and more sports entities find it difficult to establish a good and longstanding relationship with their supporters, let alone attracting new ones. Good relationships don't come for free, they normally require a lot of work and investments. The process towards healthy and valuable relationships is not an easy one, especially not for sporting organisations with few resources, but there really is no alternative in today's business of sports. The process itself consists of many different steps and involves various important tasks. Sporting organisations need to know who their customers are, where they can find them and how they can address them. Consumer research is therefore an inevitable prerequisite for relationship marketing. Once the relevant data has been obtained sports entities are able to define their target groups and build relevant customer groups. Based on segmentation sporting organisations are able to design special offers to each group and offer extraordinary services to their fans. Another important step in the process of establishing longstanding relationships with supporters is to involve them by the use of different relationship marketing instruments. The aim is, of course, to satisfy the needs of the fans. However, there will always be some unsatisfied customers who will complain. It is important to take these complaints seriously and to offer a satisfactory complaint management system. The last step of the implementation process of a systematic relationship management programme is the evaluation and control of each element. The various steps towards healthy and longstanding relationships with fans will be described in detail on the following pages.

Consumer research: understanding the fans

Understanding the fans is key in relationship marketing. But what sports entities assume is right for fans might not always be what the fans feel is right for them. In order to overcome this knowledge gap, sporting organisations need to obtain information and relevant data about their fan base. They might appoint a market research company to examine their target groups or they carry out an analysis of their fan base on their own as the example of Manchester United shows (Case study 4.2).

CASE STUDY 4.2. The Manchester United Fan Satisfaction Survey

The English Premier League club Manchester United carries out fan satisfaction surveys on a regular basis. According to the *Fan Satisfaction Survey 2004 Feedback Report*, Manchester United sees 'the survey as an important communication channel for fans to express their views about all aspects of the matchday experience'. Based on the survey results, Manchester United was able to identify so-called 'satisfaction gaps' such as the waiting time at concourse catering. Then the club consequently took appropriate action and speeded up the service in the concourse kiosks by introducing new kiosk directional signage and a queue management policy.

Surveys like the one mentioned above deliver important data on fans' attitudes and their consumption behaviour. Another source of valuable information is direct feedback from fans. Some sports entities have already realised that the opinion of a fan is an important piece of information. The example of two NBA clubs shows how sports entities can ask fans for their opinions (Case study 4.3).

CASE STUDY 4.3. Professional Sporting Organisations Asking for Fans' Feedback – Two Examples from the NBA

Example 1: The Atlanta Hawks

Fan Mail

Hey Hawks fans...we would like to hear from you, so give us a shout! Whether it is about the course of the season, or a question for one of the players, coaches and/or members of the front office staff, we welcome your thoughts.

Ask The Owners

Fans can contact the Hawks owners directly by emailing them. The owners want to hear directly from you the fans on how they can make the entire Hawks experience – from the product on the court, to watching a game at Philips Arena – even more exciting. Got a question for them? A comment? A suggestion? Let them know by emailing them directly!

Fan Feedback

The Atlanta Hawks' service goals are to exceed fan expectations and enhance fan experience by providing a consistent level of impressive service.

We value the views and opinions of our fans about their service experiences. Whether you attend a game at Philips Arena, visit one of our community-based programs or directly communicate with any of our Hawks staff, we want to hear your feedback on the experience.

What are we doing well? Where can we improve? What did you most enjoy? What more would you like to see?

Share your opinions with us in one of two ways. Call 1-866-715-1500, press option 1, or email hawks. service@atlantaspirit.com. We will always respond to your emails and calls.

Thank you,
Atlanta Hawks

Example 2: The Chicago Bulls

BULLS 6th MAN

Hey Bulls fans!

We would love to hear your ideas and we welcome your thoughts, comments or suggestions. Fill out the fields below and tell us what's on your mind. This is your chance to let us know what you think, so be as creative or as practical as you'd like!

You are our Sixth Man – we care about you and we want to hear from you. If there is a way that allows us to make your experience as a Bulls fan better, this is your opportunity to share just that.

Thank you for your support!
The Chicago Bulls

Please note: Due to the amount of emails we receive, we cannot reply to all messages, but they will all be read by a member of our staff. We cannot guarantee a response, but we appreciate your interest and support.

Apart from satisfaction surveys and direct feedback, a variety of market and consumer research instruments can be used in order to obtain data on the fan base. The most common research methods used in this context are quantitative surveys and qualitative focus groups. Once enough data has been collected, sporting organisations are able to build relevant consumer groups.

Segmentation: building relevant consumer groups

An emerging problem for sports entities is the heterogeneity of their fan base. In the early days, the vast majority of sports supporters were men aged between 18 and 50 years. Nowadays, an increasing number of women support sports clubs and more and more families can be seen in sports venues attending live matches. Furthermore, sports spectators differ not only in terms of gender and age, but also in terms of income, social class and appearance. People in business suits watch the game as well as people in replica shirts on the standing terraces. People supporting a club inside and outside the stadium are a hodgepodge of people with different needs and intentions. The heterogeneity of their supporter base makes it so difficult for professional sporting organisations to fulfil the various needs of their fans. Since it is virtually impossible to cater for every supporter's individual characteristics, professional sporting organisations are well-advised to group fans in segments by variables they have in common. These common characteristics allow for the development of a specific relationship marketing approach for all fans in a segment. All in all, fan segmentation is the basis for fan orientation and relationship marketing aiming at fans. Based on the fan segments, the sports entity is able to develop specific marketing strategies for each fan segment. Plus, the communication strategy can be adapted according to the characteristics of each segment. The basic rule in general marketing – and one that applies for relationship marketing in sports as well – is to focus on a limited number of important variables. Possible variables that could be used for segmentation are geographic, demographic, psychographic, and behavioural variables.

Geographic variables

The key question in this respect is 'where does the fan come from?' and 'where does he or she live?' Sporting organisations could segment their fans by region, countries or even continents. This segmentation criterion is a useful one because it enables the sports entity to create different marketing strategies for each geographical segment. Supporters from other countries or continents might never have been to a game of the particular club, but could be made happy by receiving exclusive information or by the opportunity to watch highlights of the games on the club's website. Furthermore, if a club identifies a considerable fan base in a foreign country it could arrange friendly matches there in order to present the team to their foreign supporters. However, domestic supporters and fans living closer to the location of the respective club might be more receptive for special ticket offers. For example, clubs could contact fans living in the surroundings of the sporting venue and inform them that there are still some tickets available for games on short notice.

Demographic variables

Clubs could segment their fans by age, gender, income or level of education. Here again, different marketing strategies are needed for different segments. If clubs segment their supporter base by age, they are able to provide special discounts for very young or very old people, for example. Segmentation by income can lead to different ticket or merchandise offers. For example, more affluent supporters might be offered very good – and expensive – seats as well as hospitality programs, whereas low-income fans might be offered seats on the standing terraces or even payment by instalment when purchasing a season ticket.

Segmentation by gender makes sense in view of the empirical fact that male and female spectators have different attendance motives as a recent study by Hall and O'Mahony (2006) shows.

EMPIRICAL DATA 4.1. Gender Differences in Sports Attendance Motives

Hall and O'Mahony (2006) found out that the factors that influence male and female attendance are different. The results of their study, carried out in an Australian sports context, indicate that emotional arousal at the sporting event and being a 'true fan' was significantly more important for males, whereas factors such as back room issues (e.g. parking, seating and stadium accessibility), front room issues (e.g. enjoyment and experiential aspects of a sports event) and social factors (e.g. sharing the event with friends and family) were significantly more important for females. Consequently, female attendance can be influenced through management and promotional strategies. Clubs could enhance the social dimensions of the experience by offering group incentives and 'friends and family' type packages, for example.

The level of education can be another important segmentation criterion because it correlates with the type of media one is using. Readers of *The Independent* or *The Times* are more intellectual than those reading tabloids only. What does that have to do with sports? Well, sporting organisations need to target their fans just as any other company. Therefore, it is important to know which channels/media a sports entity has to use in order to address and reach their target group. If a golf club, for example, places adverts or stories in tabloids it might be a waste of money. On the other hand, if it uses more intellectual newspapers or magazines, it might attract the attention of golf players.

Psychographic variables

The social status, the type of lifestyle, and the type of personality can be additional segmentation criteria. Social status and the type of lifestyle strongly correlate with income of course and therefore the above examples apply to psychographic variables as well. The type of personality can be important when it comes to the sporting event itself. Some people want to experience as much as possible at a sporting venue and therefore expect a great show before and after the actual game. Other fans want to watch the match only and do not care about a light show or loud music during sporting competitions.

Behavioural variables

The level of loyalty and commitment as a behavioural variable can be an important segmentation criterion. A sporting organisation needs to know how committed and loyal their supporters are in order to communicate with them effectively and apply marketing techniques appropriately. Fans, who are not very loyal or committed need to be motivated every once in a while to attend games or buy merchandise. Therefore, clubs and associations need to think about external motivators (e.g. a discount on tickets or merchandise) and triggers (e.g. posters advertising the next home games). Very loyal fans, on the other hand, attend games and buy merchandise because of internal motives and triggers. However, it might be sensible to award dedicated fans for their loyalty and commitment. A very effective move into the right direction is the introduction of a fan loyalty card as shown later in this chapter.

Serving different fan segments and offering the extraordinary

Once relevant segments have been identified, sporting organisations need to put their thinking caps on and design special offers for each customer group. Case study 4.4 provides some real-life examples.

CASE STUDY 4.4. Serving Different Fan Segments – Examples from the German Sports Business

The following examples illustrate the variety of offers made by professional sporting organisations in Germany to different fans before, during and after the game:

- *Hertha BSC Berlin* offers unemployed and socially disadvantaged fans the opportunity to attend live games. Against production of warrants they get discounted tickets for some low-profile games during the season.

Continued

- *Borussia Dortmund*, another club of the German Bundesliga, offers a special section on their standing terrace for kids aged 11–16 for a discounted price. In this section, the number of fans is limited in order to avoid tight squeezes. In addition, young fans are invited to play games with their friends before and after the actual match.

- The *Deutsche Bank Skyliners*, a team of the professional basketball league BBL in Germany, offers a special service for young parents during home games. A kindergarten placed within the arena takes care of children. Parents therefore don't have to find a babysitter and can watch the game calmly.

- The *Bayer Giants Leverkusen*, another BBL club, have implemented a hostesses' service for their home games. Fans will be greeted at the front door and – if necessary – accompanied to the seat. After the game,

the hostesses say goodbye and give away free sweeties.

- The German Bundesliga club *Hannover 96* offers a father–son ticket for their home games, which implies a discount for parents (fathers/mothers) attending games with their children (sons/daughters).

- *VfB Stuttgart* offers special merchandise for girls only. Female supporters can chose between 49 different articles of merchandise, such as fashion accessories (e.g. bracelets, necklaces) as well as hats, t-shirts and scarves which are held in pink instead of the usual red (the regular club colour).

- *Hertha BSC Berlin* also targets its female supporters differently with a particular website dedicated solely to female Hertha fans (Figure 4.2). The website provides private information about players, explains football rules and offers recipes.

FIGURE 4.2 *The 'Hertha Freundin' website.*
Source: http://www.herthafreundin.de

The secret of relationship marketing is not only to serve the different segments, but also to design special offers in order to fascinate the customers and give them a reason to stay with the company. A very important aspect in this context is the **consumption behaviour** of fans. Supporters often express their emotional attachment to their favourite sports club by catching special offers. Some sporting organisations soon realised that they can sell fans nearly everything and that fan loyalty can be a cash cow for sports entities. Case study 4.5 provides some examples of very special offers made by clubs of the North American National Hockey League (NHL).

CASE STUDY 4.5. Very Special Offers for Fans – Examples from the NHL

The *Anaheim Ducks* – the NHL Champion 2007 – offers an annual fantasy camp for $2500 per participant. As described on their website, the Ducks Fantasy Camp is a chance of a lifetime for 24 die-hard Ducks fans to spend four unforgettable days on and off the ice with their favourite Ducks players and coaches learning a variety of hockey fundamentals and skills. The Fantasy Camp includes professional instruction (on the ice instruction for all sessions with GM Brian Burke and Ducks Coaches), practice (2 hours of on ice instruction and scrimmage each day), uniforms (one game jersey and socks plus two practice jerseys and socks), team photo (each player receives a Fantasy Camp team photo), refreshments (provided during and after each session), golf outing (an opportunity to relax on the course with the rest of the campers and coaching staff), a video tape of the final game, a post game dinner (for each camper plus one guest) and two tickets to a Ducks home game.

NHL club *Pittsburgh Penguins*, offers special birthday and anniversary offers. By making a $20 donation to a charity fans can surprise someone with a birthday or anniversary greeting on the center ice Jumbotron at any Penguins' home game. Plus, on the day of the game, the birthday person will get a special ecard wishing them a Happy Birthday from the Penguins. Announcements are displayed during the first intermission with a public address announcement highlighting the beginning of the display.

The *Calgary Flames*, another NHL club, provides a very special offer for fans who are interested in proposing to their special someone in front of a sold out Flames crowd. The club sets up a very special night for the respective fan and his future fiancée which includes two tickets to a Calgary Flames game, at least one full minute of a TV timeout dedicated to the proposal, Energy Board full page complete with date, names, and congratulations, plus live coverage of the entire proposal taking place, a DVD recording of the proposal, one dozen roses delivered by mascot Harvey the Hound to the significant other, two Flames jerseys and a $250 Gift Certificate to Flames Central. The cost for a special night like this is $5000.

Other sporting organisations collaborate with their sponsors or other business associates in order to offer joint products and services to their fans, as will be explained later in this chapter. All these offers might be positive for fans. However, there is a fine line between doing good and exploiting fans. Sporting organisations should always remember to treat their fans fairly and not as captive consumers who don't have a choice. Fans are quite loyal to their sports club but that loyalty isn't **blind loyalty**.

Involving fans and rewarding loyalty

A very effective way to build and establish longstanding relationships with customers and fans is to offer them the opportunity to involve themselves and therefore become a part of the club. Interactive features, member clubs and fan loyalty programmes are popular relationship marketing tools in this context.

Interactive features

Interaction is a two-way process between two parties. For example, a lot of companies provide their customers with the opportunity to play games on their websites or participate in competitions. The following real-life examples show how fans can interact with their favourite clubs and therefore become part of a greater whole:

- The New York Yankees (probably the most popular baseball team in the world) provide a fan forum on their website where fans can share their favourite Yankee memories, chat about the season or any other topics.
- The All Blacks (the New Zealand's national team in Rugby Union) provides a special opportunity for their fans to interact. On their website, fans are invited to send messages of support to the team. These messages are posted regularly in the All Blacks team room and get read out to the team as well.
- NASCAR (The National Association for Stock Car Auto Racing) invites fans on their website to play 'fantasy racing'. Motorsport fans can choose from eight different car racing games which they can play online.
- FC Barcelona involves their fans directly in the decision-making process. Barca has more than 156,000 members who have the right to participate in the presidential elections which makes them direct decision makers in the club's future.

Member clubs

Another very effective tool to establish and maintain relationships with fans is the introduction of a member club. Membership schemes give fans and clubs the opportunity to strengthen their bond. Case study 4.6 describes the membership scheme of the Italian Football Club Juventus Turin.

CASE STUDY 4.6. The Juventus Turin Membership Scheme

Juventus Turin advertises their membership scheme as follows on their website:

> 'As from today, Juventus is you! Have you always wanted to see your passion for Juventus recognized? Have you always wanted to meet your favourite footballers? Do you dream of speaking and confronting yourself with them? Now all this can become reality, as Juventus' universe opens its

doors thanks to Juventus Membership, an innovative affiliation project allowing the creation of a new and stronger connection between the team and the fans: a real community enlivened by the fans themselves, their stories and their passion. By choosing one of two packages - Member and Special Member - each Juve fan will get the chance to become an active part of the Club's life and gain access to a universe of services and exclusive benefits.'

The Juventus membership costs €12 per year and includes the following benefits:

- a personal certificate signed by Chairman Cobolli Gigli and Captain Del Piero
- autographed photos of the players
- access to the JuventusMember.com website, where members are able to communicate with other members, the team and the club through the blog, the chat room
- a personalized e-mail address

- the opportunity to see the photo gallery and watch exclusive footage from Juventus Channel
- the preferential treatment with exclusive right of entry at home games and discounts on all original Juventus merchandise

Fans willing to spend €36 can become a Juventus Special member with the additional benefits:

- a personalized Special Member card
- an exclusive pin like the one worn each Sunday by Manager Ranieri
- the option to send official e-cards
- the opportunity to take part in competitions to win the chance to meet the fan's favourite players
- a discount when subscribing to Hurrà Juventus magazine
- discounts in connection with our sponsors
- the chance to star in Face to Face, the videos where they can directly confront themselves with the players!

(*Source: Juventus Turin website, http://www.juventus.com/site/eng/ JAY_juventusmember.asp*)

Member clubs are normally aimed at adult fans. However, a lot of clubs realise that they have to engage in relationships with the younger fans as well. Therefore, sporting organisations introduce so-called kids clubs. For example, the Jetstar Gold Coast Titans (an Australian professional Rugby League Football team) asks kids up to 12 years to become 'Tiny Titans'. The Tiny Titan package costs fifteen Australian dollars and includes a Tiny Titan card, a hat, a mouse pad and a t-shirt as well as the latest team poster, access to the membership website, and merchandise discount.

Fan loyalty programmes

In general, a loyalty programme is a structured relationship marketing tool that rewards, and therefore encourages, loyal buying behaviour. Such programmes are especially popular in retailing. Retailers issue loyalty cards to consumers who can then use it as a form of identification when dealing with the respective retailer. By presenting the card, the buyer is typically entitled to either a discount on the current purchase, or an allotment of points that can be used for future purchases. However, other businesses have successfully introduced loyalty programmes, too. Airlines, for example, use frequent flyer programmes in order to establish and maintain a profitable relationship with their customers. In sports, loyalty cards have long been reduced to simple season tickets. Nowadays, sporting organisations realise the benefits of structured loyalty programmes which not only benefits the loyal fan but also the sports entities and their respective sponsors as the following two examples from the NHL show. Supporters of the Anaheim Ducks receive special discounts from participating sponsors of the Ducks by presenting their fan loyalty card. In addition, supporters get a ten to fifteen per cent discount at the Anaheim Ducks Team Store. The fan loyalty card of the Columbus Blue Jackets works similarly. Valued season ticket holders of the Blue Jackets get discounts at sixteen affiliated partners such as the local theatre, the local zoo and the Columbus Crew, a member of Major League Soccer.

All of the above techniques can be used by sporting organisations in order to ensure a positive relationship with their supporters. The relationship between sports fans and their clubs might even last longer than the actual life as described in Case study 4.7.

CASE STUDY 4.7. The Relationship between Sports Fans and their Clubs – Eternal Love

'Even death can't separate us, from heaven I will cheer you on.' This famous chant among fans of the Argentinean football club Boca Juniors expresses the commitment of the Boca fans. Indeed, the relationship between sports fans and their beloved club can be a lifelong bond – and one which survives even death. Some supporters bequeath their fortune to their favourite clubs, some others let themselves bury in the club's jersey. There is also a widespread custom among dedicated football fans of adorning the graves of dead supporters with decorations in the club colours. In addition, an increasing number of die-hard fans are leaving instructions to their families to scatter their ashes on the playing field of their club. Indeed, in some countries (e.g. England and Argentina) relatives are taking the urns to the home ground of the respective football club and scatter the ashes of their beloved ones onto the pitch.

Now football clubs begin to realise that they can even make money from dead fans. For example, Boca Juniors and the German Bundesliga club Hamburger SV have opened an own cemetery exclusively for their fans. In Buenos Aires, Boca Junior fans can buy their own burial plots at the official Boca cemetery. A fountain crowned with a shield in the blue and yellow colours of the club guards the access to the cemetery where on a memorial wall (of course in the club's colours blue and yellow) small stars are inscribed with the names of former football players and committed supporters who now lie here. Even the grass has been transplanted from La Bombonera's field as the home ground of Boca Juniors Football Club is called. Prices for a burial plot range from €750 to €3000.

In Germany the law does not allow relatives to scatter the ashes of football fans across the pitch. However, a lot of football fans want to express their dedication to their clubs after the final whistle blows. Hamburger SV, the only club which has never been relegated from the German Bundesliga, has therefore created a final resting place for their supporters right next to their football stadium. It is argued that if the club is part of the fans' lives, why shouldn't it be part of their deaths as well? The entrance of the HSV cemetery is looking like a football goal and the gravestones are decorated in blue and white – the club's colours. Three hundred to 500 graves will be arranged in a semi-circle over 8000 square yards on three ascending levels to resemble a football stand. Each grave costs the equivalent of an annual season ticket.

Taking fans' complaints seriously

Only few sports entities actually care about their fans' complaints. However, complaints can be an important bit of information. Most people complain to companies because they are not satisfied with the purchased product and/ or service. In view of the fact that most complaints are justified, companies should take these complaints seriously in order to improve their products/ services and consequently satisfy their customers. A lot of companies have realised the importance of complaints and therefore have introduced a systematic complaint management programme in order to record and resolve customer complaints and thus make their customers happy. A lot of sporting organisations, however, perceive complaints as unnecessary trouble. Complaining fans are often characterised as grumblers. Indeed, some fans always nag and complain about everything. However, sporting organisations are well advised to learn from other businesses and implement a systematic complaint management programme which takes care of the fans' complaints. Of course, such a programme costs time and money. But an efficient customer complaint system leads to satisfied customers and happier fans. And who knows, maybe the old naggers will be satisfied just because a dedicated employee of the club is listening to their complaints for the first time. In order to develop an efficient customer complaint management system, sporting organisations should first define complaint policies and procedures including an accessible and visible location to receive complaints on the one hand, and a system for record keeping (in order to analyse the complaints and communicate it to the respective departments) on the other hand. Then they should assign appropriate people who take care of the fans' complaints. In addition, the sports entity should publicise the existence of such a complaint management programme in order to give fans the chance to state their complaints. Once a complaint has been stated, the complaint has to be analysed and dealt with fairly (e.g. by taking both sides of the story into consideration). Throughout the whole process, the customer should be kept informed about recent developments. Once the problem has been solved, the sporting organisation has to follow up with the fan to make sure that he/she is satisfied. The final stage of the complaint management process is the preparation of a report on how the individual complaint was resolved. Sporting organisations can then refer to the respective complaint if a similar case occurs again. The implementation of a complaint management system can be expensive because sports entities have to invest in the right technology and the right people. But it is never a waste of money because satisfied customers are the lifeblood of any organisation – even in sports.

Evaluating and controlling the relationship marketing process

The whole process of establishing and maintaining healthy and long-standing relationships has to be controlled at every level. Furthermore, the effectiveness of the implemented relationship marketing instruments needs to be evaluated on a regular basis. It is recommended to define key performance indicators (KIPs) which can be measured and compared with each other. Such a KIP could be the number of fans using a specific relationship marketing service in relation to the number of employees running it. Based on the evaluation of KIPs, sporting organisations might on the one hand, invest further in specific RM instruments which prove to be effective and withdraw ineffective ones on the other hand.

Healthy and profitable relationships between sporting organisations and their fans is an important aspect in today's professional sports as we have learned in this chapter. Case study 4.8 finally describes how the English Football Association tries to establish and maintain a healthy relationship with their fans.

CASE STUDY 4.8. Establishing and Maintaining Healthy Relationships with Fans – The Approach of the English Football Association

The English Football Association (FA) is the governing body for football in England, responsible for developing the game at every level – from the grassroots to the international game. According to their website (www.thefa.com), The FA is committed to developing an open, accountable and responsive relationship with supporters and the general public.

In 2000, The FA created a customer relations team who is responsible for collating the views of the general public and feeding those back to the key decision makers within the organisation. The customer relations team publishes an annual Customer Charter which demonstrates The FA's dedication to maintain best practice in service. The following information is obtained from the 2007 Customer Charter, a 40-page report which can be downloaded from The FA website.

On the introduction page, The FA states its aims and goals as follows:

> 'Football fans are of paramount importance to the health and future of the national game. The FA's awareness of this makes us even more determined to provide the high level of service you deserve. In order to lead the successful development of football at all levels, we must have open and accountable relationships with all stakeholders in the game; in particular football supporters.'

The Charter focuses on fan issues across the following specific areas:

Supporter Consultation
In this section, the work and purpose of The FA's customer relations team is described. Football fans are encouraged to contact The FA customer relations team via e-mail, letter or phone as follows:

> 'The FA is dedicated to developing a proactive relationship with supporters worldwide. In order for us to gain an accurate understanding of the opinions and requirements of our customers, the best thing we can do is talk to you directly.'

Interestingly enough, the FA's customer relations team points out that correspondence containing foul and abusive language will not receive a response. Furthermore, the FA notes that they want to engage in a positive dialogue with all the key stakeholders in the game and therefore meet regularly with representatives from major supporter groups (e.g. the Football Supporters Federation, Supporters Direct, The National Association of Disabled Supporters and the Gay Football Supporters Network).

The National Game Strategy
In this section, The FA introduces its new programme to develop grassroots football including detailed plans for

refereeing, child protection and governance. In order to keep modernising and improving the game at all levels, The FA has undertaken the biggest stakeholder consultation in its 143-year history and the findings will input directly into The FA's plans until 2012.

Get into Football
The Get into Football campaign was launched before the 2006 World Cup to promote its football development initiatives to children aged 5–11 years in order to inspire them to play competitive football but also to communicate a Fair Play message. The campaign seems to be successful in view of the fact that FA Learning, the educational division of The FA, trained more people than ever.

englandfans
'englandfans' is the official England supporters club which provides fans with the opportunity to purchase tickets for England home and away matches. Nearly 30,000 fans have registered for membership in 2006. With the backing of all independent fan groups and the Home Office, Alltogethernow 2006, a campaign aimed at promoting positive fan behaviour at the World Cup 2006 in Germany, was launched in March 2006. The events, which formed the backbone of the campaign, were primarily organised by the fans for the fans. The campaign was successful in view of the fact that England fans at the World Cup received universal praise for the behaviour and party atmosphere they brought to the tournament. The section on 'englandfans' also introduces five detailed commitments of The FA for 2007 in order to improve the relationship with England fans.

Merchandise
In this section, the fans learn that while The FA, unlike most professional clubs, does not sell its own merchandise it does have a large and very successful England merchandise licensing programme. The FA therefore grants licences to companies who manufacture and sell products featuring the England Crest. Currently there are around 45 FA licensees, producing hundreds of different product lines. As The FA is a non-for-profit organisation all surpluses generated

Continued

by The FA via the licensing programme are re-invested back into the game at all levels. This section further points out that if a customer is dissatisfied with the quality of an official England product they have purchased, they should address this with the retailer on the one hand. On the other hand, The FA is happy to be informed of any feedback in order to improve the quality and range of products available going forward. Finally, The FA promises that every official England kit (home and away) will continue to have a 2-year life span.

Ticketing

The FA is responsible for ticketing arrangements at all FA matches (including England Home internationals, The FA Community Shield, The FA Cup Semi-finals and Final, The FA Women's Cup Final, Women's England internationals and England men's Under-21 and Youth internationals). The FA makes the following commitments for 2007 regarding ticketing:

- We will be transparent in how tickets are allocated.
- We will make tickets available to the public for purchase via telephone and online
- We will endeavour to provide exemplary customer service to our customers

Football For All

As well as being responsible for administering the game at all levels and managing high-profile areas such as The FA Cup and the England Team, The FA has a number of staff involved in promoting football to the whole community. This section of the Charter highlights some examples of the work The FA has been involved with during 2006 to encourage people from all walks of life to get involved in football. 'Racial Equality' (projects and initiatives that open pathways for members of ethnic minority communities), 'The Goals Project' (a 5-week training course offered to unemployed and disadvantaged young people using football as a key motivational tool), and 'Disability Football' (initiatives to strengthen the relationship with disabled supporters such as the establishment of an own independent fan group) are only a fraction of examples of how The FA tries to build healthy relationships with different members of the society.

The FA's Complaints Procedure

The Charter concludes with a description of The FA's Complaints Procedure. The FA customer relations team asks fans to put their complaints relating to an issue covered by The FA's Customer Charter in writing. They promise to send a response within five working days of receipt. The following statements make clear how important complaints can be:

> 'Everyone at The FA acknowledges the fact that all football fans have the right to make their views heard and we openly seek your feedback. We aim to ensure that at all times our complaints-handling process is fair to everyone, ensuring all views are heard and taken into account in a balanced way.
>
> The customer relations team records every form of communication we receive on customer issues. This enables us to monitor particular concerns and work with the relevant departments within The FA to respond effectively to individual cases and assess any relevant future change of policy.'

The FA's Customer Charter is not only an interesting documentation of the various projects the English Football Association has created in order to build good and positive relationships with English football fans, but also a very good piece of evidence of how strong The FA is committed to relationship marketing aiming at fans.

CONCLUSIONS

Fans are the lifeblood of every sporting organisation. Without supporters the business of sports would not be a business because there would be no audience paying for tickets, no spectators watching sports on telly, no recipients reading the sports news, no fans buying merchandising, and no potential customers for the sports entities' sponsors. Nearly everything in the sports business is aimed at fans. However, fans are much more than potential income for the profit-orientated stakeholders of the sports business. Fans create atmosphere, they are part of the attraction (and sometimes they are the only attraction). All this leads to the conclusion that fans are essential for sporting organisations. That is why more and more clubs and associations realise that they have to establish and maintain a relationship with their fans in order to benefit both sides of the dyad. In this respect, relationship marketing is an important and effective tool. Sporting organisations can chose from a wide range of relationship marketing techniques. However, in order to apply such tools and techniques successfully, sporting organisations first have to understand who their fans are and what needs they have. Thus, feedback and complaint management programmes, consumer research and eventually segmentation are vitally important tools. Based on their analysis, sporting organisations are then able to provide specific offers which match the needs and expectations of their fans. Not only have such offers to be creative but – and that's very important – they have to be reasonable. Sporting organisations have to make money, no doubt about that. But there is a fine line between providing a fan something beneficial and exploiting supporters. Therefore, sporting organisations always have to bear in mind that their customers are extremely loyal, but that their loyalty is not blind loyalty. A healthy relationship should benefit both the sports entity and the fans.

DISCUSSION QUESTIONS

(1) Why can fans be considered the most important stakeholder of the sports business?
(2) What is meant by 'captive consumers' with regard to fans?
(3) How would you define a typical sports fan?
(4) What is meant by the concept of BIRGing and CORFing?
(5) Why is it so important to understand the nature and needs of fans?
(6) Which relationship marketing techniques can a sporting organisation apply in the context of fans?
(7) Imagine you are the fans' representative of a big sporting organisation and you are responsible for designing and implementing a relationship marketing programme aimed at fans. How would you do that and which aspects would you include in the programme?

GUIDED READING

We would recommend two novels which describe the nature of fans very well: Nick Hornby's *'Fever Pitch'* and Alan Edge's *'Faith of our Fathers'*. Hornby illustrates the highs and lows of a football supporter from an Arsenal fan's point of view, whereas Liverpool supporter Edge compares fandom with religion. Another book which highlights the nature of sports fans with reference to the sports business comes from Rein, Kotler and Shields and is titled *'The Elusive Fan: Reinventing Sports in a Crowded Marketplace'*.

WEBSITES

Bayer Giants Leverkusen
http://www.bayer-giants-leverkusen.de

Borussia Dortmund
http://www.bvb.de

Club Atlético Boca Juniors
http://www.bocajuniors.com.ar

Deutsche Bank Skyliners
http://www.deutsche-bank-skyliners.de

FC Barcelona
http://www.fcbarcelona.com

Hamburger SV (HSV)
http://www.hsv.de

Hannover 96
http://www.hannover96.de

Hertha BSC Berlin (general website)
http://www.herthabsc.de

Hertha BSC Berlin (website for female supporters)
http://www.herthafreundin.de

Jetstar Gold Coast Titans
http://www.titans.com.au

Juventus Turin
http://www.juventus.com

Manchester United
http://www.manutd.com

The All Blacks
http://www.allblacks.com

The Anaheim Ducks
http://ducks.nhl.com

The Atlanta Hawks
http://www.nba.com/hawks

The Calgary Flames
http://flames.nhl.com

The Chicago Bulls
http://www.nba.com/bulls

The Columbus Blue Jackets
http://bluejackets.nhl.com

The English Football Association (The FA)
http://www.thefa.com

The National Association for Stock Car Auto Racing (NASCAR)
http://www.nascar.com

The New York Yankees
http://newyork.yankees.mlb.com

The Pittsburgh Penguins
http://penguins.nhl.com

VfB Stuttgart
http://www.vfb.de

CHAPTER 5

Relationship Marketing in Sports – The Sponsor Perspective

Learning Outcomes

On completion of this chapter the reader should be able to:

- explain the nature of sponsorship
- state the importance of sponsorship for professional sporting organisations
- explain why companies engage themselves in sports sponsorship
- describe the relationship between professional sporting organisations and their sponsors
- discuss the options available for sports entities to engage in a beneficial relationship with their sponsors
- describe potential conflicts in the sponsorship dyad
- explain what professional sporting organisations and sponsors alike can do in order to make the sponsorship a success

OVERVIEW OF CHAPTER

The chapter starts off with a brief discussion of various sponsorship definitions in order to explain the nature of sponsorship. It then moves on to the description of sports sponsorship from the sporting organisation's point of view before looking at sponsorship from the sponsors' point of view. The main part of this chapter examines the relationship between professional sporting organisations and their sponsors with special emphasis on the concept of relationship quality. Subsequently, it will be explained how sporting organisations can serve their sponsors more effectively. The chapter contains a number of real life examples involving the LA Lakers, FC Barcelona and many other sports entities.

INTRODUCTION

Corporate sponsorship plays a crucial role in today's top sports. There are, of course, differences with regard to countries and sports leagues. In some countries/regions commercial sponsorship is more accepted than in others. In addition, the form of corporate sponsorship varies between countries. In Europe, for example, **shirt sponsorship** (where the name/logo of the company appears on the shirt) and **naming rights** of stadiums (e.g. *The Emirates Stadium* in London), clubs (e.g. the Austrian soccer club *Red Bull Salzburg* implemented the name of their main sponsor) or even leagues (e.g. the top English soccer league is called *The Barclays Premiership* named after one of the biggest British financial service providers) is more popular than in the United States, where corporate sponsorship is mainly limited to advertising and stadium names. The importance of sponsorship also differs between sports as some sports attract more revenues from sponsorship than others. According to *The World Sponsorship Monitor* (Sports Marketing Surveys, 2009), the top sponsored sports in a number of reported deals in 2008 were soccer, golf, tennis, rugby and basketball. In view of the fact that professional sporting organisations compete with each other for sponsorship money, relationship marketing aiming at sponsors becomes more and more important. This chapter looks at relationship marketing with regard to sponsorship.

THE NATURE OF SPORTS SPONSORSHIP

Sponsorship can take many forms. Companies can sponsor cultural, educational, social or environmental projects. However, sports sponsorship is not only the most important but also the most popular type of sponsorship. *The World Sponsorship Monitor* revealed that of the estimated global sponsorship market size of $43 billion in 2008, sports sponsorship accounted for 79% (Sports Marketing Surveys, 2009). In addition, sports sponsorship is also a highly accepted marketing tool. For example, 78% of the German population has a positive attitude towards sponsorship and attaches high quality attributes to products of sponsors (Sportfive, 2008).

Sports marketing academics as well as organisations involved in sports marketing have produced various definitions of sports sponsorship over the years. Therefore, a generally accepted definition does not exist. However, there are some patterns which can be identified in most definitions:

First, there are the protagonists of sponsorship. On the one side the sporting organisation (which can be a club, an association or an individual) and on the other side the sponsoring company (which is in most cases a business company, but which can also be a non-profit organisation, individuals or even state facilities).

Second, sports sponsorship is based on the **principle of reciprocity**, which means that both sponsor and sponsee give and receive. There is therefore a clear distinction from patronage or charity donations. In most cases, sports organisations receive financial support from the sponsor. However, sometimes sponsors also provide non-financial resources such as products, people or other services, as will be explained later. Whereas older definitions of sports sponsorship (e.g. Roth, 1990; Dibb, Simkin, Pride and Ferrel, 1994) remained vague when it came to the service in return, recent definitions (e.g. Mullin et al., 2000; van Heerden, 2001; Bühler, 2006) emphasised the commercial nature of sports sponsorship. Therefore, sponsoring companies expect a commercial relevant service in return from the sponsee. In the early days, sponsorship was mainly about sticking a logo on a shirt. Over the years, sports entities became more creative in developing sponsorship opportunities for companies. Case study 5.1 provides an example of the different sponsorship opportunities in professional sports.

CASE STUDY 5.1. Sponsorship Opportunities in Professional Sports – The Example of the Los Angeles Lakers

Los Angeles Lakers – Invest in a winner

The LA Lakers are probably one of the most famous basketball clubs in the world. Companies are prepared to pay huge sums to be associated with the Lakers and their surrounding fame. Although the Lakers, like most US sports teams, do not have a shirt sponsor, they still provide a multitude of corporate sponsorship opportunities for companies such as the following:

Signage

Companies can place their logo on the big video screen inside the arena, above the player entrance, the pole pads, the press backdrop or under the scoreboard.

Print

Sponsors can put their logo in different Laker publications such as the Lakers Magazine Game Program, the Lakers Media Guide, the Lakers Official Yearbook, the

Pocket Schedules, the Season Ticket Book or the Team picture.

Multimedia

The LA Lakers provide the following advertisement opportunities on their website which is consistently rated #1 among all 30 NBA teams: banner advertisement, home page advertisement button, online contests, skyscraper advertisements or sponsor editorials. Other multimedia opportunities include the Lakers Courtside Connection (exclusive contents, news, and video content), Lakers Inside (the official Lakers e-Newsletter delivered monthly) and the Lakers e-Mail Blast (a targeted message designed to achieve the sponsor's objective sent to all qualifying persons on the Lakers e-Mail database).

In-Arena Elements

Companies can present various entertainment events before, during and after the game such as the Camera

Continued

Kids, the Celebrity Signature Contests, the Cheer Sticks, the Game Ball Delivery, the Giveaway Nights, the Halftime Contests, the High 5 Squad, the Honorary Team Captain, the 'Kiss Me!' Cam, the Laker Girls Routines, the Lakers Opening Line-Ups, the Lobby Booths, the Lucky Row/Seat Contests, the Noise Meter, the Post-Game Court Time, the Sponsored Replay/Game Action 'Bug', the Seat Upgrades, the Video Streamers, and the Video Sports/Features.

Out-of-Arena Elements

Sponsors can also present events taking place outside the arena such as the Laker Girls Appearances, the Lakers Player Appearances, Consumer/Ticket Promotions, and the Road Trips.

Community Programs

In order to prove their social responsibility companies can engage in different community programs such as the Basketball Clinics, the Casino Night (an annual fundraiser featuring fine dining, casino games and a celebrity poker tournament), a Golf Tournament, the Read to Achieve Program (a reading initiative that encourages children's literacy), the Student &

Teacher of the Month Contest, 'Time 4 Kids', and the Thanksgiving Feeding.

Special Events

Sponsors can also present special events such as the Camp Lakers, the Chalk Talks, the Pre-Season Game Sponsorships and the VIP Tour/Practice.

Hospitality

Corporate sponsors can book various hospitality opportunities such as the Arena Club VIP Dinners, Receptions (including tickets, food and beverages, Lakers merchandise raffle, photo opportunities and Lakers players appearances) and Suite Nights (including 18 tickets, food and beverages).

Spanish Opportunities

In view of the fact that the LA Lakers have a lot of Spanish fans, companies can make use of special Spanish opportunities such as the Spanish Pocket Schedules, the Spanish section of the Lakers website and special Spanish promotions and events, e.g. the Fiesta Lakers (an annual Latino Heritage celebration featuring popular Latino artists, Lakers players, and Lakers Girls).

For many years, the sponsorship literature described sponsorship as a pure transaction. However, some recent studies (e.g. Chadwick, 2004; Farrelly and Quester, 2005; Bühler, 2006) describe sponsorship as a relational construct. Indeed, sports sponsorship is more than a transaction based on a simple contractual agreement. The modern view of sponsorship is that of a partnership where both sides trade-off advantages and reach for mutual benefit.

Based on the above patterns we consequently propose the following definition of sports sponsorship:

DEFINITION

Professional sports sponsorship is a business-related partnership between a sponsor and a sponsee based on reciprocity. The sponsor provides financial or non-financial resources directly to the sponsee and receives a predefined service in return in order to fulfil various sponsorship objectives.

The term 'professional sports sponsorship' indicates the commercial nature of sports sponsorship and therefore distinguishes it from so-called 'sweetheart-deals' (i.e. sponsorship activities where the chairman's passion is the main reason to sponsor a particular sport or sporting organisation). These sponsorships are rather based on personal and emotional involvement of the decision-maker(s) than on commercial issues, which might exist as well in professional sports. However, this chapter focuses mainly on professional sports sponsorships as these are the rule rather than the exception nowadays.

THE IMPORTANCE OF SPONSORSHIP FOR PROFESSIONAL SPORTING ORGANISATIONS

Sponsorship is an important source of revenue for professional sporting organisations. Indeed, professional sports would not be possible without the money generated from sponsorship deals these days. For example, sponsorship revenues account for more than a third of total income of professional soccer clubs in Europe (Deloitte, 2009). Furthermore, the sponsorship structure of sports entities has changed over the years. It was mostly a local company which, in the early years, backed a single sports club. However, more and more companies were attracted by mainstream sports such as football, basketball or ice hockey because it delivered wide audiences. This was even more the case, when television fell in love with certain sports. As a consequence, the sums of today's sponsorship deals have multiplied several times. For example, the average annual value of shirt sponsorship deals in the German Bundesliga in the 1981/82 season was €260 400 compared to €5.7 million in 2008/09, which means an increase of more than 2100% within 2 decades.

Furthermore, the sponsorship structure has also changed in view of the fact that the single local benefactor of the early days has been replaced by a whole pool of club sponsors as the example of Galatasaray SK shows. The sixteen fold Turkish football champion has not only a shirt sponsor (Avea) and a technical sponsor (Adidas), but also ten official sponsors (e.g. Cola Turka, Samsung), three official suppliers and more than forty licensees who pay a lot of money in order to be associated with Galatasaray. A lot of professional sports entites have structured their hotchpotch of sponsors in the form of a pyramid as indicated in Figure 5.1.

At the apex of the pyramid stands the **main sponsor**, whose name or brand logo appears on the shirts in most cases. Shirt sponsorship is just one

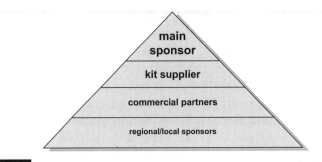

FIGURE 5.1 *Sponsorship structure of professional sporting organisations.*
(Source: Bühler, 2006, p. 27)

of various possibilities for the main sponsor to use the sports entity as a medium for his objectives. Perimeter hoardings, announcements before and after the games, PR-activities in and around the sports venue as well as business seats and executive boxes are essential parts of sponsorship deals nowadays.

In the second place usually comes the **kit supplier**, who equips the team with shirts, tracksuits, boots and other sports equipment. Besides the value in kind, manufacturers also pay a lot of money to use sports entities for promotional campaigns. In some cases kit suppliers refinance their sponsorship investments with the revenues generated from the sales of replica shirts.

Commercial partners of the sporting organisations can be found at the next level of the sponsorship pyramid. They pay usually less than the main sponsor and kit supplier, and therefore have fewer communication rights. The sponsorship packages differ from sponsor to sponsor, and the service in return depends mainly on the volume of the deal. Sponsors usually get perimeter hoardings around the pitch as well as some business seats or executive boxes. In addition, they are often named as an official partner on the club's or association's website or other publications.

The regional or local sponsors respectively build the base of the pyramid. They pay less than the three other levels above, but in total can contribute a significant part of sponsorship revenues. They usually place an advertisement in the match programme or buy a perimeter hoarding at the venue.

However, the partitioning of the pyramid can vary from club to club. Some sports entities record their kit supplier on the same level as the main sponsor, though other clubs subdivide the 'commercial partners' into 'premium partners', 'exclusive partners' or 'team partners' with clear defined services in return. Figure 5.2 illustrates the sponsorship pool of FC Bayern Munich as an example of such a sponsorship pyramid.

FIGURE 5.2

The sponsorship pool of FC Bayern Munich.

The actual fee of the sponsorship deal depends on many different factors, for example, the components of the **sponsorship package** offered by the sporting organisation (i.e. the service in return), the attractiveness and image of the sports entity (e.g. clubs and teams with a high public profile are likely to be more 'expensive' than smaller clubs) or the time on air and extent of media presence of the club. Clubs performing well on the pitch and qualifying for international cup competitions (such as the Champions League) find it easier to sell their sponsorships than other clubs. Another crucial factor determining sponsorship fees is the size of the fan base and the numbers of the clubs' members, because the more fans/members a club has, the more potential customers it can offer to sponsors. Finally, the individual negotiation skills of the people involved in the negotiations may also determine the price of sponsorship deals.

Another aspect of sports sponsorship is the area of naming rights. More and more clubs are selling the names of their venue to companies and are therefore generating significant additional income. For example, Arsenal receives £50 million for a fifteen-year-naming-rights contract with the Middle East airline Emirates from 2006 till 2014.

As we have seen, sponsorship is a very important source of revenue for sports entities. However, sponsorship offers far more opportunities for professional sporting organisations. Sponsorship partnerships can act as a branding tool not only for sponsors but also for sponsees. A sports club could benefit from the image of a well-known company in the same way as the sponsoring organisation benefits from the image of the club. Case study 5.2 provides an example where a sponsorship deal helped to boost the image of both the sponsor and the sponsee.

CASE STUDY 5.2. An Extraordinary Sponsorship Agreement – The Case of FC Barcelona and UNICEF

It was obvious that the media would cover the story extensively. For more than 100 years the biggest football club in the world could afford to leave their shirt blank while all other professional football clubs accepted shirt sponsorship because of the high revenues. But now even FC Barcelona had to realise that shirt sponsorship is an established tool in professional sports. The rumours grew fast and the media was trying to find out which company was just about to become the first shirt sponsor in the club's long and famous history. How much would they pay? Where would they come from? Which sector would they operate in? Some said that the Chinese government offered more than 20 million Euros in order to promote the Olympic games in Beijing 2008 on the 'Barça' shirts. Other sources were sure that a betting company would become the new sponsor. However, reality proved all sources wrong. It was 7 September 2006 when the president of FC Barcelona, Joan Laporta, introduced the respective shirt sponsor as follows:

> 'For the first time in our more than 107 years of history, our main soccer team will wear an emblem on the front of its shirt. It will not be the brand name of a corporation. It will not be a commercial to promote some kind of business. It will be the logo of UNICEF. Through UNICEF, we, the people of FC Barcelona, the people of 'Barça', are very proud to donate our shirt to the children of the world. We are very happy to sign this agreement with UNICEF and we are grateful for the opportunity to start this global partnership. Together, we can do a lot to improve the lives of boys and girls around the world.'

The media as well as sponsorship experts around the world were astounded because this news turned around the principles of sports sponsorship for a moment. In this case, it wasn't the shirt sponsor who paid the sponsee, but the club who paid the sponsor. Indeed, FC Barcelona makes an annual payment of 1.5 million Euros in order to support the United Nations Organisation's humanitarian aid projects around the world. In addition, 'Barça' also supports UNICEF's work by allowing them to use the club as a source of publicity. In turn, UNICEF has conceded FC Barcelona the right to use its name, logo and emblem on their football shirt and therefore has granted official recognition. The cooperation between FC Barcelona and UNICEF also finds its expression in joint projects such as the fight against HIV/AIDS in Swaziland, a country in the south of Africa, where almost half of the pregnant women have the virus.

The agreement between UNICEF and Barcelona exceeds a normal sponsorhip deal and is supposed to be a win-win-situation. On the one hand, UNICEF receives a lot of publicity through the partnership with FC Barcelona and therefore raises awareness for their mission and their work. UNICEF Executive Director Ann M. Veneman said during the announcement of the new partnership at United Nations headquarters:

> 'Barcelona shows us that sports can be a powerful, positive force for children. The team has opened a door of hope to thousands of children.'

On the other hand, the deal with UNICEF created a great deal of positive publicity for 'Barça' as well. For example, FC Barcelona received the 'International Sponsorship Award for Innovation' in 2006 for an outstanding partnership in the context of international sports sponsorship. In addition, Joan Laporta was presented with the 'Spirit of Sport Award' in recognition of the partnership with UNICEF in April 2007. The Spirit of Sport Award acknowledges those in sports who take action to create a better world. FC Barcelona's innovative decision to raise awareness about the values of UNICEF was honoured as a perfect example of how sports can help the most vulnerable children. In addition, FC Barcelona is able to reach other objectives through their association with UNICEF as Joan Laporta points out:

> *'Barça's slogan "more than a club" is open in its definition. Maybe it is this flexibility that makes it so apt for defining the complex identity of FC Barcelona. There has always been the Barça that plays every Sunday and every Wednesday, and the Barça that beats every day in the hearts of its people. The Barça of Sunday and Wednesday is already a global club. Now, we want to globalize the 'Barça' that cares for its people, we want to globalize the 'Barça' of civilian duty, solidarity and humanitarianism. We have decided that the best way to do this is to associate ourselves with UNICEF.'*

Sponsorship is also a good opportunity to improve professionalism in a sporting organisation. Sponsoring companies usually possess more marketing skills than sports entities. Some clubs and sponsors work closely together on a regular basis. The people responsible for the sponsorship, exchange ideas and might support each other. Therefore, representatives from sporting organisations with little marketing experience might learn from their more professional counterparts. Subsequently, the cooperation with sponsoring companies can lead to a knowledge transfer from the sponsor to the sponsee resulting in increased professionalism. In addition, a sponsorship partnership could be the door opener to other potential sponsors. For example, the main sponsor of a sports clubs could introduce their sponsee to some business associates who might have an interest in sponsoring the respective sports club.

In view of these opportunities, professional sporting organisations have to make sure that they do everything to attract new sponsors and keep the already existing sponsors happy.

THE IMPORTANCE OF SPONSORSHIP FOR SPONSORS

Sponsorship has established itself as a serious marketing tool for companies over the years. As long as there have been sports, there have been people who supported athletes, clubs and teams financially. In the early years, local businessmen provided money in favour of prestige and for the sake of supporting the local sports clubs. However, more and more companies soon realised that they could gain commercial advantages by sponsoring a sports entity. Nowadays 'patronage' might still be existent in professional sports but it is vanishing. A recent study shows that the vast majority of companies engage themselves in sports sponsorship for commercial motives. Only a small number of sports sponsors stated that the decision to invest in a certain sports entity was based on personal motives (Bühler, 2006).

Sports sponsorship is a popular promotional tool for companies nowadays. However, the existing marketing literature is inconclusive about where (sports) sponsorship fits into the marketing mix. Van Heerden (2001, p. 130) notes that marketing texts 'do not seemingly acknowledge that sponsorship is a new and vibrant addition to the marketing communication mix.' He also points out that sponsors have to understand where sponsorship fits into the marketing communication mix in order to maximise sponsorship effectiveness. This sub-chapter describes the importance of sponsorship as a marketing tool, the objectives of sponsors and the advantages as well as disadvantages of sponsorship for companies. We would like to emphasise that the following information is not only essential knowledge for sponsoring companies but also for sporting organisations in view of the fact that sports entities have to understand the sponsors' perspective in order to engage in a relationship which benefits both sponsorship partners.

Sports sponsorship as a marketing tool

Companies have to sell their products and/or services and prevail over numerous competitors. Since products and services become more and more alike, companies have to be creative in order to stand out from the competition. That is what marketing is all about. The marketing department has traditionally used various tactics in order to convince the consumer to buy their products. Since there is no significant difference between products, prices and distribution channels, promotion as a marketing tactic has become even more important. Companies need to get their name, their brands and their message sent directly to their customers. Advertising is not only the oldest but also the most popular promotion tool. However, there is too much advertising 'noise' and 'clutter' out there in view of numerous print advertisements and television commercials. Studies have shown that every consumer receives more than a thousand commercial messages a day, from which he or she can seldom remember a single one (Smith and Taylor, 2004). Marketers were aware of that problem and so they developed other promotional tactics. Over the years alternative tools such as sales promotion, direct marketing, public relations (PR), product placement and sponsorship have been developed. Sponsorship has been defined classically as a **below-the-line-tool** within the **promotional mix**. In order to promote the message effectively, companies have to link sponsorship with other promotional tools as outlined in Figure 5.3.

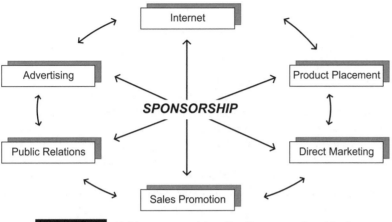

FIGURE 5.3 *Linking sponsorship with other promotional tools.*

Considering some recent examples in practice, it must be recognised that the role of sponsorship has been enhanced from that of a supporting marketing tool to the foundation of a marketing strategy, with sponsorship increasingly being a sales-oriented tool. Case study 5.3 provides some examples of how companies leverage their sponsorship properties.

CASE STUDY 5.3. Leveraging Sponsorship Properties

Sponsorship used to be very simple in the early days. Just putting a name on a shirt or on a parameter board was sufficient enough to gain some attention. But these days have gone. Nowadays, companies have to link their sponsorship activities with other promotional tools. In this respect, some companies prove to be very creative as the following examples show.

Hypovereinsbank, a German bank and premium partner of FC Bayern Munich, has introduced a special saving book for Bayern fans. With every tenth goal the team scores the interest rate increases by 0.01 per cent. If Bayern Munich wins the German Championship another five per cent will be granted for a whole month. The Hypovereinsbank offers this financial service on the club's website and advertise it with promotional tools such as advertising, PR or sales promotion. In addition, holders of the Bayern saving book

have the chance to win attractive prices such as signed merchandise or tickets for Bayern games. Since the introduction in 2003, the Hypovereinsbank has gained more than 40,000 new customers through their Bayern saving book.

Microsoft, a classic partner of Bayern Munich, does not advertise on perimeter boards but tries something else to leverage its association with the German record-holding champions. In order to promote their 'Xbox', fans of Bayern Munich play a virtual penalty shootout shortly before kick-off. The competition is shown on large video boards inside the stadium which guarantees exposure and attention. Furthermore, Microsoft promotes their association with Bayern Munich through adverts in sports magazines and various PR activities. In the pipeline are Bayern branded gaming consoles as well as an own regular 'Xbox Bayern show' on MTV in order to reach the respective target group.

The *BT Group* (former British Telecom) and the English Premier League club Everton FC have launched a loyalty card for Everton supporters that doubles as a season ticket. Fans can access the turnstiles at Goodison Park as well as collect points for a range of retail partners. BT promotes its brand by being prominently displayed on the swipe cards which are distributed to 40,000 Everton season ticket holders.

Carlsberg, the sponsor of the local rival Liverpool FC, provides Liverpool fans with a variety of opportunities to interact. For example, Carlsberg dedicated a section on their website to Liverpool FC and offer supporters a wide range of exclusive downloads including wallpapers or audio files. In addition, fans can participate in a Liverpool quiz and other competitions.

As an official sponsor of the FIFA World Cup 2006 in Germany, *McDonald's* has promoted their brand around the world through a range of activities during the tournament, including exclusive products offered at World Cup venues throughout Germany, ticket giveaways, exclusive sponsorship of FIFA Fantasy Football Online Game as well as special promotions and activities in local McDonald's markets (e.g. special sandwich promotions in Brazil, special television commercials in China, indoor table football games in India, football-themed promotions in Japan, football-related mobile phone text messaging contests in the United Kingdom, and special limited editions of FIFA World Cup beverage cups in the United States). A very special activity was the McDonald's player escort programme. Through this exclusive initiative, 1408 children aged between six and ten years were getting the chance to take part in the World Cup by walking onto the field hand-in-hand with the players. In addition, the selected children also had the chance to play friendly football matches as part of their own tournament which took place in German host cities during the World Cup.

The objectives of sports sponsors

Companies invest in professional sports sponsorship for a multitude of benefits. Various authors tried to create categories of objectives. Hermanns (1997), for example, differentiates between economic and psychological objectives. **Economic objectives** have a positive impact on monetary financial aspects (e.g. profit, turnover or expenses) and can only be achieved through **psychological objectives** such as increase of awareness levels, improvement of image, staff motivation and human relations. Pope (1998) examined the academic literature on sports sponsorship and identified the various objectives classified as corporate, marketing and media objectives of sponsors (Table 5.1).

The sponsorship of sports entities is an effective way to generate widespread **awareness** in a short period of time and to enhance the **image** of the company or the brand because sports usually attracts the attention of many people and delivers a good image. Research shows that supporters of football clubs, for example, perceive the sponsors of their club as more likeable than companies operating in the same marketplace (Seydel, 2005).

Besides awareness and image, sponsors are trying to reach other objectives through sports sponsorship. Some want to improve their relationship

Table 5.1	Aggregated Objectives for Corporations Involved in Sports Sponsorship	
Corporate Objectives	**Marketing Objectives**	**Media Objectives**
▪ public awareness	▪ business relations	▪ generate visibility
▪ corporate image	▪ reach target market	▪ generate publicity
▪ public perception	▪ brand positioning	▪ enhance ad campaign
▪ community involvement	▪ increase sales	▪ avoid clutter
▪ financial relations	▪ sampling	▪ target specificity
▪ client entertainment		
▪ government relations		
▪ employee relations		
▪ compete with other companies		

Source: Pope (1998, p. 2), Bühler (2006, p. 71)

with business associates by inviting them to games of their sponsored club. Some want to motivate their employees by giving away free tickets or special merchandising. Sponsorship can also be used to promote the company's involvement in the local community. Mack (1999), for example, revealed that small businesses are mainly into sponsorship in order to give the community something back. However, commitment to the local area is not only limited to small companies but can also be an objective of larger corporations as the example of Reebok's involvement with the English Premier League club Bolton Wanderers shows. Despite being a global player, Reebok became the main sponsor of Bolton Wanderers and title sponsor of the club's new stadium in 1997 because Reebok was founded in Bolton (Busby, 2004). Furthermore, sponsoring companies use sports sponsorship more and more as an effective networking opportunity. There are a lot of examples of companies doing business together because they sponsor the same sports club. Therefore, sponsorship is a good way to get to know other companies and to cooperate on a joint basis.

Advantages and disadvantages of sports sponsorship

Sports sponsorship as a marketing tool has its advantages and disadvantages just as any other marketing instrument. This section examines the main advantages of sports sponsorship over other marketing tools and also lists the disadvantages.

The main advantages of sports sponsorship are:

■ Sponsorship is highly accepted amongst target groups. Recent studies revealed that the vast majority of people have a positive attitude towards sponsorship and attach high quality attributes to the products of sponsors (Sportfive, 2008)

■ Gillies (1991, p. 2) explains 'the beauty of sponsorship' with the unique advantage that it 'can reach people in numerous different ways and often when they don't expect it.' Companies can target their audience at the point of consumers' attention in a highly emotional situation (Grünitz and von Arndt, 2002).

■ Sponsorship can be cost-effective considering the media exposure of shirt sponsors or companies' advertising on perimeter boards (Pepels, 2001). In addition, the desired message is likely to be spread over the view of a wide audience.

■ Sponsorship is flexible and allows a variety of audiences to be targeted (Sleight, 1989). Sponsorship packages in professional sports provide a lot of opportunities (e.g. advertising in and outside the venue, public relations, hospitality) and can therefore be used to reach a lot of various objectives.

The main disadvantages are:

■ Shirts and perimeter boards can transfer only a limited message and are often reduced to brand names or logos only (Pepels, 2001; Grünitz and von Arndt, 2002). Therefore, sponsorship has to be linked with other promotional tools in order to get the desired message right. This, of course, could be an expensive task and therefore requires a significant marketing budget.

■ Sleight (1989, p. 129) mentions the problem of clutter as the most serious disadvantage of sports sponsorship in view of the fact that 'sports that can deliver an audience of sufficient size (…) [is] already crowded with sponsors all trying to put their message across.' As Mediaedge:cia (2003, p. 1) notes in its market research report:

> 'One of the major factors driving the initial development of sponsorship was the fact that it provided a relatively clutter-free environment particularly when compared to media advertising. Success has begun to erode this critical advantage, in that increased levels of sponsorship activity have led to perceptions of a cluttered environment.'

■ Image transfer, as a desired objective, implies that a negative image can also be transferred. This can lead to problems when the image of the sponsored property becomes damaged. A prominent example is professional cycling. After a series of positive drug tests during the Tour de France 2007, some sponsors such as T-Mobile, Adidas and Audi decided to pull out of their sponsorship activities in cycling.

■ The passion and loyalty of fans of a specific club are good reasons for companies to sponsor the respective club. But sponsors must also fear a negative reaction from fans of other clubs, mainly from their direct rival (Sir Norman Chester Centre for Football Research, 2003). For example, the local Vodafone shop in Liverpool reported a significant decrease in turnover after Vodafone announced its sponsorship deal with Liverpool's archrival Manchester United (Bühler, 2005).

■ In view of the fact that sponsorship agreements run for several years, sponsors might find it difficult to change their marketing strategy whenever appropriate.

■ A main problem of sponsorship seems to be the measurement and evaluation of sponsorship effects. Isolating the sponsorship effect may be difficult because sponsorship is often linked to other promotional activities (Brassington and Pettitt, 2003; Pepels, 2001).

Despite the disadvantages, sports sponsorship still remains a popular marketing tool for companies. Therefore, sports sponsors should have a genuine interest in establishing and maintaining good relationships with the sports entity which they sponsor. The next section focuses on the relationship between professional sporting organisations and their sponsors.

THE RELATIONSHIP BETWEEN PROFESSIONAL SPORTING ORGANISATIONS AND THEIR SPONSORS

Professional sporting organisations have multiple sponsors nowadays as described earlier. Thus, sports entities have to deal with different types of sponsors and therefore with different types of relationships. For example, the relationship with the main sponsor can be more intense than with a lower sponsor. Nevertheless, sports entities have to manage the relationships with all of their sponsors properly. That also includes dealing with potential conflicts properly as the latest empirical data shows (Empirical data 5.1).

In order to manage the relationship between sports entities and sponsors properly it is very important to understand the **relational aspects** of sports sponsorship. Thus, this section will describe the relationship between sporting organisations and their sponsors in detail.

EMPIRICAL DATA 5.1. Conflicts in the Sports Sponsorship Dyad – Insights from Clubs' and Sponsors' Representatives

In order to identify potential conflicts in the sports sponsorship dyad, we carried out own empirical research and asked a number of clubs' and sponsors' representatives to give us their opinion on the matter. For reasons of confidentiality we promised to keep the statements anonymous. Nearly all interviewees admitted that conflicts regularly occur in the relationship between clubs and sponsors. All in all, four different areas of conflicts have been identified:

(1) Excessive demands and disappointed expectations by sponsors can lead to conflicts. One club official noted that some sponsors take a yard if you give them an inch. Another interviewee said that on a day-to-day-basis there are obviously some things the sponsors want and the clubs cannot give them. Again another club's representative explained:

'Sponsors think they can change things that are just not possibly to change. You can't interfere with the game and you can't interfere with the team management.'

In addition, a conflict can arise when the sponsorship does not deliver what the sponsors did expect. It is also problematic if performance of sponsorship deals has been interpreted differently. For example, one club official said:

'There had been three or four examples this year of sponsors who come on board and it hasn't delivered them the exposure they expected it to. Some sponsors think that they go on to perimeter boards around the ground and that they will get instant business from it. And as you know, that's not the case. So we have had conflict. We've had people who'd been very disappointed with what they received.'

(2) A lack of mutual understanding and clash of objectives are also potential areas of conflict. The following statement from a club's representative is exemplary:

'But it can be a problem especially if this guy from the sponsor doesn't understand the pressures that the clubs got and vice versa.'

This area of conflict is also linked with the fact that clubs and sponsors have different objectives. Sports clubs have to be successful on the pitch, whereas sponsors want to reach their objectives. The conflict occurs when these objectives clash (e.g. the sponsor needs the sports team for PR activities, but the club turns down the enquiry because it would interfere with the preparation for the next game). This problem is also due to the fact that the objectives differ within the football clubs as one sponsor noted:

'The club said, the team is there to train and not for any commercial reasons. So of course it's always quite fractious for us to gain access to players because the commercial department is in charge of making revenue for the club, the football manager is in charge of winning and they often come into conflict.'

Most of the clubs' representatives said that they try to make every enquiry possible but they have strict principles as one club official said exemplary:

'All enquiries which disturb the post-match preparation have to be rejected. The sponsors do not always show some understanding for that.'

However, most of the interviewees representing sponsors understood this problem and said that they would not want to interfere in such things because success on the pitch would be in their interest, too.

(3) Contractual conflicts have been named, especially referring to players' access. The problem of contractual conflicts takes place on two different levels. On the one hand the initial contract between club and sponsors. A club official said that conflicts occur when some parts of the contract are interpreted differently. The much bigger conflict on the other hand seems to be the problem of players' access. A lot of players have individual contracts with their own sponsors, which then leads to conflicts as the following statement shows:

'The hardest part of the problem occurs when the club sponsor has no rights to any personal

experience by any of the team players at all. If you pay somebody €3m a year, it's not unreasonable that the players turn up three or four times a year to take part to promote the sponsors.'

(4) Two sponsors were complaining that some clubs and above all some players do not realize whom they get their money from. Some sponsors feel not appreciated enough. A club official confirms this area of conflict by saying that problems occur whenever opinions differ of how players should behave towards sponsors or how they should live the sponsorship. A point which was recognised by another interviewee who said that the identification of players with the club sponsors is important for the success of the sponsorship. On the other hand, some clubs' representatives complained that they sometimes have to deal with sponsors who don't really understand their sport as the following two statements show:

'I had a meeting this morning with a new person from a company that we've done business with before. And she has no knowledge of football whatsoever. I could tell that she was anti football. I could tell that she had a version in her mind that what football is about that didn't bear any reality. And it was a difficult meeting. And I can never understand companies who spend a lot of money and then put someone in charge who don't have any interest.'

'I think some companies don't understand the culture and there are companies who believe that a football fan would buy anything I tell him to. And that's not the case. People just think blindly that football fans will do exactly what I'll tell them to do. And that's not the case.'

Finally, the interviewees made some suggestions as how to prevent or solve the conflicts. Having sensible negotiations and detailed contracts is very important according to the clubs' and sponsors' representatives. Clubs should also implement sponsorship coordinators who focus on the need of the sponsors on the one hand. On the other hand, sponsors have to make sure to put the right people on the job. The third area of suggestions refers to regular meetings and the attempt to seek for mutual understanding.

Sports sponsorship has been seen by the sponsorship literature for many years as a pure transaction based on a contractual agreement. The transactional view of sponsorship reflects reality to some extent in view of the fact that some sports sponsorships agreements are mainly transactional in nature. For example, there are definitely some sponsors looking for short-term sponsorships rather than long-term agreements, because they have short-term objectives in mind. Some sponsors also tend to be opportunistic in their behaviour by assessing the relative costs relating to the respective sponsorship deal. The same is true for sponsees. Some sports properties need short-term money and therefore look for the best deal in financial terms on a short-term basis. Support for this view comes from a study undertaken by Chadwick and Thwaites (2005), who note that many sponsorship deals in professional English football are rather short-term orientated. They also point out that many sponsors and sponsees move on to other sponsorship partners once the contractual obligations have been fulfilled. This leads to the conclusion that a lot of sponsorship deals are little more than contractual obligations between sponsees and sponsors who have convergent objectives or interests at a particular point in time. In other words, sponsees and sponsors might try to exploit each other's attractiveness for a short period of time and therefore reduce the relationship to a purely opportunistic one.

However, reducing sponsorship to a simple transaction may be somewhat limited since it ignores the consideration that sponsors and sponsees may commit resources other than money and communication rights to the sponsorship deal. For example, they invest their time, their people, and their know-how in order to make the sponsorship work. Chadwick and Thwaites (2005, p. 337) advise both sponsors and sponsees not to view 'sponsorship as an exclusively short-term transaction', in view of the fact that 'greater long-term benefits may be attainable from a closer, more strategic, network related association'. Support for this view comes from Cheng and Stotlar (1999, p. 1), who suggest that it is important to 'reconsider sport sponsorship as a durable partnership.' They even compare sponsorship with marriages and conclude that 'both require long-term commitments to assist each other in reaching mutual fulfilment'.

Therefore, sports sponsorships should also be viewed as a **business-to-business relationship** between professional sporting organisations and their sponsors. Recent studies (Chadwick, 2005; Farrelly and Quester, 2005; Bühler, 2006) established the relational aspects of sports sponsorship by examining the factors leading to a successful sponsorship partnership. In the context of the sponsorship dyad, an important issue is the concept of relationship quality as recent empirical studies show.

EMPIRICAL DATA 5.2. The Concept of Relationship Quality in the Sponsorship Dyad

There will always be sponsorship deals, which are transaction based, because sponsors and/or sponsees have short-term objectives in mind and are perfectly happy to exchange financial resources and some property rights without engaging into a proper relationship.

However, for all other sponsors and sponsees who see sponsorship not only as a transaction but also as a long-term relationship where both partners trade off advantages in order to meet long-term objectives, a deeper understanding of the relational aspects of sponsorship is necessary. In this respect, the concept of relationship quality is likely to play an important role in the context of sports sponsorship because it has been considered to be an important indicator of relationship success and business performance in other business contexts (Bejou, Wray and Ingram, 1996; Kiedaisch, 1997; Werner, 1997; Hennig-Thurau, 2000; Lee and Wong, 2001; Ivens, 2004).

Sports sponsorship has been widely ignored in the context of relationship quality research and relationship quality has been widely ignored in the context of sports sponsorship research. The need for a stronger focus on the relational aspects of sports sponsorships is therefore based on the belief that long-term relationships between sponsors and sponsees are a key element in successful sports sponsorship deals and that a deeper understanding of the concept of relationship quality in a sports sponsorship context is necessary.

To date, there are only two studies dealing with the concept of relationship quality in the context of sports sponsorship. One study (Farrelly and Quester, 2005) examined the quality of relationship between sponsors and sponsees in Australian football. The results of their study proved that trust is the essential variable in the sponsorship relationship. The second study (Bühler, 2006) examined the relationship between professional football clubs in the English Premier League and the German Bundesliga and their sponsors. The study served as a first guideline for assessing the quality of relationship between professional football clubs and sponsors by introducing the following three new dimensions to the construct of relationship quality:

- '*Relationship compatibility*' (involving a sense of understanding and fairness in dealing with each other)

- '*Long-term perspective*' (implying mutual commitment of clubs and sponsors)

- '*Collaborative behaviour*' (involving a sense of working together and doing more than needs to be done)

The above studies are a first step. However, further research into this new area is necessary in order to examine the factors determining relationship quality of partners in the sports sponsorship dyad in greater detail.

IMPORTANT FACTORS FOR SUCCESSFUL RELATIONSHIPS IN SPORTS SPONSORSHIP

Identifying the factors for successful relationships in sports sponsorship is a first step in the right direction. Based on recent studies (Chadwick, 2005; Farrelly and Quester, 2005; Bühler, 2006) we have identified five main factors which seem to be essential factors for successful relationships in the context of sports sponsorship. Figure 5.4 illustrates these five factors.

The following sections describe the respective factors and provide implications for sporting organisations in order to establish and maintain healthy relationships with their sponsors.

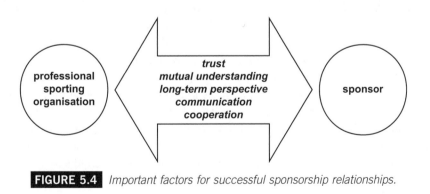

FIGURE 5.4   *Important factors for successful sponsorship relationships.*

Trust

Trust is an essential variable in the relationship between sports entities and sponsors. In order to build up trust, professional sporting organisations have to make sure that they deal fairly and openly with their sponsors. This implies that sports entities should not make any promises they cannot possibly keep as breaking promises reduces the confidence the sponsor has in the sponsorship partner. Open dealings also imply the courage to communicate unpleasant truths such as problems or conflicts. Of course, the same applies for the sponsoring company as well.

Mutual understanding

Mutual understanding of each others' objectives is another crucial factor regarding successful sports sponsorships. Thus, professional sporting organisations have to make sure that they understand the objectives and the needs of their sponsorship partner. Only then can sports entities help their sponsor to reach the partner's objectives. Sponsors, on the other hand, have to understand the requirements of the sports club primarily the financial needs, but also the focus on sporting performance and the pressure sporting organisations face in view of the public and media interest.

Long-term perspective

Sports entities should see their sponsors as long-term partners rather than as companies spending money for a few seasons. Sponsorship partners who look for long-term success would be well advised to build up a relationship with each other and to take the concept of relationship quality into consideration when doing so. The segmentation into 'transactional-orientated' and 'relational-orientated' sponsors might help professional sporting organisations in their decision whether to establish a long-term partnership based on the evaluation of their sponsor's relationship orientation. Nowadays, more and more companies seek long-term alliances with their sponsorship property. For example, the partnership between Carlsberg and Liverpool FC lasts until 1992 and is therefore seen as the most enduring brand sponsorship in football at a club level. However, every sponsorship agreement ends sometimes for various reasons (e.g. because the sponsorship partners have achieved their objectives or found better partners to do so). In this respect, it is very important to 'split up' in a professional and fair manner. The example of the German Bundesliga club Bayer 04 Leverkusen shows how sporting organisations can deal with a leaving sponsor: when their shirt sponsor RWE decided to drop out of their football sponsorships after seven years, Leverkusen put an advert in

Germany's leading sportsbusiness magazine, in which they said: "Seven years on the chest, forever in the heart – many thanks for a great partnership", in order to thank their longstanding sponsor (Figure 5.5).

FIGURE 5.5 *Bayer Leverkusen bids farewell to their longstanding sponsor.*

Communication

Successful sports sponsorships are also based on effective communication between sponsor and sponsee. Communication can take many different forms. Some sponsorship partners keep in touch on a regular basis via phone, e-mail or face-to-face meetings. In this respect, it is important that sporting organisations make sure that they provide important information about themselves and recent developments. Some professional sporting organisations have established a regular newsletter for their sponsors which includes articles about past events, birthdays of key decision makers or an outlook to future happenings. Other sports entities provide information exclusively for sponsors. For example, the main sponsors of the German professional basketball club Deutsche Bank Skyliners receive information regarding new players or other important issues before the information is made public. Therefore, sponsors gain the perception of having an exclusive information advantage. Communication between sports entities can take part on an individual basis or in a group setting where several sponsors are invited to spend an evening together in order to talk about various issues related to the sponsorship and other subjects.

Cooperation

Cooperation is another important issue when it comes to successful sports sponsorships. Involvement in each other's marketing and planning efforts is one form of cooperation and makes sense in view of the fact that it helps to achieve both partners' sponsorship objectives. Sponsors have generally more marketing skills than sporting organisations and could therefore support the sports entities in marketing issues, whereas professional sporting organisations could provide sponsors with sports-related know-how in order to improve their communication with sports fans. Case study 5.4 provides some examples of cooperation and collaboration in the context of sports sponsorship.

CASE STUDY 5.4. Cooperation in the Sponsorship Dyad

Cooperation is an important factor in the sponsorship dyad and can take many forms within and outside the context of the sponsorship agreement.

Some sports entities are trying to increase sales of their sponsors by introducing specific loyalty programmes for their fans. For example, the Italian football club *Inter Milan* has introduced a loyalty programme in cooperation with its sponsors. The programme allows Milan supporters to register their payment card details with the club in order to earn points when shopping at participating sponsors. For every purchase, cardholders can earn between one and twenty points which can be redeemed with Inter Milan for rewards including merchandising or even season tickets. Therefore all parties involved win. Fans are rewarded for their loyalty, the club strengthens its bond with their fans and the sponsors increase their direct sales.

Some other professional sporting organisations arrange specific sponsorship workshops where they meet with their sponsors in order to talk about areas for improvement and possibilities of joint activities. Such activities could be joint advertising campaigns where both the sports entity and the sponsors benefits from. For example, The New Zealand rugby team (called *The All Blacks*) as well as their sponsor *Adidas* attracted a lot of attention through their joint advertising campaign (Figure 5.6).

Cooperation can also take place outside the initial agreement and does not necessarily have to be linked to sponsorship issues as the following examples from some German Bundesliga clubs show.

VfB Stuttgart arranges an annual golf competition for their sponsors. Once a year, the decision makers of all sponsors are invited to come together and spend a day with their families on a golf course. The golf tournament is traditionally finished off by a party in the evening. This event is a good opportunity for sponsors and the sponsee to get to know each other a little bit better in a private setting.

TSV 1860 Munich invites their sponsors' decision makers and their families to spend a weekend at a chalet in the mountains once a year. Here again, sponsors and sponsees meet together in a private setting which can lead to a better and more personal sponsorship relationship.

Hertha BSC Berlin hosts a special VIP event whenever a new home or away kit is officially introduced. There, sponsors can take the opportunity to talk to the players and present themselves with the new jersey.

Some other professional sporting organisations invite their main sponsors to join the team at the pre-season training camps or at away games. Of course, the team and the sponsors stay at the same hotel which leads to a common bond. On special occasions such as away games in the Champions League, sponsors of *FC Bayern Munich* are allowed to take part in the traditional banquet after the match.

A very special event used to be organised by *Bayern Munich* and *VfB Stuttgart*. The night before the two teams were playing each other, a football match between the sponsors of both clubs was organised. Former internationals of both clubs were thereby playing in the sponsors' teams. Sources say that CEOs of major companies were happy as kids when they were travelling with the clubs' team buses to such occasions.

FIGURE 5.6 *Example of a joint advertising campaign.*

CONCLUSIONS

Sports sponsorship is an important source of income for professional sporting organisations and an effective marketing tool for companies who wish to reach commercial objectives through sports sponsorship. However, the most successful sports sponsorships are based on a good relationship between the sports entity and its sponsor. Both sponsorship partners have to work hand in hand to make the sponsorship a success. In this respect, various factors such as trust, communication, mutual understanding, cooperation and a long-term perspective are likely to improve the relationship. Overall, it is the sports entity's responsibility to make the sponsorship a success. Sporting organisations should therefore proactively work on the relationship and commit significant resources (such as time and people) to the sponsorships. A key factor in this respect is the appointment of appropriate people who look after the club's sponsors. They should have the necessary marketing and personal skills in order to communicate with the sponsors' key decision makers at eye level. In addition, the whole sporting organisation should be service orientated. In view of the fact that sports sponsorships should be considered as a two-way partnership, both sides should commit themselves in the long-term and cooperate fairly and trustfully.

DISCUSSION QUESTIONS

(1) What is sports sponsorship and how does it differ from patronage?
(2) Discuss the following statement: 'Sports sponsorship is only a source of income for sports entities.'
(3) What are the main objectives of companies engaging in sports sponsorship?
(4) What are the main advantages and disadvantages of sports sponsorship?
(5) Why can sports sponsorship be viewed from both a transactional and a relational view?
(6) What are the main factors contributing to a successful relationship between professional sporting organisations and their sponsors?
(7) What can professional sporting organisations do in order to improve the relationship with their sponsors?

GUIDED READING

Regarding sports sponsorship we would like to recommend the following two academic journals which regularly publish papers on sports sponsorship: *The International Journal of Sports Marketing & Sponsorship* and *Sports Marketing Quarterly*. In addition, Sam Fullerton comprehensively covers the area of sports sponsorship in his textbook titled *Sports Marketing*.

WEBSITES

Bayer 04 Leverkusen
http://www.bayer04.de

Carlsberg & Liverpool FC
http://www.carlsberg.co.uk/LiverpoolFootballClub.aspx

Emirates Stadium
http://www.arsenal.com/emiratesstadium/

FC Barcelona Fundació
http://www.fcbarcelona.cat/web/Fundacio/english

FC Bayern Munich
http://www.fcbayern.de

Galatasaray SK
http://www.galatasaray.org

Hertha BSC Berlin
http://www.herthabsc.de/

Inter Milan
http://www.inter.it

Karen Earl Sponsorship
http://www.karen-earl.co.uk/

Red Bull Salzburg
http://www.redbulls.com

Sport + Markt
http://www.sportundmarkt.com

The All Blacks
http://www.allblacks.com/

The Barclays Premiership
http://www.premierleague.com

The Institute of Sports Sponsorship
http://www.sports-sponsorship.co.uk/index.htm

The LA Lakers
http://www.nba.com/lakers/

TSV 1860 Munich
http://www.tsv1860.de

VfB Stuttgart
http://www.vfb.de/

CHAPTER 6

Relationship Marketing in Sports – The Media Perspective

Learning Outcomes

On completion of this chapter the reader should be able to:

- describe the various types of media with respect to sports
- explain the importance of the media for professional sporting organisations
- illustrate how sports entities and the media relate to each other
- explain the main problems and challenges sporting organisations face in dealing with the media
- provide examples of relationship marketing techniques aimed at the media

OVERVIEW OF CHAPTER

First, we will describe the various types of media and their connection to sports. We then explain the importance of the media for sporting organisations before looking at the relationship between sports entities and the media in detail. Subsequently, we will provide some examples of relationship marketing techniques aimed at the media. Finally, a case study illustrates how even a relatively small sporting organisation can establish effective media relations.

INTRODUCTION

Imagine the Olympic Games taking place unnoticed in some part of the world without any coverage of the most important sporting event on earth. Imagine no football games on television, no sports stories in the tabloids and

115

no sporting news on the internet. Such a scenario is unthinkable as the coverage of sports by television channels, newspapers, radio stations and any other kind of media is an essential part of our modern life. Case study 6.1 shows the dimension of media coverage of a global sports event such as the Football World Cup. However, sports and media interaction is more than collaboration. Both need each other. Both benefit – and sometimes suffer – from each other. The relationship between professional sporting organisations and the media is a special one as this chapter will show. In view of the fact that the media is not only an important stakeholder of the sports business but also a very special customer, establishing and maintaining a healthy relationship with the media becomes more and more important for professional sports entities.

CASE STUDY 6.1. Media Consumption FIFA World Cup 2006™

In 2006, the 18th FIFA World Cup took place in Germany and broke all records in media consumption as the following figures show impressively. The sixty-four games were broadcasted by 376 channels in 214 countries. Each 90-minute match received on average 858 hours of dedicated coverage resulting in more than 73,000 hours of total coverage. In other words, if the World Cup had been broadcasted by one channel only, people would have enjoyed 8 years of football coverage without a break. A total of 43,600 programmes dedicated to football were shown around the world during the World Cup. A cumulative TV audience of 26.29×10^9 viewers followed the games with an average 259.9 million viewers per game. The highest viewing figures were recorded for China (with a cumulative audience of nearly 4×10^9 viewers), Brazil, Vietnam and Germany. The final between Italy and France attracted a total cumulative audience of 715.1 million viewers.

A total of 18,850 media representatives (including 4250 print/internet journalists and editors, 1200 photographers, and 13,400 TV commentators, camera teams and technicians) were accredited. The FIFA World Cup website was the most successful sports event website in 2006 with 4.2×10^9 page views in the four weeks of the competition and 73 million page views on the FIFA World Cup mobile web portal. In addition, a vast number of football-related articles have been published in thousands of newspapers around the world before, after and during the World Cup 2006.

THE DIFFERENT TYPES OF MEDIA IN THE CONTEXT OF SPORTS

Media is an overall term for many different things. In the context of communication, media is a means by which information is distributed. Media can take many forms such as:

- print media: communications delivered via paper or canvas
- electronic media: communications delivered via electronic or electromechanical energy

- multimedia: communications that incorporate multiple forms of information content and processing
- published media: any media made available to the public
- mass media: all means of mass communication in order to reach a very large audience
- broadcast media: communications delivered over mass electronic communication networks
- news media: mass media focused on communicating news

The **mass media** plays a special role in the context of professional sports because of its ability to reach a wide audience through various mediums such as newspapers, magazines, television, radio and the internet. These mediums – with special regard to sports – will be explained in the following.

Newspapers

In general, a newspaper is a publication containing news, information and advertising, usually printed on low-cost paper. Newspapers may be of general interest or special interest, most often published daily or weekly. Most nations have at least one national newspaper that circulates throughout the whole country (e.g. *The Times* and *The Guardian* in Great Britain; *USA Today* in the United States of America; *Frankfurter Allgemeine Zeitung* in Germany; *Le Monde* and *Le Figaro* in France). In addition, there are local newspapers serving a city or region. Most newspapers are either broadsheets (generally associated with more intellectual newspapers such as *The Independent* in the UK) or tabloids (often perceived as sensationalist such as *The Sun* in Great Britain or the *BILD-Zeitung* in Germany). General-interest newspapers usually include current news such as political events, crime, business, and culture. However, there are also some special-interest papers such as *The Financial Times*. In the context of sports, the most famous **sports newspaper** are *La Gazetto dello Sport* (Italy), *AS* and *Marca* (both Spanish). Furthermore, nearly every newspaper includes a more or less comprehensive sports section. In view of the fact that various newspapers have various customers (with distinguishing levels of interest and intellect) and differing levels of competitive pressure, the layout and content of the sports sections differ from each other. Intellectual newspapers are trying to cover sports in a serious way and with reasonable diligence. In contrast, tabloids present sports in a sensational (and often unserious) manner. It seems that sometimes the background stories are more important than the actual sports event.

Magazines

Magazines (also called periodicals or serials) are publications which are generally published on a regular schedule (weekly, monthly, bimonthly or quarterly). They contain a variety of articles either covering general subjects or focusing on special subjects. Current magazines are generally available at bookstores and newsstands, while subscribers can receive them in the mail. Some magazines are available both in hard copy and on the internet, usually in different versions, though some are only available in hard copy or only via the internet (the latter are known as online magazines). Most magazines are available in the whole of the country in which they are published, although some are distributed only in specific regions or cities. Others are available internationally (e.g. *The Economist*), often in different editions for each country or area of the world, varying to some degree in editorial and advertising content but not entirely dissimilar. Magazines fall into two broad categories: business magazines and consumer magazines. Similar to a magazine, in some respects, is an **academic periodical** (also called academic journal), which features scholarly articles in specialised fields. The most important **academic journals** in the context of professional sports are:

- The *International Journal of Sports Marketing & Sponsorship*
- The *European Journal for Sport and Society*
- *Sport Marketing Europe*
- *Sport Marketing Quarterly*
- *European Sport Management Quarterly*
- The *Journal of Sport Management*

Although academic journals and **sports business magazines** (such as *SPONSORs* and *Horizont Sport Business* in Germany or *Sport Business International* in the UK) have only a limited audience, they have an important impact in view of the fact that they are mainly read by key decision makers in the field of sports business. However, the majority of sports magazines are consumer magazines aimed at the ordinary sports fan. There are **sports magazines** which cover a variety of sports (e.g. *Sport-Bild* in Germany) and there are sports magazines which focus on one sport only (e.g. *FourFourTwo* in Great Britain or *11 Freunde* in Germany are famous football magazines published on a monthly basis).

Radio

In the early radio age, content typically included a balance of comedy, drama, news, music and sports reporting. By the late 1950s, radio broadcasting took on much the form it has today – strongly focused on music, news and sports. Indeed, radio still plays an important part in sports coverage in view of the fact that a lot of radio stations provide live coverage of sports events. Listening to the radio conference switching of football games on a Saturday afternoon is a legendary and popular habit of numerous football fans across Europe. A special form of radio is **sports radio**, which is devoted entirely to discussion and broadcasting of sporting events. Sports radio is characterised by an often-boisterous on-air style and extensive debate and analysis by both hosts and callers; political commentary is rare. The format is very popular amongst an almost exclusively male demographic. Many **sports talk stations** also carry play-by-play of local sports teams as part of their regular programming. For example, the Boston-based sports radio station *WEEI 850 AM Sports Radio* broadcasts Boston Red Sox games (baseball), Boston Celtics games (basketball), and provides extensive coverage of the New England Patriots (American Football).

Television

Television has become a source of entertainment and news since television sets first became commercially available in the late 1930s. Television genres include a broad range of programming types that entertain, inform, and educate viewers. Popular entertainment genres include action-oriented shows and comedy. The least expensive forms of entertainment programming are game shows, talk shows, variety shows, and reality TV. Television genres that aim to educate and inform viewers include educational shows such as DIY programmes on gardening, home renovation or cooking as well as history shows, performing arts programmes, and documentaries. Other genres which inform viewers include news and public affairs programming. The television landscape of a single country consists of many different channels nowadays. People in Germany, for example, are able to receive around fifty different channels free-to-air. At least twenty of them cover all kinds of sports on a regular basis.

Indeed, sports, is a genre which both informs and entertains viewers. Sports can deliver wide audiences and is therefore an effective driver for many TV stations. Nearly every main TV station covers sports to some extent, either through live coverage or by broadcasting highlights of a game. In addition, there are special TV stations focusing exclusively on sports (e.g. *Sky Sports* in the UK, *Deutsches Sport Fernsehen* in Germany, *FOX Sports* and *ESPN* in the USA, or *Eurosport* in Europe). Sports programmes on TV may be general (featuring different sports in one programme) or may focus on individual sports (e.g. the football programme *BBC Match of the Day* in the UK or the *Golf Channel* in the US and the *Rugby Channel* in New Zealand). Nearly all **sports programmes** include extensive analysis and debates by the so-called TV pundits, who are often former sportsmen (e.g. the former English internationals Gary Linker and Alan Hansen at the BBC's *Match of the Day*). Television stations covering sports can be classified as **Free TV stations** (e.g. the *BBC* in Great Britain) or **Pay-TV stations** (e.g. *BSkyB* in the UK and *Premiere* in Germany). Free-to-air TV stations are financed mainly by advertising or by public fees as in the case of TV stations which are subject to public law (just as *ARD* and *ZDF* in Germany). Pay-TV stations are financed by their subscribers who pay a fee for the whole package (including various channels and/or programmes). A special form of Pay-TV is Pay-Per-View-TV (PPV) where subscribers pay for a specific match or competition. All in all, television seems to be the most important form of media for the business of sports as we will see later.

Internet

The internet has dramatically shaped our world and changed our lives with new opportunities emerging. Of course, sports is a popular content of the internet. Countless websites covering sports from all angles have been set up in the last years, most of them privately run. In addition, there are **commercial sports websites** such as *Sport1.de* in Germany which provide sports news and sports related content. Increased transmission speed has made video and audio streaming more practical. Consequently, more and more providers offer not only information but also live coverage of sports events. This is especially important for smaller sports that cannot make it on television, but need to reach wide audiences in order to be attractive for sponsors. Consequently, the internet as a medium for sports becomes more and more important. Therefore, a lot of media companies as well as sporting organisations are looking for ways to make use of the internet. For example, nearly every professional football club in Europe offers a so called **club.TV** to which fans can subscribe in order to watch the highlights of their favourite teams' matches. Furthermore, some companies provide **PPV formats** for sports fans. The German sports right agency SPORTFIVE, for example, established an internet channel called Sportdigital.TV where they provide live coverage of handball, basketball and volleyball games. For 2.99 Euros subscribers can purchase the specific game which they can watch live in real-time on their computer. Once the game has been bought it can be watched over and over again. This might be an interesting feature for fans who have attended the game live at the venue but want to watch it again at home. With the internet, sporting organisations are able to grow their international fan base because the internet has given supporters around the world the opportunity to follow their team and to watch the games.

Mobile communication

In a world where mobile phones, PDAs (personal digital assistants) and podcasts (a collection of digital media files which is distributed over the internet) are a crucial part of everyday life, mobile communication becomes more and more important. Through new technological standards such as WAP (Wireless Application Protocol) or UMTS (Universal Mobile Telecommunications System) people can access the internet from a mobile phone or PDA and therefore receive information and entertainment wherever they are. Content providers (e.g. media companies, telecommunication companies or sporting organisations) can provide a wide range of mobile content. Sports fans are now able to follow a game live on their mobile phone, they can read sports news or access the sports entities' websites. In view of the fact that an increasing number of sports fans are prepared to pay considerable fees for such offers, a new source of revenue becomes available for content providers. In addition, marketers as well as sporting organisations are able to communicate with their target group one-to-one by sending text messages and engaging the users in interactive competitions.

As we have seen above, media includes many different forms of publication and means of communication. In addition, the communication behaviour of sports fans changes. More and more people, especially the younger ones, consume news and information through modern means of communication such as the internet or mobile devices. As a consequence, companies have to advertise in new media in order to reach their target groups. Media companies are aware of the media variety on the one hand and the **changing communication behaviour** of sports fans on the other hand. Thus, a lot of media companies are trying to include many different forms of media in their portfolio in order to reach as many target groups as possible and to generate additional advertising revenues. For example, ESPN (the US-American Entertainment and Sports Programming Network) communicates with sports fans through a number of different communication channels such as television networks (e.g. ESPNEWS, ESPN2, ESPN Classic and ESPN Deportes), radio stations (e.g. ESPN Radio), magazines (e.g. ESPN the Magazine), an interactive website with audio and video streamings (ESPN. com) and a mobile phone content provider (ESPN Mobile). Their European counterpart Eurosport has also established a media portfolio in order to provide sports fans with their favourite means of communication as Case study 6.2 shows.

CASE STUDY 6.2. The Media Portfolio of Eurosport

Eurosport was founded in 1989 as the first European TV station exclusively focusing on sports. The programme philosophy was and still is a simple one: Eurosport covers all Olympic sports – summer as well as winter sports – and thereby provides the best live coverage of sports. Indeed, 44% of the programme is dedicated to live sports – mostly at full length. Another important aspect is the multilingualism of Eurosport which offers its content in 20 different language versions, including English, German, French, Italian, Dutch, Swedish, Finish, Spanish, Czech, Russian, Hungarian, Danish, Polish, Portuguese, Romanian, Norwegian, Turkish, Greek, Bulgarian and Serb.

Over the last years, Eurosport (which is solely owned by the biggest commercial broadcaster in France, TF1) has established itself as the leading multimedia platform in sports. The media portfolio includes – in addition to the main programme Eurosport – the following media:

Eurosport 2

Eurosport 2 is the digital programme of Eurosport which can be received by cable or satellite in 40 countries thereby reaching more than 22 million households. Eurosport 2 complements the main programme by additional 1500 hours of live sports such as motor sports, handball, basketball, football, extreme sports, and winter sports. The programme selection of Eurosport 2 focuses deliberately on a younger target group.

Eurosportnews

Eurosportnews is a digital news channel which covers sports news in six different languages. It can be received in more than 70 countries around the clock.

Eurosport Mobile

Eurosport makes use of WAP and UMTS in order to enable sports fans to receive sports news and live coverage of sports events on their mobile devices.

Eurosport.com

Eurosport provides websites in seven languages across Europe which record more than 26 million visits per month. In Germany, UK & Ireland, Spain and Italy, Eurosport cooperates with Yahoo in order to offer one of the leading sports websites in Europe. According to the agreement, Yahoo provides its leading Web 2.0 know-how as well as the respective community services, whereas Eurosport offers high-quality content and editorial expertise. Sports fans are able to watch live scores as well as interviews and selected live events on the website. A media archive with more than 15,000 interviews and highlights as well as a game zone with more than 400 online sports games are additional features of the co-branded website. In total, 60 full-time and 100 part-time employees are responsible for the Eurosport websites.

Eurosport Events

The Eurosport group also seeks opportunities in the market of sports rights. Eurosport Events, an affiliated company of Eurosport, takes care of various sports rights. For example, there is a direct involvement in motor sports (FIA World Touring Car Championships) and football (global rights of the French national team). Furthermore, a new media cooperation with SailingOne (a French media company) was established in order to promote a new sailing regatta called SolOceans.

All in all, Eurosport reaches 110 million households and 240 million people in 59 countries with different means of communication.

THE IMPORTANCE OF THE MEDIA FOR PROFESSIONAL SPORTING ORGANISATIONS

Sports is an important driver for the media as we have seen above. However, the media is equally important for professional sporting organisations for various reasons. First, revenues generated from the sales of broadcasting rights are an essential income stream for sports entities. Second, the media can help to boost the image of a sports club or association. And finally, the media can be an effective political tool for sporting organisations as we will see in the course of this section. Let us have a look at the monetary aspect first.

Media companies are keen on sports because it delivers wide audiences. A lot of sporting organisations are blessed with so much mass appeal that the media is compelled to cover sports entities on a daily basis. Of course, the media turns the popularity of sports teams into money by selling more papers, magazines or generating more income from advertising. However, in order to show games or competitions – either live or as highlights – the media has to buy the respective broadcasting right first. In general, the sporting organisations sell their rights to the media, who then refinance their expenditures by revenues from subscribers and/or advertisers. The broadcasting rights market is a booming business. For example, the recent deal for Indian cricket ($612 million for cable, broadband, internet and radio rights) was eleven times the price of the previous TV rights deal. However, a number of television channels have suffered serious losses as a result of unprofitable acquisitions of sports rights in the last years. A key problem seems to be that rating figures for international tournaments within a country are highly dependent on the success of either domestic clubs or the national team. For example, the French broadcasting group TFI purchased the rights for the 2002 World Cup in which the French team was eliminated in the first round. As a consequence, TFI suffered a direct loss of twenty to thirty million Euros as well as decreasing stock prices (Desbordes, 2006). Another problem is that a lot of fans watch sports events free of charge on the internet. For example, approximately more than a hundred thousand people, especially younger ones, are watching live games of the English Premier League on illegal websites each week without paying for it. Besides these problems, sports broadcasting is becoming an increasingly valuable property for media companies, as its real-time nature makes it an anomaly among programming types and a powerful lure to advertisers. For professional sporting organisations, the sale of broadcasting rights is an essential part of their business. Revenues from sales of **broadcasting rights** (including TV rights, radio broadcasting, internet rights and rights for multimedia usage) have become the most important income stream for the majority of professional sporting organisations. In European football, for example, broadcasting revenues account for nearly forty percent of the clubs' total turnover. The English Premier League has secured two broadcasting deals worth around £2.325 $\times$ 10^9 (£1.7 $\times$ 10^9 for domestic television rights and £625 million for overseas rights).

Apart from the financial aspect, the media can be very important for professional sporting organisations in terms of publicity and image. The media plays an important role when it comes to promoting the sports entity. Newspapers, magazines, radio, television and the internet transport the name and the image of the club whenever they cover a game or publish a story about the respective sporting organisation. A sports entity which is prominently displayed in various media can boost its image and reach new target groups and therefore grow its fan base. Television thus serves as a marketing tool for sports entities, since they are in the focus of public attention through the media. In addition, the media can be seen as the gateway for the sponsors and advertisers. A sports entity which attracts a lot of publicity and media contacts might find it easier to attract potential sponsors and advertisers.

In addition, the media can serve as an effective weapon when it comes to politics. Whenever sporting organisations need public backing they can use the media to promote their opinion. For example, the local media often plays a crucial role in sports venue developments because they have the power to influence the public opinion and put pressure on local politicians and decision makers who would rather oppose projects in view of the financial risks involved. With the help of the media, sporting organisations might push their needs through.

THE RELATIONSHIP BETWEEN PROFESSIONAL SPORTING ORGANISATIONS AND THE MEDIA

The relationship between professional sporting organisations and the media can be best described with the picture of Siamese twins: both need each other to survive. In view of this **interdependency** both parties are well advised to seek for a positive relationship in general. In this section we will have a closer look at the relationship between sports entities and the media by describing the different relational levels in the sports entity – media dyad, as well as examining the relationship from both perspectives.

The different relational levels in the sports entity – media dyad

Cooperation between sports entities and the media can take place on different levels (i.e. the personal and the organisational level) and often involves different representatives of both sides.

The personal level

Cooperation between sporting organisations and the media mainly takes place on a personal level involving close contacts and even amicable relations between representatives of sports entities and the media. In general, the media is represented by journalists, commentators, editors, chief editors and the owners of media companies. People representing the sporting organisation can be the owners or the presidents of the sports entity, members of the management, coaches, players and employees responsible for media relations. The different personal relationships will be described in the following.

The most obvious relationship exists between journalists and the official spokesmen of a sports entity. A lot of sporting organisations have established their own press or communication departments with an official press spokesman at the top of it. The communication managers within the sports entities' press departments make up and release press handouts, organise their own press conferences and coordinate interview requests. They also check and evaluate the coverage and try to sort out problems whenever they arise. Most communication managers and press spokesmen have known the local editors for many years and have established a personal relationship which is characterised by a sense of mutual understanding. Communication often takes place on an informal level. Should problems occur they can be solved easily with a phone call or a brief face-to-face meeting. One of the most important issues in these relationships is trust. Journalists have to trust that the sports entities' press spokesmen provide them with correct information and deal with them fairly and openly, and communication managers of clubs and associations have to trust that editors do not misuse the given information.

Another relationship exists between journalists and the top management of sporting organisations. Presidents, managing directors or commercial managers of sports clubs often maintain longstanding relationships with (chief) editors of the local media or even the owners of media companies. Here again, the relationship is supposed to be mutually beneficent in view of the fact that both parties exchange information and news. Known journalists might find it easier to get an interview with clubs' representatives than those who do not engage in positive relationships. On the other hand, members of a sporting organisation's top management might prevent the publication of a problematic story because of a longstanding relationship with the chief editor of a newspaper.

On a sporting level a number of different relationships exist. Coaches and managers, for example, often maintain friendly contacts with journalists. Therefore, those journalists might receive exclusive information in return for less critical coverage. However, sports is a fast moving business and coaches are hired and fired very often, which makes it difficult for media representatives to establish trusting relationships. That is also true for relationships between journalists and players. Some journalists try to establish amicable relations with players in order to get exclusive information. In turn, players might make use of such a relationship when it comes to contract or transfer negotiations. A positive article in the newspaper can boost the image and the personal market value of the respective player.

All these relationships – especially those that take place on a personal level – might benefit both sides but could also lead to potential conflict of interests. Objectivity and trustworthiness is a key issue in journalism and therefore must always be guaranteed. On the other hand, sports entities and their representatives should be professional enough to maintain a certain balance in dealing with the media.

The organisational level

Besides the more personal level, cooperation between sporting organisations and the media can take place on an organisational level. More and more sports entities are seeking specific media partnerships. This special form of collaboration is a combination of media cooperation and sponsorship. Often local and regional companies act as 'the official media partner' of a certain sports club. For example, *XFM Radio* (a local radio station in Manchester) acts as the official radio partner of Manchester United and is allowed to provide full and uninterrupted match commentary on all Manchester United games. Media partnerships like these are based on contractual agreements which define both sides' tasks and obligations. Sometimes, media partners even have to pay a fee for their association with the respective sports entity.

The ultimate form of media partnerships is the acquisition of sporting clubs by media companies. In the late 1990s Rupert Murdoch, the famous Australian-American global media tycoon, and his media network (including News Corporation, Fox Entertainment, BSkyB) bought considerable shares of major sports entities as the following examples show. In 1998, Fox Entertainment purchased the Los Angeles Dodgers (baseball) for $311 million and gained foothold in the US-American sports franchise market with a 40% interest in both the New York Rangers (ice hockey) and the New York Knicks (basketball). In 1999, BSkyB tried to buy Manchester United for £623 million but the bid was eventually blocked by the Mergers and Monopolies Commission. Instead, BSkyB gained part-ownership in individual English football clubs such as Chelsea FC, Leeds United, Manchester City, Manchester United and Sunderland FC with a 9.9% stake at each club, which was the maximum percentage allowed for ownership in multiple clubs in the

UK at the time (Andrews, 2003). Acquisitions like these are a clear commercial investment and involve some logic: media companies owning sports entities (partly or entirely) can influence the clubs' media strategy and, most of all, have a say when it comes to broadcasting negotiations. Furthermore, having a sporting organisation in the portfolio is a prestigious thing for media companies. However, collaboration on this level should be viewed critically. The relationship between a sports entity and a media corporation is unlikely to be a healthy one if the media company cares more about its short-term profits than about the long-term future of the respective sports club or organisation. Jerry Colangelo in his book 'How You Play the Game' (1999) rightly stated that owning a professional sports team should not be a right, but a privilege.

The relationship between sporting organisations and the media from both perspectives

In order to present a realistic picture of the relationship between sports entities and the media we have spoken with a number of journalists and editors on the one hand and with communication managers and official press spokesmen of sports clubs and associations on the other hand. In this section we will present their points of view and describe how they perceive the relationship between sporting organisations and the media.

The relationship as perceived by sports entities

In general, the relationship between sporting organisations and the media is described as a positive one by the representatives of sports entities. Trust and mutual understanding were named as the most important aspects of a healthy relationship. Some press spokesmen told us that they maintain close and nearly amicable relations with a small number of journalists and that long-standing relationships help in daily work with the media because they know the business and they know how to use delicate information. For example, some years ago a key decision maker in German sports had a sexual affair with his secretary and she eventually became pregnant. A number of journalists knew about it but did not cover the story because they had established a longstanding relationship with the respective official and therefore respected his private life. However, one tabloid eventually broke the silence and one paper after the other then covered the story. This case shows that close relations can not always prevent a story but can delay its publication. Another benefit of positive relationships with the media is the exchange of information. Managers of sports entities often receive important pieces of information from close journalists who talk to each other. Some representatives of sporting organisations explained that they use particular journalists as messengers in order to deliver important messages. Other journalists (often those who have a reputation for gossiping) are used for spreading rumours which benefit the own sports entity and/or damage the competitor. However, nearly all sporting organisations we spoke with admitted that there are problems, difficulties and conflicts in the relationship with the media from time to time. The following statement of the press spokesman of a professional sports club reflects the widespread opinion:

> 'We and the media are in the same boat. However, sometimes it seems that we are rowing in different directions.'

Although the majority of journalists seem to be fair and serious in doing their job, there are some journalists and papers who make things up, exaggerate stories or simply spread lies in order to increase the circulation of their papers. In this respect, each sporting organisation sets its own acceptance limit. Hertha BSC Berlin, for example, does not allow any unauthorized home stories of their players published in tabloids because they want to protect the private life of their players, especially the younger ones. If such a story were published, the club would seek a legal response. Communication managers of other sports entities told us that they work with lawyers (specialising in entertainment law) who take legal steps resulting in injunctions against media companies, whenever a story is incorrect or totally fabricated. However, legal steps are the ultimate measure because clubs seek the direct dialogue with problematic journalists or papers in the first place whenever a problem occurs. A number of our interviewees on the club side noted that some editors need to be reminded that their jobs depend, at least to some extent, on the success of the sports entity they are writing about. Therefore, bad publicity would not do them any good. In summary, all of the sporting organisation's representatives emphasised that the relationship with the media is a professional one. Now let us have a look at the relationship between sporting organisations and the media from the perspective of the media.

The relationship as perceived by the media

All editors and journalists we have spoken with, named the interdependency as the main characteristic of the sports entity – media dyad. During our interviews we realised that the sports journalists show not only a professional attitude but also a strong affinity towards sports which can result in a deep emotional attachment towards a specific club. The resulting problem described by the interviewees is the balancing act between being objective and being a fan. One journalist told us that it is very difficult to obtain an objective and critical attitude after twenty years of reporting about a certain club because one has known the club's representatives for many years and established real friendships. Objectivity, however, is a key factor for every editor and commentator. For example, the German public television stations ARD and ZDF stopped their live coverage of the Tour de France 2007 following a number of positive drugs test. The decision was a difficult one because both stations and their commentators had established tight links with officials and racing cyclist over the years. However, in order to remain credible both stations dropped the live coverage of cycling competitions.

The overall relationship between sporting organisations and the media was described as a good and relatively healthy one, in general. Some editors, however, said that the quality of the relationship depended pretty much on the individual people involved. For example, some managers and players know how to deal with the media and show understanding and respect which then leads to a decent working relationship. Some other players, managers or officials simply do not collaborate with the media which in turn leads to rather negative stories. Mutual respect and some sense of understanding have been named as the most important factors for positive relationships. The interview presented in Case study 6.3 provides additional points describing the relationship between sporting organisations and the media.

CASE STUDY 6.3. The Sporting Organisation – Media Relationship: Views from the Inside

One of the media we were talking to was *SPONSORs*, Germany's biggest magazine on sports business. They allowed us to reprint the interview with editor Michael Weilguny who deals with sports entities on a daily basis for many years now.

How would you describe the relationship between the media and sporting organisations from your point of view?

Generally, it is a mutual dependence. The media depends on sports. Sports is one of the main drivers of the media and a major reason why people watch television, read newspapers and surf the internet. In turn, sports is dependent on the medial reporting. No sports becomes big without television, without radio, without newspapers and without the internet. The best example in Germany is ski jumping. First, it has been extensively promoted by a TV station and therefore gained huge publicity. Then it has been abandoned and

subsequently disappeared. Again, sports and media greatly depend on each other.

What's the relationship between editors and the press spokesmen of sports entities like?

It differs, I think. Both sides are aware of the mutual dependence. Sometimes cooperation works better, sometimes worse. I can't make general judgements, it depends on the single case.

Where do conflicts occur in such a relationship?

Some conflicts occur because press spokesmen want to read a different article from the one that the editors write. Of course, the press spokesman takes care of his company, his club or his association and wants his organisation to be shown as best as possible. The editors, on the other side, are interested in the story. And the editors, especially those

Continued

from tabloids, benefit more from a critical headline or super-latives, positive as well as negative ones, than from a boring story. However, in our case it's different because we benefit more from stories with profound content than from big head-lines. Having said that, there might be some conflict poten-tial whenever we critically cover some key people.

There are some sports entities which invite editors to join their training camps in Dubai in order to get a positive story. Where should editors draw the line?

Some magazines and newspapers do not accept any invi-tation at all. If they want to write something about a specific sponsor they would not accept an invitation in the VIP box of the sponsor but would rather pay for the tickets on their own.

Does the invitation of a sports entity influence the coverage at all?

In no way! I am strongly convinced that it does not influ-ence our coverage at all. The only benefit a sports entity or a sponsor gets, is the contact. And a good contact can be worth a lot for companies. However, a good contact doesn't have any influence on the story itself. If I – as an editor – would be influenced by that, then I would score an own goal. Objectivity is above everything else.

How would you assess the media relations of sporting orga-nisations from your perspective?

The general problem is that a lot of sporting organisations are very defensive in terms of media relations. The main part of media relations at sports clubs consists of preventing a headline rather than thinking about how a story could be placed within a medium. They should better focus on the brand and try to make it into lifestyle magazines. Football, for example, is not only a sports, it is also some kind of

lifestyle. Therefore, football clubs should try to place their stars and icons in the respective magazines. That just doesn't happen enough. Some sporting organisations simply don't have enough people or the right people to do that. Sporting organisation employ less people in media relations than ordinary companies do. However, I notice that sports clubs and associations begin to invest more resources for communication nowadays. But that should have been done earlier and to a greater extent.

Let us imagine you are the media representative of a sports club. From your experience as an editor, what would you do in order to ensure an effective cooperation with the media?

Well, I should chose my words carefully because I am the editor of a special interest magazine and therefore I am not as close to clubs as editors of regular newspapers who attend training sessions and press conferences on a daily basis. As for me, I would like clubs to consider our wishes to a greater extent. And that they cater for our needs. That they proactively think about stories which could be placed in our magazine. Within the last five years almost none German sports club made a suggestion as how to place a story in our magazine. It could be so easy. They could come and say 'Hey, we do have a new sponsor who has a lot of new ideas. Couldn't you make a story and tell your readers about our new sponsor and his ideas?' No move. Nothing. Sporting organisations do not have a proactive atti-tude when it comes to media relations. On the other hand, there is an agency which calls us at least three times a year asking whether we could do a story about a certain baseball association. Baseball might not have such a high sporting status here in Germany, but they are proactive and they approach us.

All in all, the relationship between sporting organisations and the media as perceived by both sides can be described as a mostly professional one. Both parties are aware of the interdependencies and therefore both the sports entities and the media try to collaborate in a professional manner. Personal or even amicable relations between representatives of sporting organisations and the media can lead to mutually beneficiary relationships as long as trust and friendship is not misused by one side or the other. In the next section we will have a look at what sporting organisations can actually do in order to establish and maintain healthy relationships with the media.

RELATIONSHIP MARKETING TECHNIQUES AIMING AT THE MEDIA

There are many options available for sporting organisations to establish and maintain a good relationship with the media. First of all, the working conditions for the media (including journalists, editors, commentators, cameramen and technicians) have to be of good quality. The flow of information is an essential factor in this context. Most sports entities distribute press releases on a daily basis. The bigger sports clubs hold press conferences featuring managers, selected players or officials nearly every day, the smaller clubs provide such an opportunity before and after each game, at least. In this respect, a growing number of sports entities provide a special service for smaller papers or stations enabling them to follow the press conference live on the internet and thereby giving them the option to ask questions online. Furthermore, press spokesmen and communication managers of sporting organisations chat with the media on the phone every day in order to provide information and answer questions. In addition, more and more sports entities provide an own password-protected media section on their website where registered journalists can log in and download information and pictures. A very important point in terms of information flow is the availability of players for individual interviews. Of course, some players are more in demand than others and therefore star players can not meet every enquiry. The press department of a sports club has the difficult task of balancing the number of interviews without disappointing the media. They also must make sure that their players deal with the media professionally. After all, dealing with the media is part of the players' job and therefore some clubs even provide journalists with the players' mobile numbers. With regard to access to players', it is important that clubs establish and communicate a strict policy. The preparation for a game should not be disturbed and the private life of players should not be covered without prior authorisation. In order to establish and maintain positive relationships with the media, a lot of sporting organisations invite media representatives on special occasions. For example, some clubs invite close journalists to attend their summer or winter training camps at the clubs' expenses. Some other sports entities invite editors to social events such as gala dinners or charity balls hosted by the respective sporting organisation. Another opportunity to strengthen the bond between the sporting organisation and the media are 'away games' in international cup competitions. For example, some football clubs invite the local media to travel with them to UEFA Champions League games taking place in major European cities where the media then stays in the same hotel as the team and takes part in the post-match gala. Although such events are a good opportunity to maintain good relationships they can also damage relations with the media in case the journalists perceive such invitations as some kind of bribe. In this respect, sporting organisations should be sensible and always emphasise that they do not expect a service or a favour in return. Another – and less expensive – relationship marketing tool is the establishment of a data base including personal and professional data of each journalist, editor, commentator or other media representative the sporting organisation is dealing with. An individual birthday card or seasonal greetings as well as small birthday presents for the kids are small tokens which contribute to a positive relationship. Often it is not the present or gift itself, but the fact that the sporting organisation remembered and cared about the individual media representative that counts. Case study 6.4 describes what even a small sports entity can do in order to establish and maintain a good relationship with the media.

CASE STUDY 6.4. Media Relations at the Deutsche Bank Skyliners

The Deutsche Bank Skyliners are a professional club of the German top basketball league (BBL). The club was founded in 1999 and won the German Cup final in its first year and the German Championship in 2004. The Skyliners are a relatively small sporting organisation in terms of annual turnover (around 3.5 million Euros in 2007) and number of staff (41 full-time and six part-time employees, including players and coaches have worked for the club in 2007). However, the Deutsche Bank Skyliners are seriously managed with professionals at the top management level. This becomes apparent in the area of media relations where the club is collaborating on many different levels with the media. The Deutsche Bank Skyliners cooperate with various media partners; among them a local radio station (radio fortuna) which provides live coverage of every Skyliner game home and away. In addition, they broadcast a 30-minute radio show on a weekly basis. The topics and guests of each show are scheduled in consultation with the club. The Skyliners also cooperate with Eurosport which broadcasts all home games of the European Cup competition (ULEB Cup) live. Another media partner, the production company GOTV!, produces video highlights and interviews for the club's website. In order to be a professional partner for the media, the club has appointed a full-time media expert who is responsible for establishing and maintaining a positive and healthy relationship with media representatives as well as fulfilling their needs. In order to keep the media informed, a press release is distributed at least three times a week and a press conference is held before and after each game. Furthermore, communication between the club's press spokesman and the most important editors takes place on a daily basis in order to exchange information. Regular meetings, including an evening meal, are held between the media and club's representatives (top management, coaches) to speak about issues which cannot be covered in press conferences. On match days, the club provides excellent working conditions for the media. The press room of the arena and the press seats on the sidelines are equipped with state-of-the-art features such as DSL, ISDN, phone and fax terminals.

Media representatives also receive all kinds of information such as statistics and line-ups once they have entered the venue. Half an hour before the game, journalists have the chance to attend a tactic session in the players' dressing room where the head coach explains the tactical plans for the respective game. After each match, photographers and cameramen have the opportunity to take pictures in the dressing room. In addition, selected representatives of big newspapers, television channels and radio stations are invited to join the team and coaches for dinner in the VIP area. Whenever an away game takes place, the club takes care of the transportation of journalists, commentators and editors. In

2005 and 2007, the club invited the media to Istanbul and Valencia where the team played European Cup games.

At the beginning of each year, selected journalists have the opportunity to take part in a special new-years dinner where the head coach provides background information for the forthcoming games. The head coach is also involved in a special workshop where he explains basketball tactics to journalists who are new in the field. At the end of each season, a basketball match between representatives of the club and the media takes place. Events like that strengthen the bond between club and media.

The example of the Deutsche Bank Skyliners shows that media relations are a difficult task and hard work for a club, but leads to a positive relationship between the sporting organisation and the media.

CONCLUSIONS

The relationship between sporting organisations and the media is based on the fact that both need each other. The media needs sports as content for its publications and programmes and sports entities need the media in order to grow their publicity and their brand on the one hand and to generate significant revenues from broadcasting rights on the other hand. Sporting organisations face the challenge of dealing effectively with a variety of different types of media (e.g. papers, magazines, television, radio, internet). In addition, collaboration takes place on different relational levels. First, on the personal level involving individual journalists, editors, commentators and other representatives on the media side and owners, presidents, managers, coaches, players as well as communication managers and press spokesmen on the part of the sporting organisation. Secondly, collaboration can take place on an organisational level. More and more sports entities seek official media partners, for example. In order to deal with the media in a professional manner on all levels sports clubs and associations should have a dedicated team of people taking care of media relations. The tasks of such a press or communication department involve an effective flow of information, the provision of good working conditions for the media and the establishment and maintenance of positive relations with the media. In this respect, sports entities can apply a range of different relationship marketing techniques. However, objectivity is (or at least should be) an essential issue for every journalist and therefore sporting organisations have to be careful when inviting media representatives to various events or giving away gifts, because such activities can be easily misperceived as an attempt at bribery. With regard to this delicate manner and with regard to relationships between sporting organisations and the media in general it can be concluded that trust and a sense of mutual understanding are key factors.

DISCUSSION QUESTIONS

(1) Please name the most important types of media with regard to sports.
(2) What opportunities does the internet provide for sporting organisations?
(3) Why are sports entities so important for the media?
(4) Why is the media so important for sports entities?
(5) How would you describe the relationship between sporting organisations and their media?
(6) What problems and conflicts might occur in the relationship?
(7) Imagine you are the communication manager of your favourite sports team. What would you do in order to establish and maintain a good relationship with the media?

GUIDED READING

For a closer look at the relation between sports and the media we would recommend a textbook by Matthew Nicholson called *Sport and the Media: Managing the Nexus*. The book covers the historical development of sports and the media, explains the current commercial and contextual relationships between the media and sports industries, explores ways in which audiences and advertisers drive the media coverage of sports, describes ways in which the media industry generally and the sports industry more specifically are structured to produce content/news/products, and finally introduces ways in which the media represents sports in order to sell it. Another textbook we would recommend comes from Claude Jeanrenaud and Stefan Késenne called *The Economics of Sport and the Media*. In this book various authors from different countries examine a number of issues relating to the broadcasting of sports on the one hand and the sale and purchasing of sports media rights on the other hand.

WEBSITES

11Freunde
http://www.11freunde.de

AS
http://www.as.com

Deutsche Bank Skyliners
http://www.deutsche-bank-skyliners.de

Deutsches Sport Fernsehen
http://www.dsf.de

European Sport Management Quaterly
http://www.easm.net

Entertainment and Sports Programming Network (ESPN)
http://espn.go.com

Eurosport
http://www.eurosport.com

FIFA Media
http://www.fifa.com/aboutfifa/media/index.html

FourFourTwo
http://info.fourfourtwo.co.uk

FOX Sports
http://msn.foxsports.com

HORIZONT SPORT BUSINESS
http://www.sportbusiness.horizont.net

La Gazetta dello Sport
http://www.gazzetta.it

Marca
http://www.marca.com

The European Journal for Sport and Society
http://www.ejss.de

The Golf Channel
http://www.thegolfchannel.com

The International Journal of Sports Marketing & Sponsorship
http://www.im-reports.com/SM/IJSM

The Journal of Sport Management
http://www.humankinetics.com/JSM/journalAbout.cfm

The Rugby Channel
http://www.skytv.co.nz

Sky Sports
http://www.skysports.com

SPONSORs
http://www.sponsors.de

Sport1.de
http://www.sport1.de

Sport-Bild
http://www.sportbild.de

SPORTFIVE
http://www.sportfive.com

Sport Marketing Europe
http://www.sportmarketingeurope.com

Sport Marketing Quaterly (SMQ)
http://www.smqonline.com

WEEI 850 AM Sports Radio
http://www.weei.com

CHAPTER 7

The Extended Marketing Mix of Relationship Marketing in Sports

Learning Outcomes

On completion of this chapter the reader should be able to:

- explain the '7 Ps' or extended marketing mix
- characterise the additional instruments of the service mix
- apply the extended marketing mix of relationship marketing to sports
- recognize the interdependencies of the different instruments
- examine existing sports events with regard to the extended marketing mix in relationship marketing

OVERVIEW OF CHAPTER

First we will look at the development of the traditional marketing mix and how it has been extended and applied to relationship marketing. Then we will describe and analyse each instrument in detail. We will start with the classical '4 Ps' of marketing and continue with the additional '3 Ps' of service marketing which are of special importance in the context of relationship marketing. For each instrument examples and best practices of implementation in the sports sector are provided. Finally we will present a summarizing case study about the extended marketing mix of the Formula One Grand Prix in Melbourne.

INTRODUCTION

Marketing mix is the term traditionally used to describe the ingredients of a marketing programme. The origins of the concept lie in a work done by

Borden (1965) at the Harvard Business School. He suggested that companies should consider twelve elements when formulating a marketing programme:

- product planning
- pricing
- branding
- channels of distribution
- personal selling
- advertising
- promotions
- packaging
- display
- servicing
- physical handling
- fact finding and analysis

The marketing mix concept has become widely accepted since some years later, this long list was condensed and simplified into a much shorter list usually known as the '4 Ps' of marketing. These four categories, which have been enshrined in marketing theory and practice, comprise (Christopher, Payne and Ballantyne, 2008):

- **Product:** The product or service being offered.
- **Price:** The price charged and the terms associated with the sale.
- **Promotion:** Advertising, promotional and communication activities.
- **Place:** The distribution and logistics processes involved in fulfilling demand.

This traditional marketing mix model was primarily designed and useful for tangible products. But the 4 Ps model tends to oversimplify the thought of relationship marketing, particularly in today's more complex and fast-moving climate. This has led to the suggestion that an expanded marketing mix is needed. The '7 Ps' (or extended marketing mix as it is often called) was first introduced by Booms and Bitner (1981) and comprises seven elements: the traditional 4Ps (product, price, promotion, place) plus three additional elements (people, processes and physical evidence) (Figure 7.1).

The 7 Ps model is more adequate for service industries and arguably also for knowledge-intensive environments. This is how Booms and Bitner (1981) characterise the three additional Ps:

- **People:** All people directly or indirectly involved in the consumption of a service (knowledge workers, employees, management and consumers often add significant value to the total product or service offering).

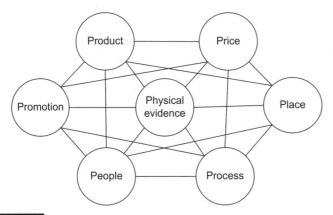

FIGURE 7.1 *The 7 Ps or extended marketing mix of relationship marketing.*

- **Process:** Procedures, mechanisms and flow of activities by which services are consumed (customer management processes).
- **Physical evidence:** The ability and environment in which the service is delivered (tangible goods that help to communicate and perform the service, the intangible experience of existing customers and the ability of the business to relay customer satisfaction to potential customers).

People and process are explicit factors, whereas the physical evidence is an implicit factor.

For sports marketing, this opens up a new perspective which values people (both customers and employees) as a sporting organisation's most important asset and addresses the need to create viable strategies for meeting customer needs profitably. The possible application of relationship marketing to the different elements of the extended marketing mix for sports will therefore be explored in this chapter.

The example of the German Football Club 1899 Hoffenheim introduced in Case study 7.1 indicates how a sports club can improve its image and the mutual understanding between the club and the community it is operating in, and also with its own employees.

CASE STUDY 7.1. Building Sustainable Relationships: The Example of 1899 Hoffenheim

Anne Schall

Only a couple of years ago 1899 Hoffenheim just operated in the lower amateur leagues of German football. However, since Dietmar Hopp (co-founder of SAP) offered himself as a financial backer, the club has seen a fairytale rise. In 2007, Hoffenheim entered the second German football league and only 1 year later Hoffenheim was promoted to the German Bundesliga. In autumn 2008, the newcomer

Continued

team surprised again and finished the first half of their first Bundesliga season at the top of the table.

While it is undeniable that the sporting success of Hoffenheim would not have been possible without the substantial financial resources of Hopp, it is believed that the recent extraordinary success of Hoffenheim is also based upon their philosophy. Team spirit is especially important. Expensive experienced players are mostly rejected in favour of young talents who fit better into the overall team structure. Furthermore, recruitment is also focusing on searching for talent in the own ranks and in the surrounding region. Hoffenheim and Hopp have understood that the surrounding community can be important stakeholders of a sporting organisation, and efforts should be made to build up relationships with them because this can benefit both parties. Therefore, 1899 Hoffenheim and Hopp do not only invest significant resources into social work, such as the training of youngsters and young talented players, but also into other social projects such as community, education or health care programmes. Hopp says: 'The region has given me much, and I would like to pay this back now' (cited in Träber, 2008, w.p.).

There have been a couple of incidents when opposing fans have blamed Hoffenheim and especially Dietmar Hopp to follow the same strategy as Roman Abramowitsch (owner of the English club FC Chelsea London and said to support the club only for his own benefit and reputation). However, Hoffenheim's fans and the local community reject such accusations and rather value the efforts the club and Hopp make, as many fans benefit themselves from the offered programmes. Ticket sales for the newly built stadium go very well and even some of the away games of Hoffenheim are already sold out. Media exposure for 1899 Hoffenheim is also increasing and free publicity for them is created. Articles and reports frequently praise the achievements of Hoffenheim and Hopp, not only in terms of games but also in terms of social work, which contributes to a more and more positive attitude of people towards the club in general and obviously contradicts the allegations against Hopp.

Anne Schall graduated at ESB Business School of Reutlingen University and wrote her bachelor thesis on relationship marketing under the supervision of Prof. Dr. Gerd Nufer.

Even though 1899 Hoffenheim is a good example of how a club can build up sustainable relationships with its stakeholders, this can obviously not be copied to the same extent by many other sporting organisations because a significant amount of money is needed in the beginning. There are, however, other strategies requiring less investment and still profitable. Sports marketers have to provide a well balanced marketing mix focusing on the development of ongoing relationships. Different suggestions and examples of how relationship marketing can be implemented within the marketing mix of sporting organisations will be explained throughout this chapter.

PRODUCT

The sports product exists both as a **physical good** and as a **service**. The four basic factors that differentiate services from goods are intangibility, consistency, perishability and inseparability (Smith, 2008; Harness and Harness, 2007). In practice, most sports products are a combination of goods and services. For example, during a football match fans might buy the merchandising articles of their favourite team. Likewise goods are often bought because of the intangible benefits they deliver, such as the brand image or the celebrity endorsers that are related to the sporting good. In sports marketing it is common to combine the tangible and intangible elements of goods and services in order to provide a more flexible, textured and appealing set of materials to sell to sports consumers (Smith, 2008; Bühler and Nufer, 2006).

The **core product** represents the product itself and the principal service or benefit that a consumer receives from buying the product. Due to the fact that in a sporting context the core product is normally a competition, the quality of the core product can vary significantly every time it is produced. Approaches to overcome this uncertainty are important to maintain a good relationship with consumers and have been developed in the form of product extensions (Smith, 2008). **Product extensions** refer to all goods or services that are added to the actual features of the core product. These product components enhance the value of the core product. Nowadays product extensions or value-added services often represent the only factor that differentiates one's own product from that of the competition. Examples for product extensions are surrounding entertainment, hospitality packages, catering, merchandising articles or information brochures, but also the improvement of the facility infrastructure or adequate and helpful service personnel, as we will see later.

Branding

Branding is the strategy to heterogenise homogeneous products (Ramme, 2004). The existence of a brand enables consumers to differentiate one sports product from another. An effective way of enhancing the brand image is for example to sell merchandising articles with a constant and easily recognizable design that represents the corresponding sporting organisation. The higher the perceived quality of a brand, the more attractive the product becomes for consumers and the higher the number of people who want to purchase related products. In sports this also means becoming more attractive to sponsors and other sources of income. Successful sports brands are for example the association NBA (National Basketball Association), the club Real Madrid or the sportsman David Beckham.

Positioning

The positioning process involves three steps (Harris and Elliott, 2007):

- **Segmentation:** Market segmentation is the process of categorising groups of consumers, based on their similar needs or wants. The total group of consumers in a market is broken down into smaller groups with similar characteristics that differ from other groups with different needs. Sports consumers are not that easy to classify given the fact that people have different reasons for consuming sports as described in Chapter 4.

- **Targeting:** Once market segments have been identified, each segment's attractiveness has to be evaluated in terms of profit potential. After that it has to be decided how many segments to focus on.
- **Positioning:** The aim of positioning products is to provide an appealing offer to special target markets in order to satisfy their needs in a superior way, and to create a differentiated image and advantage in comparison to competitors.

Product programme strategies

The aim of product programme strategies is both to manage existing products and markets to effectively meet the needs and wants, perceptions and attitudes of consumers, and to look for new products and new markets for future growth in order to reduce the risk of being dependent on one single type of product or market. The Ansoff approach combines present and new products as well as present and new markets in a 2×2 matrix (Table 7.1). This can help sporting organisations to determine whether any opportunities exist for improving their existing business performance.

Table 7.1 The Ansoff Matrix for Sports		
	Existing Products	**New Products**
Existing Markets	*Market Penetration or Expansion:* Attempts to persuade existing customers to consume at a higher rate or to convert non-users to users of the product, e.g. sale of season tickets or incentives like two-for-one offers.	*Product development:* Involves marketing to the same consumers with a new version of the product or service. The new or modified product is sold to the same target market as the existing product, e.g. beach volleyball.
New Markets	*Market development:* Aims at expanding the target market to reach a wider range of consumers. The product or service is promoted to existing markets, but to a wider range of consumers, e.g. variations of seating options with complementary hospitality packages.	*Diversification:* Means to market a new product to a new target market. This is the most risky option, but when successful also the most rewarding, e.g. modified-rules versions of sports for children.

(*Source*: Adapted from Smith, 2008, pp. 74 f.)

PRICE

As to the sports industry we are faced with a constantly changing demand curve that includes elastic, inelastic and unitary components (Mullin, Hardy and Sutton, 2007). Research shows that the **price elasticity** for tickets to sports events is rather inelastic (Breuer, Wicker and Pawlowski, 2008). This means that a price increase for tickets will not decrease demand proportionally, rather most fans will be willing to pay a surcharge for a ticket in order to attend a specific sports event. Consequently a strong brand loyalty has in many cases led to price premiums that are realised (Meir and Arthur, 2007).

The consumer's **sensitivity** to price changes is also influenced by the perceived value of the sports product. If consumers believe that a sports product has substantial benefits or provides them with social status, then they might be willing to pay higher prices than the market average. For example, the often very strong attachment of football fans to their teams has a big influence on the decision of buying related sports products such as season tickets. It should also be noted that organisations providing spectator sports in general set their ticket prices rather lower than they actually could because first they want to fill up the event-facility to create an adequate atmosphere, and secondly they hope to generate additional revenue with service extensions such as merchandise articles or food and beverages.

Pricing methods

The determination of a minimum price that a sporting organisation needs to charge in order to break even should always be the starting point of the pricing process. There exist several approved pricing methods that can be applied (Freyer, 2003):

- A standard approach to determine a price is **cost-orientated pricing**. This is the classic form of price calculation and is still used in many industries. The total costs for producing and providing a product should be covered by the selling price of the product. In the end a certain percentage mark-up is added in order to make a profit. While this method might be effective for businesses such as fitness studios, where costs can be calculated pretty accurately. Freyer (2003) notes that for other sporting organisations, especially in the non-profit and spectator sports sector, this approach is difficult as some accounts are not easy to determine.

- For **competitor-orientated pricing**, a sporting organisation bases its price largely on that of competitors. When using this method, the sporting organisation sets its price higher, lower or on the same level as that of competitors. This method can be a useful tool for the sports industry in cases where costs might be difficult to measure or competitive response is uncertain.

Therefore the reason for charging the same price as successful competitors, often could be the expectation of getting similar revenue and success.

- **Demand-orientated pricing** is based upon ascertaining the perceived value of a sporting organisation's product in customers' minds and upon what particular target markets are willing to pay for it. The factors that influence demand are perceived value, personal income, the market volume and the price elasticity of demand. An example of demand-orientated pricing is the variation of ticket prices for premium packages sold to corporations and for 'regular' tickets at certain events, such as the Football World Championship or the Olympic Games.

Sports marketers prefer a pricing approach that considers the existing market conditions in terms of competitors and demand. But there is no general recommendation which method to choose, because the environment for each sporting organisation is different.

Pricing strategies

When deciding on pricing strategies, other variables of the marketing mix and how they position the product or brand in the minds of consumers have to be considered. For example, choosing a low-price strategy might result in the product being perceived as a commodity, but more people are able to afford it. A high-price strategy can position the offer as a premium product, but fewer customers will be able to afford it. Meir and Arthur (2007) suggest a number of pricing options and quality levels and explain the images associated with them (Figure 7.2).

Level of Quality	Price Level: Low	Price Level: Medium	Price Level: High
High	**Steal:** For consumers the best possible option, but mostly hard to find.	**Good Value:** Can be used as part of a penetration strategy. Good price and high quality can impress consumers and make them repeat purchasers.	**Premium Product:** For prestigious or exclusive products and demanding consumers that are prepared to pay for quality.
Medium	**Bargain:** This is often the case when discounts are applied.	**Equitable Buy:** Here, consumers get what they pay for. This is a reliable product that delivers what it says.	**Fad Buy:** Especially important to new products were consumers are ready to pay more in order to get the latest innovation.
Low	**Cheapie:** When quality is not the issue, then for many consumers this alternative will be fine.	**Brand Buy:** The brand name is enough to convince a consumer to buy a product, even if it is not the best quality.	**Rip off:** Price makes consumers believe that they purchase good quality, but product fails to deliver on the promise. For companies, this market is only profitable for a short time.

FIGURE 7.2

Different pricing options and images associated with them.
(*Source:* Adapted from Meir and Arthur, 2007, pp. 324 f.)

PROMOTION

Because of the long-term nature of sports commitment and the lifetime value of customers, it is argued that relationship building and management form the foundation on which all other communication activities should follow. While one-way or one-time communication is not designed to get feedback, two-way symmetrical communication is established to support relationship building and to create a direct dialogue between the sporting organisation and the consumer (Hopwood, 2007; Bee and Kahle, 2006; Stavros, Pope and Winzar, 2008; Bühler and Nufer, 2008).

Integrated marketing communications

The most effective communication strategies are those that adopt an integrated approach in which each of the tools of the communications mix is used synergetically. With an integrated marketing communication strategy a consistent, unified image to the marketplace is communicated. Because of the special nature of sports, the traditional tools of marketing communications (especially advertising) are too limited and often inappropriate for the sports product (Hopwood, 2007; Nufer, 2007). Especially younger and more interactive promotional elements (such as event marketing) open up large possibilities for sporting organisations to build up relationships with customers and thus increase customer lifetime value. Figure 7.3 shows the integrated communications mix in sports, while the next section analyses the different communication instruments in greater detail.

Communication instruments

The objective of a **corporate identity policy** is to establish a favourable reputation by developing credibility and trust between an organisation and its stakeholders (Jobber, 2004). The corporate identity policy can be seen as the roof of all communications because it determines the message which is to be delivered to the public and which all other promotional mix elements are built upon (Nufer, 2007). If well managed, the corporate identity can affect an organisation's performance by attracting and retaining customers, recruiting high-quality staff, maintaining strong media relations and strengthening the identification of the staff with the company.

Advertising is used to reach large audiences, create brand awareness, help differentiate a brand from its competitors, and build an image of the

FIGURE 7.3   *The integrated marketing communications mix.*

brand (Hopwood, 2007). Advertising used to be the most important communication tool. In recent years however, the reliance on advertising has diminished in favour of other forms of communication. The reasons for this are the high costs associated with it and the advertising message overload for consumers, who become more and more resistant to its appeal.

Public relations have the unique ability to build relationships, establish credibility and create understanding between the organisation and its public (Jobber, 2004). Therefore public relations are closely linked to relationship marketing. Most of the processes employed can benefit the company in multiple ways. In order to create a dialogue and acceptance among the local community, sporting organisations can become socially engaged. Youth work and training of youngsters is an example frequently practiced by sporting organisations. This creates goodwill among the local population and at the same time positive word of mouth endorsement is created.

Sales promotions are usually incentives that are designed to stimulate purchase (either by consumers or by the trade). They can be useful supplements to other promotional activities as they can boost sales during promotional periods and tend to draw attention to a brand or organisation, thereby providing other activities with more exposure (Smith, 2008).

Incentives for interested or existing customers, e.g. family or children's discounts, can increase the number of sold-out games which in turn will boost average attendance (Shilbury, Quick and Westerbeek, 2003). Other examples for sales promotion are a free trial for first time visitors to fitness studios or an open day in a sports club.

Whereas mass advertising reaches a wide spectrum of people and often not the target audience, **direct marketing** uses media that can target consumers more precisely and request an immediate direct response (Jobber, 2004). Examples are direct mailing, direct selling or direct response advertising. In this context online marketing via the internet represents a new form of direct communication which presents an opportunity to communicate to global audiences interactively and cheaply. In a sporting context, direct marketing is greatly enhanced in supporting consumption and communication, as sports consumers seek to be involved and are extremely committed to their sports club. One of the most effective ways of managing customer information for direct marketing activities is the creation and continuous management of a database.

BACKGROUND INFORMATION 7.1. The Importance of a Marketing Database for Relationship Marketing

Anne Schall

Since direct marketing depends on customer information for its effectiveness, a marketing database has to be at the heart of the process. This mostly electronic customer information system contains a list of names, addresses, telephone numbers and other known information and transactional data about all current and prospective customers who got into touch with an organisation via various touch points. Upon these data a good database can determine which customer will receive certain types of offers, can reactivate customer purchase and identify patterns and trends within the data (data mining). The more personalised the interactivity is, the more effective and persuasive it is.

Many professional sporting organisations use their marketing database to send out personalised birthday or Christmas cards which make customers feel that the club cares for them and that they are not just a number in the crowd. It is a must for sporting organisations to create and maintain such a database in order to develop ongoing direct marketing relationships with customers and differentiate themselves from competitors via personalised communication (Turner, 2007).

Sponsorship can be seen as a business relationship between a provider of funds, resources or services and an individual or organisation that offers in return some rights and association that may be used for commercial advantage (Jobber, 2004; Nufer, 2002). This definition shows that **sponsorship** is a bilateral agreement from which both parties want to benefit. The objectives for both parties have to be well defined prior to any agreement, so that the link between a sponsor and a sponsee becomes clear to the target audience. Other factors that influence the success of a sponsorship are the communication, cooperation and mutual understanding between both parties as already explained in Chapter 5.

In order to sum up all the activities a sporting organisation initiates to directly interact in the form of events with consumers, prospective employees and sponsors, the term **corporate events** has been created. When corporations are using an existing event to associate a product with it, this is referred to as event sponsorship. When corporations are creating a special event of their own, we talk about event marketing. The initiation of corporate events has become very popular in recent years, as marketers develop integrated marketing communications including a variety of promotional tools that create experiences for consumers in an effort to associate their brands with certain lifestyles and activities. Examples are sports events or festivals, but also grassroots events like streetball competitions. Ambush marketing campaigns are an alternative for event sponsorship (Nufer, 2007; Nufer and Bühler, 2008).

PLACE

A distribution channel is an organised series of intermediaries or individuals passing a product from the producer to the final consumer. Distribution channels have different lengths and therefore occur in different forms (Smith, 2008). In the case of **direct distribution**, the producer sells the product directly to the consumer and the distribution channel is quite short. An example would be a tennis lesson where the tennis teacher sells his product directly to the customer. For sporting goods, this can mean that they are sold directly via internet or via mail. **Indirect distribution** is longer as there are a number of intermediaries involved before the product is bought by the consumer. A tennis racket, for example, is produced by a manufacturer and then distributed to a wholesaler who passes it on to a retailer where the tennis racket is finally purchased by a consumer.

Special distribution channels in sports

In addition to these traditional distribution channels, Freyer (2003) mentions a number of special channels that are unique for the sports business that we will focus on.

- **Sponsors as distribution channels:** Sponsors can work as a useful tool to popularize the sponsored organisation such as a sports club or a sports team in the eyes of the general public. The sponsor could for example inform his customers via his website about the sponsee. Sponsorship agreements should therefore be seen as bilateral agreements from which both organisations can profit in numerous ways.

- **Distribution via marketing agencies:** This form of distribution is becoming increasingly important in the professional sports sector. Marketing agencies serve as intermediaries between sporting organisations and sports consumers and have different tasks: In today's professional sports sector there are transfer markets for professional athletes and players, in which agencies arrange negotiations dealing with player transfers to other clubs. Besides, these agencies care for the asset management of their clients. Another task fulfilled by agencies is the distribution of rights for sports events. Here, the agency mediates between the organiser of the sports event and interested companies , about possible broadcasting rights or the right for advertisements during the event (sponsorship).

- **Distribution via the media:** This form of distribution is increasingly important for big sports events such as the Olympic Games or the World Championships, but also for popular sports such as football or the Formula one. Media broadcasting and the internet give sporting organisations the opportunity to deliver their events to the masses and reach people far beyond the normal catchment area of the stadium. TV spectators benefit from media broadcasting because they do not need to travel long distances in order to watch an interesting sports event. This fact makes sports events also increasingly interesting for sponsors as the awareness for their company or product can be enhanced enormously.

Ticket distribution

As ticket sales are the most important sources of revenue for many sporting organisations, the distribution of tickets is extremely important. Tickets can either be sold face-to-face, via phone or online. Larger sporting organisations often tend to distribute their tickets via a ticket agency. Smaller sporting organisations would rather sell their tickets directly or via an event organiser. However, the old box office sale still exists. Other channels for ticket distribution are partnerships with consumer retail outlets, payroll deduction especially for season ticket holders or even the home delivery of bought tickets.

Logistics

Physical products such as equipment, merchandise articles or tickets, but also intangible items like information have to be moved, so issues of stock handling and transport turn up. Major events such as the Olympics or other forms of one-time competitions are especially challenging, because of the complex organisational and logistical processes that have to be thought of (Sparks, 2007). Specialist logistics service providers have been engaged increasingly to manage, coordinate and undertake the various distribution activities of the logistical mix.

PEOPLE

According to Zeithaml, Bitner and Gremler (2006, p. 26) people participating in the delivery of a service are 'all human actors who play a part in service delivery and thus influence the buyer's perception: namely, the firm's personnel, the customer, and other customers in the service environment.' This means that human resources are of critical importance to a sporting organisation. Hence, personnel policy is not regarded as an isolated part of the management of a sporting organisation, but seen as an integral part of the mix in relationship marketing – and included as the fifth 'P' for people or personnel.

Taylor, Doherty and McGraw (2008) summarize that attracting, recruiting, developing, motivating, retaining, rewarding and managing of the right, talented people, and also the dismissal of the wrong people, can provide a sporting organisation with the resources it needs to gain a competitive advantage. The right coach or manager, a dynamic CEO or a new key player can transform the fortunes of a sports club in a short period of time from a bottom-line team into a champion. Moreover, increased globalisation has changed the face of sporting organisations; there is nowadays a big transnational movement of athletes, coaches and even management personnel.

In this context it is important to distinguish between employees who produce a product (such as a team or a trainer) and those who support its production (e.g. a hospitality or security employee). Literature has recognized that customers may themselves be co-producers of the product and actively contribute to how others experience service performances (Lovelock and Wirtz, 2007). We will give an overview on these perspectives in the next sections.

Employees as producers of services

The core sports product is being performed by sports professionals who work in multiple roles: first of all they are the performers of the sports service being offered, such as a sporting competition (e.g. a football match). Second they are also testimonials for the sporting organisation and role models for many consumers because of their inherent visibility and the public interest in them both on the field and in their private lives. Thus sports professionals link the inside of an organisation to the outside world (Smith, 2008).

According to a study by Frick (2005), the performance of professional team sports athletes depends significantly on the remuneration of players, the brand value of a team and the salary of the coach. Furthermore a strong cohesion of the team members has a major impact on the success of teams. Despite the variable quality of the core product, sporting organisations also have other possibilities to create passion, emotional attachment and customer loyalty: From a customer perspective, the encounter with sports professionals can have a major impact on the perception of a sports service. This is an excellent opportunity for sporting organisations to introduce relationship marketing. As fans often see players in the arena or on TV only, it is for many fans the biggest thing to meet their 'stars' in person. Making sports professionals accessible and approachable by organising meet-and-greets with fans or giving fans the possibility to join training sessions, can have an enormous impact on customers' perception of a sporting organisation and can increase loyalty and long-term structural bonding.

Frontline work is also performed by sports trainers working either in for-profit organisations like fitness studios, or in not-for-profit organisations like local clubs. Sports trainers and coaches interact directly with customers of a sporting organisation because they manage and coordinate training programs, provide the necessary training plans and give advice on further improvements in the training process. Customers and employees work so closely together that they might even become friends. The development of such relationships decides how profitable and beneficial the bond between the organisation and the customer will be.

Employees as supporters of service production

For sporting organisations it is often not possible to deliver a constantly high-quality core product. However, product extending services have the possibility to increase and maintain the quality and perception of the whole product/service bundle. For example, for a sports event the hospitality services, cleaning services, ticket sales and also the administrative work in the back-office are performed by support staff. Whether these people are paid employees or unpaid volunteers, they will often make or break the experience that a customer gets. High-value customers' assessment of front- and back-office staff affects the level of service quality and the satisfaction they perceive. The behaviour and friendliness of employees play a key role in delivering customer experience effectively. A quick purchasing process for tickets or food, a friendly and helpful service staff and a pleasurable, clean and friendly environment might result in an overall positive and satisfying perception of service delivery in customers. Consequently, it could turn a certain percentage of temporary fans and event goers into constant loyal supporters of a sporting organisation, and thus increase customer lifetime value (e.g. repeat purchase of tickets, continued attendance at sporting events and purchase of sports-related products) (Lovelock and Wirtz, 2007).

Sporting organisations frequently employ former players for management or administrative tasks. This has obvious benefits, but can also represent problems for an organisation. Former sportsmen certainly know a lot about the business they are working in and are highly committed; however, they often lack the fundamental economic knowledge required to assure effective management.

BACKGROUND INFORMATION 7.2. The Role of Volunteers

Anne Schall

Due to their overall small operating budget many sporting organisations, especially in the non-profit sector, are highly dependable on voluntary work. Examples are support staff during match day, the fulfilment of administrative tasks, the coaching of athletes and juniors or fund-raising for events. Volunteers are therefore sometimes referred to as the 'life-blood' of a sporting organisation, because they dedicate hours of time and energy working in a variety of ways without receiving remuneration. Without them most sports clubs and associations would cease to exist.

The motives that drive people to assist sporting organisations without receiving remuneration have to be well explored in order to reward and retain these invaluable human resources. Many volunteers are members, friends, parents, students or spectators. Their motivation factors to do voluntary work are involvement with the club, self-actualisation, prestige and recognition or just the possibility to do something different then the daily job.

It is very costly to lose experienced volunteers and recruit and train new ones. Therefore, time should be spent on retaining existing staff. It is already a good start to just recognize volunteers' work and thank them for their support. In order to value their contributions and to keep them motivated and enthusiastic, special reward programmes such as 'volunteer of the year' can be implemented. Considerable time should also be spent on training, mentoring and managing each volunteer to ensure that he or she is being deployed effectively and that they are enjoying their role. By managing and preparing volunteers in an appropriate way, sporting organisations can reduce the risk of failure in service delivery for customers and improve overall service perception.

Customers as co-producers of services

Customers of a sporting organisation are participants, spectators, fans and also sponsors. Spectators and fans especially influence the quality of the sports product and hence their own satisfaction. An example of a co-produced service experience is the atmosphere of a football game which is actively created by the participating audience (for example by clapping or shouting), and can influence the spectators' entire perception of the game. Atmospheres can however also have negative impacts. Tensions between supporters of rivalling teams have often led to violence and brawls. Hooliganism has also to be mentioned in this context. The management of such unruly fans or hooligans is nowadays a major issue that sporting organisations have to think about. The police has to attend sports events and special security personnel has to be employed to ensure the safety of spectators and participants (Smith, 2008).

There are other ways in which sporting organisations can actively contribute to a positive perception, for example, by playing music during breaks or when something special happens, by organising entertainment such as dancing girls, fairground attractions, family-friendly activities or by providing international cuisine. By creating a memorable event, one can increase customers' regular attendance and spread positive word of mouth. Successful customer relationship management is in most cases rewarded by loyalty. Not lastly due to its relationship marketing practices, the German Bundesliga Football Club Borussia Dortmund has the highest average attendance of fans in Europe with nearly 80,000 spectators per match on average.

PROCESS

The steps that a consumer passes through in order to receive a service, and the actions a provider has to perform in order to deliver a service are referred to as the process in the marketing mix (Smith, 2008). It is important that these processes are conducted in an appropriate way so that they do not hamper a customer's positive perception of quality. Additionally consumers should be educated to understand and anticipate the processes they have to experience to receive a service. For example, in order to attend a basketball game, a sports fan might have to queue for a ticket, wait again in queues to enter the arena, go through security screening, search for his allocated seat, locate some food and beverage and eventually exit. As the example shows, a service can be divided into different steps. Badly designed processes lead to slow, bureaucratic and ineffective service delivery, wasted time and a disappointing experience for customers (Lovelock and Wirtz, 2007).

The sports service delivery system

In order to identify key activities involved in creating and delivering a service experience, Lovelock and Wirtz (2007) propose the development of a 'blueprint' of the processes employed. Figure 7.4 displays a blueprint of the service

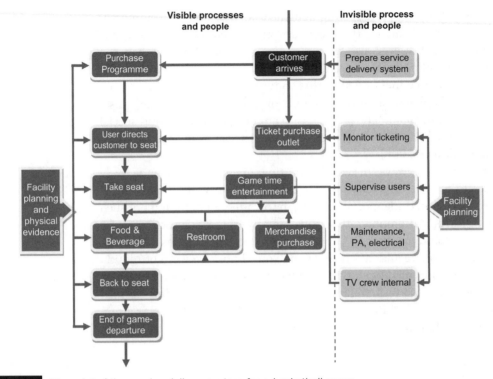

FIGURE 7.4 *Blueprint of the service delivery system for a basketball game.*
(*Source:* Shilbury, Quick and Westerbeek, 2003, p. 125)

delivery system for a basketball match. The visible part of a sports service (front-office) means the environment where the sports service is produced and consumed and the contact people that support and produce the service on the day of the performance. The invisible part of the service (back-office) is for example the facility management that cares for a working electricity supply during games or for the cleaning of toilets. Service blueprints clarify the interactions between customers and employees. Thus they can facilitate the integration of marketing, operations and human resource management within an organisation. Blueprinting gives sports managers the possibility to identify fail points within a process, which means areas where there is a higher risk of things going wrong, but at the same time it opens up opportunities to prepare preventive measures.

Levels of customer participation

Blueprinting also clarifies whether the customer's role in a given service process is primarily that of a passive recipient or entails active involvement in creating and producing the service. Some degree of customer participation in service delivery is inevitable in people processing services, especially in the context of sports. However, the extent of participation varies widely and can be divided into three broad levels (Lovelock and Wirtz, 2007):

- **Low participation level:** At this level of customer participation, employees and supporting systems do all the work. Products tend to be standardised. Payment may be the only required customer input. Taking public transport to a sports event or routine cleaning and maintenance of sporting facilities are example of services where the customer mostly remains uninvolved with the process.
- **Moderate participation level:** Here customer inputs are already required to assist the organisation in creating and delivering the service and providing a degree of customization. These inputs may include provision of information or personal effort. An example is the atmosphere of a sports event which is actively created by the participating audience and influences the spectators' whole experience of the game.
- **High participation level:** At this stage, customers work actively with the provider to co-produce the service. The service cannot be created without the customer purchasing it and participating in it. If the customer fails to perform the required process steps, the whole quality of the service outcome will be jeopardised. This is especially true for B2B services where customers and providers closely work together as a team, but also for coaching and health care services like fitness or physiotherapy studios, in which customers work under professional supervision (see section people).

Process characteristics

The degree of personalisation is an important characteristic of a service and determines whether a service should follow a standardised approach or whether it is customized (Zeithaml, Bitner and Gremler, 2006).

In the context of mass spectator sports it is important to provide the same service to all or at least to most customers. The success of **standardising processes** lies in the speed of the process, the number of customers that can be dealt within a given time period and the reduction of servicing costs to a minimum. According to Zeithaml, Bitner and Gremler (2006) standardisation of services can take three forms:

- Substitutions of technology for personal contact and human effort (e.g. online ticket sales, gate entry machines, computer designed training plans in fitness studios).

■ Improvements in work methods (e.g. different queues for food and beverage, different entrances for different ticket holders, reducing waiting and walking times).

■ Combinations of these two methods.

Standardisation does not mean that the service is performed in a rigid, mechanical way. Rather customer-defined standardisation ensures that the most critical elements of a service are performed as expected by customers. A problem of many standard procedures is that they are company-defined, which means primarily based on internal objectives such as increased productivity, efficiency, technical quality or less costs. But standards set by companies must be based on customer requirements and expectations, rather than just on internal company goals. If a sporting organisation is able to identify what customers value and require, it can focus on these activities and eliminate all other features that customers do not notice or will not pay for (Harness and Harness, 2007).

While many sports events can be delivered with a customer-defined standard service, specialist sports services such as working with a fitness trainer or physiotherapist require **customized processes**. If a fitness trainer provides a standardised service and gives every customer the same training programme, the service will be perceived as being impersonal, inadequate, and not in the customer's best interest. The ability to vary the service according to the needs of the customer is essential to address individual requirements and provide the expected quality and customer satisfaction. The usually higher price of a customized service is also due to the fact that the number of customers that can be dealt with in a certain time is limited. For many sporting organisations the most important and critical customers from a financial point of view are B2B customers such as sponsors. These clients require individual attention. By paying attention to particular needs, providing extra service personnel for particular wishes, and also coming up with helpful and creative ideas for fast problem solving, a sporting organisation can create a competitive advantage and increase lifetime value of B2B customers (Zeithaml, Bitner and Gremler, 2006).

PHYSICAL EVIDENCE

The environment in which the service is delivered, in which the organisation and customers interact, and any tangible component facilitating performance or communication of the service is called physical evidence (Zeithaml, Bitner and Gremler, 2006). Physical evidence is important to service quality because consumers use tangible elements of services as a cue to support their judgement of the organisational performance. So physical evidence influences the flow of experience, the meaning customers attach to it, their satisfaction and their emotional connection with the company delivering the service.

The sports facility

The place where sports participants carry out their activities or where the sports competition is delivered, where spectators are entertained is most important. Designing a sports facility to fit in with the local area can help to make the sports service more attractive and support media exposure. Many sports facilities have a special architecture so that they create substantial attention and can even become attractive tourist destinations, e.g. the Allianz Arena in Munich or the Sydney Olympic Park.

In order to maximize the function of the sports facility as a distribution element, features and design should reflect the intended value proposition to customers. To give clients a unique experience, a number of factors should be considered:

- **Location and accessibility:** Both are critical to the experience of every sports consumer, whether participant or spectator. Especially for participating sports in sports clubs or fitness studios, and also for spectator sports like basketball, football or tennis, the location of a sports facility and its accessibility are crucial to success and revenue for the sporting organisation. Mullin, Hardy and Sutton (2007) note here that up to 90% of a sports facility's customers live within 20 minutes' travelling time. The location should be readily accessible by major highways and public transport. The latter is especially important when customers are mostly senior citizens, youth or lower economic groups. Other factors that should be taken into account are a good signage and directions to the facility, the facility should be easy to enter and exit and should provide a disabled access.

- **Design and layout:** Planning for sports facilities should involve a long-term perspective in terms of the prospective usage of the facility because it is extremely costly to redevelop and redesign existing facilities (Shilbury, Quick and Westerbeek, 2003). Sports marketers should consider the opportunities and limitations a prospective sports facility offers to them. Most sports facilities can be adapted to various needs and wishes. For spectator sports, the arrangements of seats and the view from them can also have a strong influence on sports consumers' experience. Here organisations have the possibility to differentiate their offering by providing business lounges or VIP areas and normal sitting areas at different price levels. The exposure to the weather should be minimised. Safety and security issues such as surveillance systems, emergency procedures or fire detection systems have to be thought of.

Facility infrastructure

The infrastructure of a sports facility and the environmental features included can be combined to a complex mix that influences the response and behaviour not only of customers, but also employees. Zeithaml, Bitner and Gremler (2006) classified this extensive mix of potential elements involved in three different categories:

- **Ambient conditions:** Includes background characteristics, such as temperature, lighting, music, scent and colours, which affect how people feel.
- **Spatial layout and functionality:** Tangible parts of the service that exist to fulfil the specific purpose of a customer, such as seats for watching sports events, or facilitate the accomplishment of his or her goals, such as training equipment in fitness studios.
- **Signs, symbols and artefacts:** Tools serving as explicit or implicit signals to their users. Signs can be used as labels, for directional purpose and to communicate rules. Symbols and artefacts like photos or cups may communicate cues about the meaning of the place and the norms and expectations for behaviour and help to form first impressions about the sporting organisation.

The provision of well maintained equipment or facilities to practise their sports, such as the playing field, a sports track, swimming pool or ice rink, will encourage individuals to use a certain facility instead of another (Harness and Harness, 2007). Providing light for night-time outdoor sports can increase participation rates especially in the context of after-work recreational activities. The high-quality perception of a facility will result in higher levels of satisfaction with the service experience and hence customers are more likely to return. For spectator sports, banners, photographs or statues of sporting heroes can decorate the outside or inner walkways of a facility, supporting motivation, excitement and the overall experience of the sports service. The way in which seats, aisles, hallways and walkways, food service lines, restrooms, entrances and exits are designed and arranged also influence fan comfort at sports events (Shilbury, Quick and Westerbeek, 2003). In addition, positions for food and beverage outlets and merchandise stands have to be chosen wisely because they are amongst the most lucrative services that can be offered at a sports facility (Smith, 2008). Given the rising number of female fans, sports venues will also have to adapt their offering to be appealing to women. Other infrastructural issues include the positioning of scoreboards and promotional signage, emergency medical service as well as broadcasting and media requirements.

Customer service is closely related to people and also processes. In order to give sports spectators a great experience and entertainment during the event, the service personnel should be well trained. Staff should be friendly, helpful and efficient. Information stands can be provided for bigger events and suffi-cient security and emergency staff has to be employed. To help customers to recognize staff, easily recognizable uniforms that are consistent with the area of responsibility the service staff is working in can be used. For big interna-tional events, the name and even the spoken languages of service employees can be tagged to uniforms. Furthermore, assistance to people with restricted mobility like elderly or disabled customers which reflects good service, should be provided; some facilities even provide childcare services (Smith, 2008).

APPLYING THE EXTENDED MARKETING MIX TO SPORTS EVENTS

The following Case study of the Formula one Grand Prix in Melbourne serves as both illustration and summary about the application of the '7 Ps' or the extended marketing mix of relationship marketing in sports. Accord-ing to the event operator who assigned an external market research institute to measure satisfaction among the attendees. 96% of the participants rated their satisfaction with the overall event as good or even very good.

CASE STUDY 7.2. The Extended Marketing Mix of the Formula one Grand Prix in Melbourne, Australia

Constantino Stavros

Product

The Australian Formula one Grand Prix (AGP) is usually the first race of the F1 season. Managed by the Australian Grand Prix Corporation (AGPC), the event is held in the city of Melbourne and operates over 4 days, from Thursday to Sunday, with the last day being the official race day. The event typically attracts a cumulative crowd of around 300,000 people over the whole period, including many visitors from interstate and overseas. These visitors are a particularly important revenue source as they bring new money into the local economy, thus helping to justify the large costs of staging the race. As the commercial rights of F1 are managed by an international group of companies, known collectively as the Formula One Group, the AGPC is particularly reliant on gate receipts and a number of limited

Continued

sponsorship agreements to produce revenue to operate the event. Shortfalls in meeting costs, which can be as high as AUS$40 million, are made up through public funds provided by the State Government, who justify this expenditure with estimations that Melbourne receives economic impact benefits generated by the event worth more than AUS$100 million. In contrast with attendees at F1 in Europe, many AGP attendees come to the event in order to celebrate the festival atmosphere across the 4 days and are not only interested in the main race itself. Therefore a critical marketing strategy employed by the AGPC focuses on creating activities and entertainment around the actual F1 race in order to meet consumer expectations of being part of a much larger spectacle. Aside from the actual F1 race, the event includes numerous other classes of car racing, including the very popular V8 Supercars, free concerts featuring international acts, live broadcast of television programs from the track, celebrity appearances, aircraft flyovers, product demonstrations, merchandise stands and extensive corporate hospitality areas. The race track adds to the atmosphere as it is a street circuit situated at Albert Park, a parkland precinct within an inner suburb of the city of Melbourne.

Price

The AGP has three broad types of consumer attendees. The grandstand ticket holders are generally seen as wealthy, white-collar motorsport enthusiasts, comprising both private and corporate 4-day ticket holders; prices for these start at AUS$379 for a single seat to several thousand dollars for corporate hospitality packages. Furthermore, there are the 4-day general admittance attendees who likely cannot afford the grandstands and tend to be blue-collar males who select the AUS$175 ticket on offer. The last category is the single-day general admittance purchasers who are seen as event-goers and tend to be both male and female; their ticket prices range from AUS$39 on Thursday to AUS$99 on race day. Further revenue is generated via different food and beverage facilities ranging from the classic chip shop to exclusive bars, lounges and dining areas specially targeted at corporate clients who are responsible for a significant proportion of the total generated revenue during the Grand Prix.

Promotion

Big crowds are encouraged by the promotion and hype generated by the event and also by the marketable elements of F1 motorsport itself. The highly popular drivers, the well-known teams and the glamour of F1 racing itself are key components used to attract customers and develop and maintain relationships with them. As Melbourne considers itself a highly passionate sporting city, there is a considerable inherent interest in the event amongst the local community, especially with the excitement and enthusiasm generated by the media. This provides the Grand Prix with excellent publicity. However, the AGPC itself also heavily invests in integrated marketing communications campaigns to promote the spectacle throughout the year, especially prior to the event in order to capture interest from casual fans that may still be undecided about attending. Communications are of a particularly high standard and advertisements are designed to appear in the print media, on radio, TV and on the internet in such a way to reflect the high quality and entertainment character of the event. The message of the campaign is generally a balancing act between trying to retain the core audience (predominantly males aged 20–39 years interested in sport) and appealing to newer or more casual audiences. Women are seen as a particularly important future growth market, so there are ideas to attract additional media partners like female fashion magazines in order to generate interest and excitement about the event for this group. Particular interest is given to the retention of previous event goers through a loyalty program called 'GP Advantage'. This program allows patrons who buy grandstand tickets in 1 year to access a priority-booking period for the following event and also gives them regular information about motorsport and the event. By purchasing a ticket via GP Advantage, attendees also receive additional rewards such as a chance to walk through the pit area, the option of timed payments and various merchandise articles.

Place

The commercial exploitation of customer information via GP Advantage and the value that consumers receive by joining the program is arguably somewhat limited because ticket distribution and purchases occur through an external ticket agency, rather than the AGPC itself. In the past the database management system used by the ticketing agency has been partly incompatible with that used by the AGPC. However, there is hope that updated systems will be put in place in order to better monitor individual consumers' purchasing and usage habits and consequently provide them with specially tailored offers. As for the event location itself, the choice of a street circuit at Albert Park is preferred rather than other possible fixed race track locations in Melbourne. Albert Park, a cosmopolitan and relatively prosperous area, is only a short tram ride from the central business district of Melbourne and provides excellent access and facilities that are aligned to the tourist and festival focus of the event.

People

Personnel employed during the event have to attend a customer service and cultural awareness programs to deal with both overseas and local visitors. Event staffs carry with them an array of information to assist fans and are encouraged to smile and approach people looking lost. Besides easily recognizable uniforms, employees have also worn language flags on their lapels to indicate if they can speak a language other than English. Within the diverse F1 race personnel, any link to Australia is used to stimulate interest and attract more people to the track. This has occurred primarily with Australian driver Mark Webber, whose emergence on the F1 scene helped to reinforce local interest in the event.

Process

The AGPC has blueprinted all occurring processes during the event in extensive documentation for ongoing reviews and future reference. One example of this is a manual that breaks down every activity occurring at the event over the 4-day period on a minute-by-minute basis. Because of the busy and diverse festival character of the race, efforts are made to educate consumers by providing them with the necessary material so that they can efficiently enjoy a relaxed and entertaining day at the track and then return home satisfied, irrespective of race results. A package of information is therefore given to ticket purchasers. Not only does it contain a standard ticket-wallet, but also a high-quality fold-out map, public transport guide and lanyard. Portable radios, ear plugs, sunscreen and various other amenities are also distributed to some ticket holders, or available for access throughout the event area.

Physical evidence

As the event takes place on regular streets in a parkland area, most of the infrastructure has to be carefully constructed and deconstructed each year. Thus the management of the physical evidence of the Grand Prix is one of the most important issues facing event organisers. In order to increase customer satisfaction in a large crowd situation, over 20 giant video screens are placed around the race course, allowing almost every patron to have a view of all the track action. Giant murals of former F1 drivers are put in place on grandstands named after them to give the temporary structures a high-quality look. In a further effort to produce a visually spectacular site, grassed areas have been groomed to appear uniformly even and Albert Park Lake in the centre of the circuit is carefully maintained to appear especially picturesque. On the lake itself, a series of yachts have been put in place some years to create a 'Monte Carlo' harbour look. The yachts were also a source of revenue as they could be rented as vantage points to groups. Signage to and within the event is also excellent; toilets and food stalls are in abundance, and all staffs wear clearly identifiable uniforms.

Dr Constantino Stavros is a senior marketing academic in the School of Economics, Finance & Marketing at RMIT University in Melbourne, Australia.

As a yearly event the Australian F1 Grand Prix is in a special situation because it is marketing a single event, whereas other sports have season-based structures and therefore a more long-term focus in their marketing strategy. The challenge for the future will be to find the balance between a mass market strategy that focuses on the creation of hype, and an adequate relationship marketing approach with a good database management system as the basis to get more insight into customer purchase behaviour and improve customer retention.

CONCLUSIONS

All 7 Ps or components of the extended marketing mix contribute to the evaluation of the total experience. A well-blended mix of the three service elements in addition to the general four marketing mix instruments is essential to achieve the goals of relationship marketing. To achieve full effectiveness, all elements of the marketing mix have to be balanced and in harmony with each other. The challenge for sports marketers is to picture a consistent view of all elements and to determine where to invest their limited resources to create the best outcome.

We cannot deny that the ultimate factor of success for every sporting organisation is dependent on the sporting performance achieved during the competition. However, the universal nature of sports can stimulate such a strong emotional response in its consumers that many of them will still support their team or athlete even though sporting success is not given. This opens up great opportunities for relationship marketing. The surrounding services can significantly affect the perception of the sports activity in the eyes of consumers and hence provide opportunities for sporting organisations to improve the perceived quality of their offering and consequently the overall satisfaction of customers with the sports product.

DISCUSSION QUESTIONS

(1) What do the '7Ps' in relationship marketing stand for?
(2) Apply the Ansoff matrix for relationship marketing to sports!
(3) What images are associated with certain pricing options in sports?
(4) What does an integrated marketing communications mix in sports look like?
(5) Who are the people that participate in the delivery of a sports service?

(6) Describe why customer service is a combination of physical evidence, people and processes.

(7) Characterise the extended marketing mix of a self-selected sports event.

GUIDED READING

We would like to recommend a textbook edited by Beech and Chadwick titled *The Marketing of Sport*. In addition, Lovelock and Wirtz especially cover the 3 Ps of service marketing in detail in their book *Services Marketing. People, Technology, Strategy*.

WEBSITES

Adidas
http://www.adidas-group.com

Borussia Dortmund
http://www.bvb.de

City of Melbourne, Australia
http://www.melbourne.vic.gov.au

FC Bayern Munich
http://www.fcbayern.de

Forum Database Marketing and Data Mining
http://www.data-mining.de

Sport Volunteers
http://www.sportvolunteers.org

The Official Formula 1 Website
http://www.formula1.com

TSG 1899 Hoffenheim
http://www.tsg-hoffenheim.de

VfB Stuttgart
http://www.vfb.de

CHAPTER 8

Relationship Marketing in Sports – Today and Tomorrow

Learning Outcomes

On completion of this chapter the reader should be able to:

- recall the key aspects of this book
- describe the current status of relationship marketing in sports
- explain the main issues professional sporting organisations have to consider in order to establish and maintain healthy relationships with their primary customers
- name some relationship marketing trends
- explain the challenges professional sporting organisations are likely to face in the future

OVERVIEW OF CHAPTER

In this final chapter we will first look back at the previous seven chapters and summarise their key aspects. We have also incorporated three brief 'To-do-lists' with regard to fan relations, sponsor relations and media relations in order to emphasise the most important steps for professional sporting organisations again. Furthermore, this chapter brings together the individual relationship marketing approaches aimed at the various stakeholders of sporting organisations as presented in the preceding chapters and ultimately presents a holistic approach which already works in practice. With regard to the future perspectives of relationship marketing in sports we will look at general trends in relationship marketing first. Then we will identify the main trends and challenges of relationship marketing in the context of sports and

165

provide our vision of how relationship marketing in sports will develop over the next years. Finally we will have a look at Gary Smith again and see what the Marketing Director of our fictional football club has learned from this book and how he turned his newly gained knowledge into a strategic relationship marketing programme at Nowhere FC.

INTRODUCTION

In the previous seven chapters we have learned how relationship marketing can be applied to the field of sports these days. We have presented various practical examples from the past and the present. Besides looking at the current status of relationship marketing in sports we also want to take this final chapter as an opportunity to look ahead by addressing the main trends and challenges of relationship marketing in the context of sports. It would be great to have a crystal ball which tells us the future, but unfortunately we don't have one. Therefore we base our predictions on general trends in relationship marketing on the one hand and on our intuition as sports marketing academics and practitioners on the other hand. Although we will try to be as realistic as possible we will also try to be visionary because visions shape our future and the success of sports is partly based on the right vision. However, only history - and hopefully many future studies by fellow academics - will tell whether we had the right vision for relationship marketing in sports.

SUMMARY OF THE PREVIOUS SEVEN CHAPTERS

Before we look at the future, we will now take a look back at the previous chapters in order to summarise the current status of relationship marketing in sports.

In **Chapter 1** we identified the need for relationship marketing in sports. We concluded that many sports-related organisations still do not appear to maximise their marketing potential or leverage their ability to exploit the relationship dimension. Therefore, a new paradigm in the context of sports marketing is needed. Indeed, relationship marketing provides sports marketers with the opportunity to establish, develop and maintain meaningful and mutually beneficial long-term associations with fans, sponsors, and the media as well as internal and external stakeholders. The effective management of all these relations is one of the main challenges a professional sporting organisation faces nowadays.

In **Chapter 2** we introduced the principles of relationship marketing and explained the basic concepts and theories of relationship marketing in general. We have also described the shift from a transactional marketing approach to relationship marketing and explained the key variables for relationship success. Furthermore, we proposed our own definition of relationship marketing in sports (i.e. the establishment and maintenance of positive, enduring and mutual beneficial relations between professional sporting organisations and their stakeholders) and subsequently highlighted the benefits that may be associated with the adoption and implementation of a relationship marketing approach within a professional sporting organisation. Finally, we have shown that the implementation of sophisticated marketing strategies is an absolute precondition for any sporting organisation in order to be able to compete not only with other sporting organisations but also with the large variety of leisure time activity offers.

Chapter 3 first introduced the business of sports as the context in which professional sporting organisations operate. We concluded that the sports business can be seen as an independent and very serious business, in terms of income and number of employees. We also emphasised the unique characteristics of the sports industry (e.g. the uncertainty of outcome, the attitude towards profits and the extraordinary public perception) and highlighted the need for marketing people to take these specific characteristics into consideration when dealing with sports. We then introduced the main stakeholders of the sports business and subsequently identified fans, sponsors and the media as primary customers of any professional sporting organisation on the one hand. On the other hand we defined other stakeholders such as suppliers, agencies and the sports entities' employees as secondary customers of professional sporting organisations. The key message of this chapter was that sports clubs, associations and teams have to deal with many different customer groups and therefore with many different relationships. The professional application of relationship marketing therefore seems to be the logical consequence for any sporting organisation, in order to make and keep the primary and secondary customers happy.

In **Chapter 4** we have focused on the relationship between professional sporting organisations and their fans whom we defined as anyone who is emotionally attached to a specific sport, club or team. Therefore, the term 'fan' involves not only supporters attending games but also people watching games on television or the internet. When dealing with fans professional sporting organisations face various challenges, bearing in mind that fans are a heterogeneous group of people with different backgrounds, motives and needs who need to be targeted and treated differently. In the course of the chapter we provided a number of examples as how sports entities can apply relationship marketing techniques to fans and how they can establish and maintain a good relationship with their supporters. 'To-do-list–1' summarises the key points for professional sporting organisations with regard to fan relations.

To-Do-List 8.1   How to Improve Fan Relations

- Segment your fan base into useful segments (e.g. kids, die-hard supporters, regular spectators, once-a-season ticker buyer) using demographic, sociocultural and psychographic factors.

- Find out about the needs and wishes of your fans base through consumer and market research (e.g. fan satisfaction surveys).

- Be creative in what you offer your fan base. Supporters have a good sense when it comes to differentiating original ideas from bad copies.

- Provide value-added offers tailored to the specific customer segments, but do not exploit your fan base. Always keep in mind that fans might be loyal but that their loyalty is not a blind one.

- Solve problems with fans by consulting them personally, but drive a zero-tolerance policy when it comes to troublemakers such as hooligans.

- Establish loyalty programmes such as member schemes or kids clubs to reward and encourage the loyalty of your fan base.

Chapter 5 dealt with the relationship between professional sporting organisations and their sponsors. First we introduced the nature of sports sponsorship before we explained the importance of sponsors for sport clubs, associations and teams. The relationship itself was examined from both the sponsors' and the sponsees' perspectives and potential areas of conflict, where identified. We also incorporated recent research on the concept of relationship quality in the sponsorship dyad and thus identified a number of variables which are likely to make the relationship a success (e.g. trust, mutual understanding, long-term perspective, communication, and cooperation). Finally we provided numerous examples and suggestions for sporting organisations to establish and maintain healthy relationships with their sponsors. In 'To-do-list–2' we have summarised the main steps which help professional sporting organisations to build and maintain a healthy relationship with their sponsors.

To-Do-List 8.2   How to Improve Sponsor Relations

- Find out as much as you can from potential sponsors and the businesses they operate in. Your insight knowledge might not only impress the sponsor in question but also shows that you try to understand the other side.

- Find out what the sponsor tries to achieve with the sponsorship of your sporting organisation and try to find ways in order to help the sponsor achieving those objectives.

- Be committed to the sponsorship and do not risk a long-term partnership just because a competitor of the sponsor leads you in temptation with a better offer. However, if there is an offer you cannot possibly deny, talk to your long-term sponsor in an open and frank way about it.

- Conduct negotiations openly and sincerely. Do not make any promises you cannot possibly keep. Be realistic about what you can offer or not.

- Try everything to keep to the promises you made.

- Do more than what is expected from you or what is stated in the contract.

- Implement and establish regular get-togethers with your sponsors, e.g. workshops with representatives of your sponsorship partners in order to improve the sponsorships together. Remember that a leisure programme should always be a part of such workshops in order to give your sponsors the opportunity for bonding and networking in a more relaxing atmosphere.

Chapter 6 looked at the relationship between professional sporting organisations and the media, which is mainly characterised by interdependence. The simple rule in this relationship is: 'sports needs the media and the media needs sport'. Therefore both parties are well-advised to aim for a healthy relationship. In this respect, relationship marketing offers a number of concepts and techniques which should be applied by sports clubs and associations. In 'To-do–list 3' the key points with regard to media relations are summarised for professional sporting organisations.

To-Do-List 8.3   How to Improve Media Relations

- In order to deal with the media in a professional manner you should have a dedicated team of people taking care of media relations.

- Always provide the best possible working conditions for the media at your events. The provision of a specific media section with state-of-the-art technology at the venue is a clear must for any professional sporting organisation.

- Response to media enquiries immediately and ensure an effective flow of information. However, if a media request cannot be met explain your reasons for it.

- Design and establish a media relation policy involving rules and regulations for a better and more effective cooperation between your organisation and the media. It might be a good idea to involve media representatives in designing such a policy.

- Point out the importance of healthy media relations to your staff, especially the players and managers of your team. Being available for the media nowadays is part of their job. Whenever needed organise media trainings for them.

- Establish regular meetings with the media in different settings and for different purposes (e.g. press conferences before and after games, background information meetings in a private setting with selected journalists).

- Try to establish a private – but also professional – relationship with journalists and engage them in unique events (e.g. a game between the sports entity's managerial staff and the representatives of the media at the respective sporting venue).

- However, the implementation of relationship marketing techniques comes with a warning note because some journalist or editors could perceive well-intentioned approaches (such as invitations to away games) as some kind of bribery. Indeed, journalists need to remain objective in their coverage and therefore should not be influenced strongly by sporting organisations.

In **Chapter 7** we explained how the marketing mix might be used in a relationship marketing approach and in the context of sports marketing. We strongly believe that the extended marketing mix (i.e. the 7Ps) should be used as a tool to stimulate relationship marketing thinking in a professional sporting organisation. We thereby concluded that a well blended mix of the three service elements in addition to the general four marketing mix instruments is essential to achieve the goals of relationship marketing. However, we also emphasised the challenge for sports marketers to picture a consistent view of all elements on the one hand and to determine where to invest the limited resources to create the best outcome on the other hand. In the course of the chapter we also provided a range of examples as how sports entities can apply the various marketing instruments in combination with a relationship marketing approach and thus make and keep their customers happy.

All the previous chapters have more or less focused on specific elements of relationship marketing in sports. In this final chapter we are now presenting a holistic approach which considers all relevant customer groups and brings together individual elements.

IMPLEMENTING A HOLISTIC RELATIONSHIP MARKETING PROGRAMME

So far, most professional sporting organisations have failed to implement a coherent relationship marketing programme which targets not only one but all customer groups of a club. This is mainly due to a lack of resources. Sports clubs and associations seldom have the money (and the right people) to implement a systematic relationship marketing programme; and even if they commit considerable resources to relationship marketing, they find it difficult to manage the relationships efficiently due to a clear lack of supporting IT-programmes. Of course, there are many CRM programmes available, but most of them are not applicable to the needs of sports entities. Case study 8.1 describes one of the few CRM solutions which have been adapted to the context of professional sports and which is affordable even for sports entities with limited resources.

CASE STUDY 8.1. Tailormade CRM Solutions for Professional Sporting Organisations

Martin Lochmüller and Hartmut Voss

Sports clubs need more than sporting success to be successful in the long run. The professional handling with sponsors, members, fans and the media is becoming more important. Therefore professional sporting organisations need a minimum of human resources who are not only interested in sports, but who also have a good business understanding. They should consider sponsors, fans, members and the media as real customers and need to use new technologies and media for the clubs success. On the other side, sports entities need systems which can represent every process in a sports club. They should be easily understood, easy to handle and should offer the best communication possibilities for different groups of customers.

Normally, most clubs have persons who meet the demands mentioned above. In the periphery of nearly each club there are many persons who are extremely interested in working for their preferred club. In addition, many graduates from degree programs like sports marketing, sports economy and sports management are looking for these types of jobs. They have a qualified education and are highly skilled. The administrative management's first task is to engage such high potentials.

The second aspect is more difficult to fulfill. In spite of intensive research during the last 3 years, the authors could not find a system which allows for the various demands of sports clubs. Indeed there are a lot of first class CRM systems, but these systems generally neither know memberships, fan clubs, sponsors, ticketing systems, catering areas

Continued

nor VIP lounges. But these aspects are relevant for professional sporting organisations.

Combining a state-of-the-art CRM tool with soccer club specific needs – VMC Sports

The most important point of efficient customer service is a central database. Normally sports clubs use a mingle-mangle of different systems of databases which don't match and cannot communicate with each other. In addition, various persons apply and maintain them or members of staff have to keep up with customer information in different Excel sheets. In fan shops it is seldom known if a buyer is member of the club. Season tickets are maintained in other databases than day tickets, and newsletter subscribers are known only as an e-mail-address but not as individuals. Another problem is that many addresses exist twice or even more often. Furthermore, information about staff members from sponsors or the media exists rudimentarily or not at all. Overlapping contents between the involved target groups are hidden. The data situation of most sports entities is shown schematically in the following diagram.

The solution to the above mentioned problems is presented by Voss Management Consulting which extended a repeatedly prizewinning CRM-software for medium-sized enterprises with functions allowing to represent each target group in a database and which masters the specific requirements of these segments in the sports business.

Technically, data management is based on a Microsoft SQL or Oracle database system. A central data archive allows access for every authorized user from each workstation. Further important features are, to a large extent, free customising to individual requests as well as the possibility to exchange data via interfaces between other systems like inventory management, ticketing or accounting. Integrated office applications and e-mail clients facilitate not only standard letters, but also offer individualised serial-e-mails. Due to CTI (Computer Telephony Integration) every phone call can be recorded. This guarantees a complete verification of all customer contacts (members, fans, sponsors, media, etc.).

The unique aspect about VMC Sports is that in comparison to other CRM systems VMC Sports is fairly priced, easy to learn and to handle and can be customised

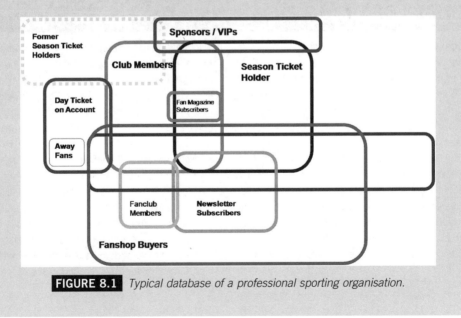

FIGURE 8.1 *Typical database of a professional sporting organisation.*

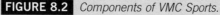

FIGURE 8.2   *Components of VMC Sports.*

individually to the sports club's needs. Based upon the open and approved architecture of CAS AG's base software the sporting organisation benefits from many realisations of other branches completed with typical solutions for sports clubs which have not been existent until yet.

Professional fan (and member) management

The central point of the VMC Sports solution is the member management, consisting of member and fee administration. Depending on the chosen member class maximised flexibility is guaranteed. Yet, slightly bigger sports clubs have a lot of member classes with different service bundles. For example, there are lifetime memberships, premium memberships, supporting memberships and gift memberships. For non-permanent members, membership can be developed otherwise and active junior players pay different fees, depending on their team. The software must and can represent each of these alternatives.

Efficient fee administration is another specific requirement from medium-sized to big (professional) sports clubs. The number of members is often lying in a four or five digit range. Therefore an automatic accounting of incoming fees is urgently required. The quality of dunning processes is increasing thanks to a club-specific CRM system because defaulters can be reached more easily within their preferred communication channels.

In general, VMC Sports supports each management task along the customer's life cycle, starting from the acquisition of members and fan support to measures of longstanding relationships (e.g. integrated bonus programme), cross- or up-selling activities (ticket sale, fan merchandising) until cancellation of the membership. Every contact (letter, phone call, fee payment, tribute, etc.) with a member or fan will be registered and will be available for each member of staff in the electronic customer file. Therefore sports entities can target members and fans, inform them in an optimal way and offer them suitable products of the club or their partners. A CTI-able telephone-system and a scan-to-PDF solution guarantee the completeness of the customer file.

Multiplexed information of ticket sale and fan shop will give an integrated view on the club customer and will provide the opportunity of a significant segmentation of fans and members. The classification of fans and members to different target groups will then offer the possibility of an efficient campaign management.

Figure 8.3 shows a typical description of a fan target group.

Professional management of sponsors

Today a professional support of sponsors is essential for most professional sporting organisations. Therefore a significant database is indispensable. At any time a club requires updated data of the sponsor's contact persons and their responsibilities, the subject matters and terms of contracts as well as an immediate summary of fulfillment of contract or possible changes. In addition, it is important to document the relations between club and sponsor and between sponsor and its members of staff in a preferably simple way.

The sponsorship contract presents the main issue of contract management. It provides all necessary information of the contract like performance, consideration, responsibility and duration. Great importance is attached to the permanent recording of performance and consideration

Continued

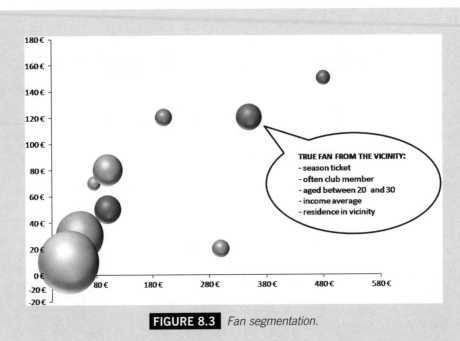

FIGURE 8.3 *Fan segmentation.*

which many clubs actually do not control. In addition, agreements will often be modulated or marginally changed with the result that neither the sponsor nor the club's responsible person knows an actual agreement. A central database can help to check changes and fulfillments anytime. Besides a real time warning system is implemented (e.g. when a contract is expiring) so that crucial deadlines or periods can be noticed in advance. As a matter of fact different rules and periods for these warning functions can be defined (e.g. warnings once a month or once a quarter).

Updated information as well as other important features (numbers of members, merchandising turn over, sales of tickets, etc.) offer predefined analyses in the so-called cockpit which can be configured in a task-related way for all responsible persons of management or agency. So important indexes are available anytime and important decision processes can be pre-structured and managed.

Professional management of media contacts
Also the handling of external media (television, radio, print, internet) always requires updated and short response time.

In the module media management all contact persons of the different media as well as the respective contact history are lodged. Press distribution lists facilitate the contact to media representatives and standardised patterns help to answer requests quickly.

The module naturally supports the organisation of press conferences, the coordination of interview appointments or visits on practice fields as well as the accreditation of journalists for match days.

For inquiries, the document archive in which press reports and also statistics are stored could be used. The permanent actualised knowledge of all matters concerning the club (numbers of members, activities of sponsors, etc.) is helpful when it comes to writing press releases and to present the sports entity in the media optimally.

VMC Sports in practice: the case of 1. FC Lokomotive Leipzig
VMC Sports expands the classical membership administration of sports clubs with real functions in customer management. The support service of members, fans and fan clubs

Continued

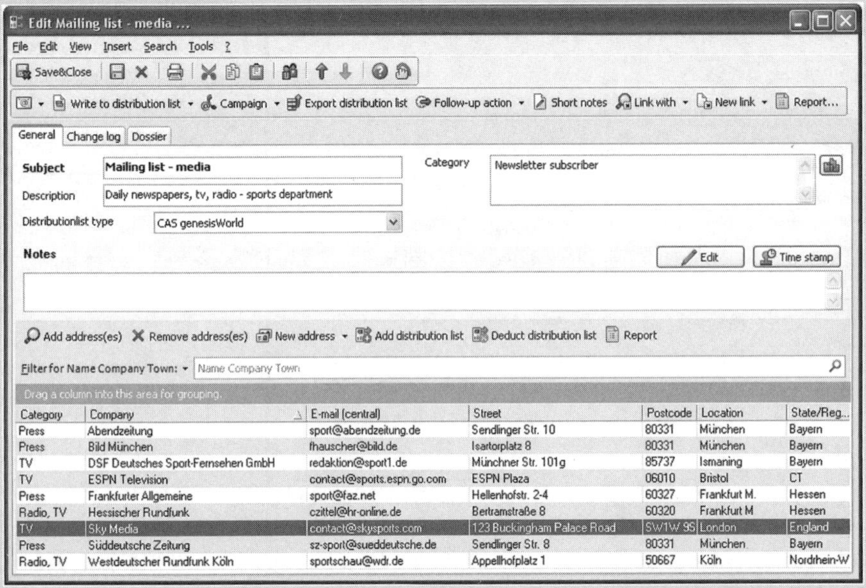

FIGURE 8.5

Mailing list 'representatives of the press'.

as well as sponsors and media representatives can be performed individually and always traceable. At the same time all members of staff have easy access to updated information and personalised addresses are prepared quickly and economically. In addition, cross- and up-selling-potentials can be realized easily.

The first German football champion 1. FC Lokomotive Leipzig has been convinced by all these arguments and has established VMC Sports in their organisation. Lokomotive Leipzig as one of the most traditional clubs in German football has about 1.600 members and ranks among the top 100 clubs in Germany concerning attendance. Because of some financial problems in the past, the club has decided to develop an efficient administration infrastructure in order to utilize the enormous potential of fans and sponsors in a better way.

Lok Leipzig intended to achieve the following primary aims by the installation of VMC Sports:

- Increase efficiency in the administration of members by automated booking of membership fees (significant economy of time)

- Traceability of all contacts with members using the "customer file"

- CTI-support and scan-to-PDF system in order to scan applications for membership and link them with the address using the document port

- Access to members for all office staff members and all trainers

- Prevention of data duplication

- Review of all information concerning sponsors' contracts

- More efficiency in administration of season tickets

Katrin Pahlhorn, treasurer of Lok Leipzig, stated: 'For a long time we have been in search for a system which could help us to improve activities in office and, at the same time, serve all fans, members and sponsors in a more efficient way. Now we gather all club information in one central data base and all authorized members of staff can access. Hereby we are enabled to help fans and fan clubs faster, to inform members in a better and more updated way and to advise our sponsors more competently. The system also facilitates the teamwork with media enormously and different, otherwise time-killing jobs (e.g. messages for associations) can be done automatically – thus the members of staff have more time left to serve fans, members and sponsors much better.'

Step by step Lokomotive Leipzig intended to link the merchandise management system of the fan shop in order to achieve better information of all former buying decisions and to increase sales using target-group specific activities. Furthermore, the club thinks about introducing a bonus system in order to increase the number of members and, closely connected, also membership fees and incomes of provisions.

The example of Lok Leipzig shows the opportunities linked to the implementation of a professional customer

management in a midsize sports club – even with limited financial resources. Clubs which are prepared to create professional structures in administration and to develop individualised and target-group specific activities for serving fans, members, sponsors and the media will be more competitive in the future.

Dr. Hartmut Voss is the founder and owner of Voss Management Consulting (a German based consultancy with special focus on strategic marketing, international marketing and relationship marketing), Martin Lochmüller works as a CRM Consultant for VMC.

Now that we have looked at the previous chapters and summarised the status quo of relationship marketing in sports we can focus on the future. What are the general trends and challenges and where are the main opportunities and threats for sports marketers in the future? On the following pages we will aim for some answers.

TRENDS AND CHALLENGES IN RELATIONSHIP MARKETING AND IN SPORTS

Marketing is a consistently developing subject with new trends and challenges emerging on a regular basis. A few decades ago, marketing was a simple task because it was directed towards all customers. There was no segmentation, no differentiation. Mass marketing and a transaction-orientated marketing strategy did the job. However, new challenges such as the shortening of product life cycles, an increasing variety of products and – most of it all – higher customer expectations emerged. Therefore, a new marketing paradigm was needed because the transactional paradigm couldn't cope with the challenges anymore. Companies had to become more customer-oriented in order to stay competitive and subsequently applied a relationship-oriented strategy. Some companies were struggling and never succeeded in this process, some others are still struggling and again some others successfully achieved the turn around. However, as the process towards relationship-oriented marketing still goes on, marketing develops further and new marketing trends are emerging. As a consequence, companies in general and professional sporting organisations specifically have to face new challenges in the near future. In the following we will name and describe five trends we think will be crucial both in general marketing as well as in sports marketing.

Personalisation of products and services

Nowadays, marketing is more and more directed towards specific customer groups which have been differentiated on the basis of segmentation. The focus is on establishing and maintaining good relationships with customers. Companies now use relationship marketing instruments such as CRM programmes, databases, and direct marketing. Personalisation is a key issue in this respect and becomes even more important. In the future, marketing will be directed towards each individual customer and companies will offer unique products which are tailored to each individual customer. They will distribute the products individually and they will communicate with the customer on an individual basis. Of course, some companies already use such an approach, but in the future individual approaches will become more effective and efficient and therefore applicable for many more companies. However, there still will be mass marketing and transaction-oriented strategies as we know it from the old days, but from our point of view this will vanish sooner or later.

With regard to sports, personalisation of products and services will be an important issue as well. As we have seen before, professional sporting organisations have to deal with a growing number of heterogenic customers. For example, the spectatorship in a football stadium becomes more and more heterogenic. Different supporters have different needs which have to be satisfied by the sporting organisation. Consequently relationships in sports will become more and more individual and therefore more difficult to manage. One-to-one-marketing techniques such as personalised communication will be a crucial factor in identifying and subsequently satisfying the individual fan's personal needs, wishes and desires. In addition, demand for personalised products (such as **customised merchandising**) and personalised services (such as unique events for individuals) will increase, and needs to be satisfied. Knowing and understanding the individual customer (e.g. individual fans or sponsors) is a precondition for personalising products and services and therefore consumer research becomes even more important in the future. Furthermore, professional sporting organisations need to be more creative when designing such personalised products and services.

The focus on C2C relationships

So far relationship marketing has mainly focused on relationships between organisations (B2B) and between organisations and customers (B2C). However, relationships between customers (C2C) have been widely neglected. Therefore, a new approach could be the study of C2C relationships and the impact of such relationships on the B2C relationship. **Customer-to-customer relations** can be of vital importance bearing in mind that word-of-mouth is one of the most powerful marketing tools these days. The personal recommendation of other customers might sometimes be the key factor when it comes to purchasing decisions. Therefore, companies need to develop a stronger interest in the relationships between their customers.

In the context of sports, relations between fans need to be studied in more detail in order to make use of supporters' opinions. We are strongly convinced that most professional sporting organisations still don't understand the full benefits consumer research is able to offer in this context. For example, **qualitative consumer research** approaches such as **focus groups** can help sports entities to gain a better understanding of how fans interact and how they communicate with each other. This knowledge then has to be translated into creative relationship marketing approaches.

The increasing importance of strategic partnerships

Strategic partnerships are long-term orientated and aim for mutual benefits. However, they are nothing new in the world of business. The Walt Disney Corporation and McDonalds, for example, have been engaged in a 10-year marketing partnership until recently in order to benefit from each other. McDonalds was allowed to use characters of Disney movies for promotional activities which, in turn, generated more publicity for Disney. The importance of such strategic partnerships will further increase from our point of view. In order to make the relationship a success, companies need to understand each other and need to be clear on what the partnership should achieve for both parties.

One of the most popular examples of a **strategic partnership between professional sporting organisations** is the alliance of Manchester United and the New York Yankees. In order to exchange know-how & expertise, to help one another and to develop joint products and services for their fans, both clubs successfully engaged themselves in a strategic partnership. We believe that more and more sports entities will understand the benefits of such strategic alliances and will start looking for the right partner across different sports and/or across different countries. However, in order to make the partnership a success, sporting organisations need to do more than just bringing their brands together. They need to design and offer creative and useful products for their fans. Furthermore, they need to generate business for each other (e.g. by introducing potential sponsors or investors).

The internationalisation of relationship marketing

Globalisation brought a lot of change to humankind in the last twenty years and it is a process which still goes on and on. As a consequence the internationalisation of relationship marketing will further develop. At the same time the importance of **cross-cultural issues** will increase further as Flambard-Ruaud (2005, p. 53) notes:

'The environment is and remains multi-cultural. In that sense, the dangers of ethnocentrism must be avoided and, on the contrary, the phenomena of acculturation and local appropriation must be embraced. To be successfully implemented, relationship marketing should reflect the value system of the population to which it is targeted.'

The internationalisation of relationship marketing not only demands specific knowledge about cultural differences between various target groups but also a new cultural setting and understanding of relationship marketing. So far the classical relationship marketing theory has been determined by the Western perspective. However, an Eastern perspective as well as their understanding of relationships, might develop relationship marketing as a whole. In Chinese society, for example, conducting business is based on the concept of **guanxi** (which describes the basic dynamic in the complex nature of personalized networks of influence and social relationships). From our point of view, Western and Eastern orientated relationship marketing approaches have to be seen as complementary rather than contrary concepts.

The **internationalisation of sports** and of the sports business is an ever growing process. It started slowly with the signing of a few foreign players. Nowadays, professional sports teams consist of a hotchpotch of players from all over the world. The variety of international star players as well as media exposure and clever marketing strategies led to the development of international (and in the case of Manchester United or Real Madrid even global) fan bases. This process will develop further and relationships in sports will become more and more international (e.g. international sponsors or fan bases outside the domestic market) and therefore cross-cultural issues will become more and more important. Sports marketers need to be aware of cultural differences in the first place. However, they should also be able to apply different marketing approaches to different cultural markets.

The shift from relationship marketing to network marketing

A very important shift – and one which has already begun – is the shift from a relationship marketing approach to a network marketing approach. This might sound dramatic, but it is a logical advancement in view of the fact that networks are nothing more than a complex web of many relationships. However, network marketing has already gained a bad reputation because it is often associated with direct selling organisations which are characterised by multilevel organisational structures. Such marketing approaches have to be viewed critically because they are similar to so-called **'pyramid schemes'** (a non-sustainable business model that involves the exchange of money primarily for enrolling other people into the scheme, usually without any product or service being delivered). From our point of view, network marketing could be the new paradigm in marketing if it is seen as a marketing approach which aims at networks and focuses on the relationships involved.

In sports, too, relationships will transform more and more into networks. For example, the sponsors of one sports property could do business together, thereby creating one network. Another network could consist of various fans. The sponsors' network could then do business with the fans network. Or sponsors of one sports property could form a network in order to do business with a network of sponsors from another sports entity. The more networks involved and the bigger the individual networks, the more complex it becomes. Therefore, sporting organisations need to manage these networks properly. Again, a deep understanding of the nature of networks as well as the dynamic processes behind and between such networks is needed to successfully apply network marketing approaches in the future.

CONCLUSIONS

Relationship marketing in sports is not only a very interesting topic but also an area which develops further and further. Professional sporting organisations need to keep up-to-date with developments in order to be able to successfully adapt general relationship marketing trends to their specific context and needs. We are strongly convinced that the successful management of relationships as well as the useful application of relationship marketing techniques will contribute to the overall success of any sporting organisation. In contrast, sports properties which neglect the importance of healthy relationships and/or are not able to implement a systematic relationship management programme will find it more difficult to stay competitive in the business of sports. We therefore hope that this book has provided professional sporting organisations with the necessary basic concepts of relationship marketing on the one hand and that it has generated a lot of new ideas on the other hand. We are looking forward to the further development of relationship marketing in general as well as in the context of sports. And we will keep our eyes open for new and innovative ideas in the field of sports marketing as long as it remains our passion and profession.

DISCUSSION QUESTIONS

(1) How would you describe the status quo of relationship marketing in sports?

(2) How can professional sporting organisations establish and maintain healthy relationships with their fans, sponsors and the media?

(3) Explain the main aspects of a holistic CRM programme such as the one by Voss Management Consulting.

(4) Which of the five general relationship marketing trends presented in this chapter is the most important one from your point of view?

(5) What are the main challenges professional sporting organisations have to face in the future?

(6) How will relationship marketing develop in the context of sports?

(7) What exactly have you learned from this book?

GUIDED READING

For further reading we would like to recommend an empirical paper called *The Past, Present and Future of Relationship Marketing* by Michael John Harkern and John Egan. The paper, which has been published in the *Journal of Marketing Management* in 2006, concludes that relationship marketing is here to stay, whether or not it is recognised as the dominant logic/paradigm of marketing.

WEBSITES

Voss Management Consulting
http://www.voss-mc.de

Nowhere FC – Their Learnings from this Book

After reading this book, Gary Smith developed a sophisticated relationship marketing strategy for Nowhere FC. His first step was to persuade the Board of Directors that the club needs to manage its relationships with the club's stakeholders more effectively and more professionally in order to stay competitive. Gaining the directors' commitment was the first achievement in Gary's strategy; the second one was negotiating a considerable budget for his relationship marketing programme. After some weeks of further planning and negotiating he changed the organisational structure of the club and introduced single units focusing on Human Resource Management, Media Relations, Investor Relations, Fan Relations and Sponsor Relations. Gary also hired a dedicated relationship marketing consultant who had to keep himself up to date with latest trends and research in the field of relationship marketing in order to support the other departments and coordinate the different relationship marketing activities within the club

The main task of the *Fan Relations Department* was to engage the club and its fans in a deeper relationship. Therefore a worldwide membership scheme was developed which provided the club's supporters around the world with unique benefits and a wide range of offers. The Nowhere FC Membership Scheme gained a lot of publicity and became very popular because the income generated by the annual membership fees was used to finance an international star player who was then promoted as 'the fans' player'. Nowhere FC soon became a very popular and attractive football club for fans worldwide because of their approach to view fans not as captive consumers but as an important and integrative part of the club.

In order to run the *Media Relations Department* a former journalist was hired as the new Media Relations Director. He soon implemented regular meetings with the media and established some professional standards (e.g. regulations with regards to player access). The major challenge for the Media Relations Department was to find a healthy balance between offering the best service available and remaining a professional distance. However, extraordinary events such as a post-season match between the managerial staff of the club and media representative at the club's home ground led to a deeper relationship between the club and the media on a personal level.

On an organisational level, the club entered into a number of media cooperations with various local and regional newspapers, radio stations and TV channels.

The *Sponsors Relations Department* is run by a dedicated team of marketing professionals taking care of the club's sponsors and partners. Their daily work is based on the question as what they can do for their sponsors and how they can find ways to make the sponsorship a success. This rather proactive approach was a huge success factor for the club because the sponsors felt that their investment in the club was the right decision. As a consequence more and more companies wanted to engage themselves in the club and therefore revenue streams from sponsorship increased significantly. The club eventually became a prominent case study when it came to mutual benefiting cooperation models in sports sponsorship and servicing the sponsorship partner.

The *HRM Department* contributed to the overall success story of Nowhere FC because it put the club's employees first, cared for their needs and supported their skills. The club was soon awarded with the Best Employer of The Year Award and had no difficulties in attracting high potentials any more which, in turn, led to a further professionalisation of the whole club.

The *Investor Relations Department* was implemented in order to establish and maintain healthy relationships with internal stakeholders of the club (e.g. the club's shareholders) as well as external stakeholders such as the local community, suppliers and the governing bodies of football (i.e. the National Football Association, UEFA and FIFA). With regard to the local community, Nowhere FC was able to establish a joint project with various non-for-profit-organisations in order to keep young people with deprived backgrounds away from the street. This and other social projects won the club many sympathies in and around Nowhere and led to a stronger bond between the local community and its club.

Two years after the introduction of a systematic relationship marketing programme, Nowhere FC was able to significantly increase all of their revenue streams because the healthy and mutually beneficial relationships with all their stakeholders paid off. As a consequence, the club was investing heavily in the team and soon became one of Europe's top clubs.

References

Andrews, D. L. (2003). 'Sport and the Transnationalizing Media Corporation'. *The Journal of Media Economics, 16*(4), 235–251.

Banks, S. (2002). *Going Down – Football in Crisis*. Edinburgh: Mainstream Publishing.

Barnes, J. G. (1994). 'Close to the customer. But is it really a relationship?'. *Journal of Marketing Management, 10*(7), 561–570.

Bee, C., & Kahle, L. (2006). 'Relationship Marketing in Sports: A Functional Approach'. *Sport Marketing Quarterly, 15*(2), 102–110.

Beech, J., & Chadwick, S. (2004). *The Business of Sport Management*. Harlow: Prentice Hall.

Beech, J., & Chadwick, S. (2007). *The Marketing of Sport*. Harlow: Prentice Hall.

Bejou, D., Wray, B., & Ingram, T. N. (1996). 'Determinants of Relationship Quality: An Artificial Neural Network Analysis'. *Journal of Business Research, 36*, 137–143.

Berry, L. L. (1983). 'Relationship Marketing'. In L. L. Berry, G. L. Shostack, & G. D. Upah (Eds.), *Emerging Perspectives on Service Marketing* (pp. 25–28). Chicago: American Marketing Association.

Berry, L. L. (1995). 'Relationship Marketing of Services – Growing Interest, Emerging Perspectives'. *Journal of the Academy of Marketing Science, 23*(4), 236–245.

Booms, B., & Bitner, J. (1981). 'Marketing strategies and organizational structures for service firms'. In J. Donnelly, & W. George (Eds.), *Marketing of services* (pp. 47–51). Chicago: American Marketing Association.

Borden, N. (1965). 'The Concept of the Marketing Mix'. In G. Schwartz (Ed.), *Science in Marketing* (pp. 386–397). New York: John Wiley.

Brassington, F., & Pettitt, S. (2003). *Principles of Marketing* (3rd edn). Harlow: Pearson.

Breuer, C., Wicker, P., & Pawlowski, T. (2008). 'Der Wirtschafts- und Wachstumsmarkt Sport'. In G. Nufer, & A. Bühler (Eds.), *Management und Marketing im Sport. Betriebswirtschaftliche Grundlagen und Anwendungen der Sportökonomie* (pp. 23–47). Berlin: ESV.

Bruhn, M. (2002). *Integrierte Kundenorientierung. Implementierungen einer kundenorientierten Unternehmensführung*. Wiesbaden: Gabler.

Bruhn, M. (2009). *Relationship Marketing: das Management von Kundenbeziehungen* (2nd edn). München: Vahlen.

Bruhn, M., & Homburg, C. (2005). *Handbuch Kundenbindungsmanagement* (5th edn). Wiesbaden: Gabler.

Bühler, A. (2005). 'Fans und Fanverhalten im Profifußball: Ein Vergleich zwischen England und Deutschland'. In G. Schewe, & P. Rohlmann (Eds.), *Sportmarketing* (pp. 221–236). Schorndorf: Hofmann.

Bühler, A., & Nufer, G. (2006). 'The Nature of Sports Marketing'. *Reutlingen Working Paper on Marketing & Management 2006-06*. Reutlingen University.

Bühler, A., Heffernan, T. W., & Hewson, P. J. (2007). 'The Soccer Club – Sponsor Relationship: Identifying the Critical Variables for Success'. *International Journal of Sports Marketing & Sponsorship, 8*(4), 291–309.

Bühler, A., & Nufer, G. (2008). 'Marketing im Sport'. In G. Nufer, & A. Bühler (Eds.), *Management und Marketing im Sport. Betriebswirtschaftliche Grundlagen und Anwendungen der Sportökonomie* (pp. 325–357). Berlin: ESV.

Busby, R. (2004). *'Sports sponsoring and the English markets at present and in the future'*, Heidelberger Sportbusiness Forum. Heidelberg. 29 April 2004.

Buttle, F. (1996). 'Relationship Marketing'. In F. Buttle (Ed.), *Relationship Marketing. Theory & Practice* (pp. 1–16). London: Paul Chapman Publishing.

Cashmore, E. (2003).'The marketing Midas with a golden boot', *The Times Higher*, London, (26 September 2003), p. 22–23

Chadwick, S. (2002). 'The Nature of Commitment in Sport Sponsorship Relations'. *International Journal of Sport Marketing & Sponsorship, 4*(3), 35–53.

Chadwick, S. (2004). Determinants of commitment in the professional football club/shirt sponsorship dyad, unpublished thesis, University of Leeds.

Chadwick, S., & Thwaites, D. (2005). 'Managing Sport Sponsorship Programmes: Lessons from a Critical Assessment of English Soccer'. *Journal of Advertising Research, 45*(3), 328–338.

Cheng, P.S.T., & Stotlar, D.K. (1999). 'Successful Sponsorship: A Marriage between Sport and Corporations for the Next Millenium'. *The Cyber-Journal of Sport Marketing.*

Chiu, H.-C., Hsieh, Y.-C., Li, Y.-C., & Lee, M. (2005). 'Relationship Marketing and Consumer Switching Behaviour'. *Journal of Business Research, 58*(12), 161–168.

Christopher, M., Payne, A., & Ballantyne, D. (1991). *Relationship Marketing. Bringing Quality, Customer Service and Marketing Together*. Oxford: Butterworth-Heinemann.

Christopher, M., Payne, A., & Ballantyne, D. (2008). *Relationship Marketing. Creating Stakeholder Value*. Oxford: Elsevier.

Cialdini, R. B., & Richardson, K. D. (1980). 'Two indirect tactics of image management: Basking and blasting'. *Journal of Personality and Social Psychology, 39*, 406–415.

Colangelo, J. (1999). *How You Play the Game: Lessons for Life from the Billion-Dollar Business of Sports*. American Management Association.

Conn, D. (1999). 'The New Commercialism'. In S. Hamil, J. Michie, & C. Oughton (Eds.), *A Game of Two Halves? The Business of Football* (pp. 40–55). London: Mainstream.

Conn, D. (2001). *The Football Business* (5th edn). Edinburgh: Mainstream Publishing.

Daumann, F., & Berlin, A. (2008). *CRM im Profifußball. Eine empirische Analyse des Status Quo*. Friedrich-Schiller-Universität Jena.

Deloitte. (2009). *Annual Review of Football Finance - 2009*. Manchester: Sports Business Group at Deloitte.

Dempsey, P., & Reilly, K. (1998). *Big money, beautiful game – saving soccer from itself*. London: Nicholas Brealey Publishing.

Desbordes, M. (2006). 'The Relationship between Sport and Television: The Case of TF1 and the 2002 Football World Cup'. In C. Jeanrenaud, & S. Késenne (Eds.), *The Economics of Sport and Media*. Cheltenham: Edward Elgar Publishing.

Dibb, S., Simkin, L., Pride, W. M., & Ferrel, O. C. (1994). *Marketing: Concepts and Strategies*. Boston: Houghton Mifflin.

Diller, H. (2000). 'Customer Loyalty: Fata Morgana or Realistic Goal? Managing Relationships with Customers'. In T. Hennig-Thurau, & U. Hansen (Eds.), *Relationship Marketing. Gaining Competitive Advantage Through Customer Satisfaction and Customer Retention* (pp. 29–48). Berlin: Springer.

Dittrich, S. (2002). *Kundenbindung als Kernaufgabe im Marketing. Kundenpotentiale langfristig ausschöpfen* (2nd edn). St. Gallen: Thexis.

Dobson, S., & Goddard, J. (2001). *The Economics of Football*. Cambridge: Cambridge University Press.

Edge, A. (1998). *Faith of our Fathers – Football as a Religion*. Edinburgh: Mainstream Publishing.

Ehrke, M., & Witte, L. (2002). *Flasche Leer! Die New Economy des Europäischen Profifussballs*. Bonn: FES Library.

Farrelly, F., & Quester, P. (2003). The effects of market orientation on trust and commitment: The case of the sponsorship business-to-business relationship. *European Journal of Marketing, 37*(3/4), 530–553.

Farrelly, F., & Quester, P. (2005). 'Examining important relationship constructs of the focal sponsorship exchange'. *Industrial Marketing Management, 34*(3), 211–219.

Flambard-Ruaud, S. (2005). 'Relationship Marketing in Emerging Economies: Some Lessons for the Future'. *Vikalpa, 30*(3), 53–63.

Freyer, W. (2003). *Sport-Marketing. Handbuch für marktorientiertes Management im Sport* (3rd edn). Dresden: FIT.

Frick, B. (2005). '… und Geld schießt eben doch Tore'. *Sportwissenschaft – The German Journal of Sports Science, 35*(3), 250–270.

Friedrichs, S. (2005). 'Nachhaltigkeit als Impulsgeber für ein Relationship Marketing'. *Forschungsbeiträge zum Strategischen Management*. Universität Bremen. Bd. 7.

Fullerton, S. (2009). *Sports Marketing* (2nd edn). Maidenhead: McGraw-Hill.

Gensmüller, M. (2008). 'Customer Relationship Marketing im Sport'. In G. Nufer, & A. Bühler (Eds.), *Management und Marketing im Sport. Betriebswirtschaftliche Grundlagen und Anwendungen der Sportökonomie* (pp. 417–441). Berlin: ESV.

Gillies, C. (1991). *Business Sponsorship*. Oxford: Butterworth-Heinemann.

Greenfield, S., & Osborn, G. (2001). *Regulating Football – Commodification, Consumption and the Law*. London: Pluto Press.

Greuel, W. (2007). *CRM im Sport. Wie der Club mit dem Kunden gewinnt*. Saarbrücken: VDM.

Grönroos, C. (1994). 'Quo Vadis, Marketing? Towards a Relationship Marketing Paradigm'. *Journal of Marketing Management, 10*(5), 347–360.

Grönroos, C. (1995). *The Rebirth of Modern Marketing: Six Propositions About Relationship Marketing*. Helsinki: School of Economics and Business Administration. Working Paper 307.

Grossman, R. P. (1998). 'Developing and managing effective consumer relationships'. *Journal of Product and Brand Management, 7*(1), 27–40.

Gruen, T. W., Summers, J. O., & Acito, F. (2000). 'Relationship Marketing Activities, Commitment, and Membership Behaviours in Professional Associations'. *Journal of Marketing, 64*(3), 34–49.

Grünitz, M., & von Arndt, M. (2002). *Der Fußball-Crash*. Stuttgart: RRS.

Hall, J., & O'Mahony, B. (2006). 'An empirical analysis of gender differences in sports attendance motives'. *International Journal of Sports Marketing & Sponsorship, 7*(4), 334–346.

Harness, D., & Harness, T. (2007). 'Managing Sport Products and Services'. In J. Beech, & S. Chadwick (Eds.), *The Marketing of Sport* (pp. 158–185). Harlow: Prentice Hall.

Harris, K., & Elliott, D. (2007). 'Segmentations, Targeting and Positioning in Sport'. In J. Beech, & S. Chadwick (Eds.), *The Marketing of Sport* (pp. 123–142). Harlow: Prentice Hall.

Harwood, T., Garry, T., & Broderick, A. (2008). *Relationship Marketing. Perspectives, Dimensions and Contexts*. London: McGraw Hill.

Heinemann, K. (2001). 'Grundprobleme der Sportökonomie'. In A. Hermanns, & F. Riedmüller (Eds.), *Management-Handbuch Sportmarketing* (pp. 15–34). Munich: Vahlen.

Heitmeyer, W., & Peter, J.-I. (1988). *Jugendliche Fußballfans*. Weinheim/ München: Juventa.

Hennig-Thurau, T. (2000). 'Relationship marketing success through investments in customers'. In T. Hennig-Thurau, & U. Hansen (Eds.), *Relationship Marketing: Gaining Competitive Advantage Through Customer Satisfaction and Customer Retention* (pp. 127–146). Berlin: Springer.

Hennig-Thurau, T., & Hansen, U. (2000). 'Relationship Marketing – Some Reflections on the State-of-the-Art of the Relational Concept'. In T. Hennig-Thurau, & U. Hansen (Eds.), *Relationship Marketing. Gaining Competitive Advantage Through Customer Satisfaction and Customer Retention* (pp. 3–27). Berlin: Springer.

Hermanns, A. (1997). *Sponsoring*. München: Vahlen.

Hermanns, A., & Riedmüller, F. (2008). *Management-Handbuch Sportmarketing* (2nd edn). Munich: Vahlen.

Hirt, E. R., & Zillmann, D. (1992). 'Costs and benefits of allegiance: Changes in fans' self-ascribed competencies after team victory versus defeat'. *Journal of Personality and Social Psychology, 63*, 724–738.

Hopwood, M. (2007). 'The Sport Integrated MarketingCommunications Mix'. In J. Beech, & S. Chadwick (Eds.), *The Marketing of Sport* (pp. 213–238). Harlow: Prentice Hall.

Hornby, N. (1996). *Fever Pitch*. London: Indigo.

Irwin, R. L., Sutton, W., & McCarthy, L. (2008). *Sport Promotion and Sales Management* (2nd edn). Champaign: Human Kinetics.

Ivens, B. S. (2004). 'How relevant are different forms of relational behaviour? An empirical test based on Macneil's exchange framework'. *Journal of Business & Industrial Marketing, 19*(5), 300–309.

Jackson, B. B. (1985). 'Build Customer Relationships That Last'. *Harvard Business Review, 63*(6), 120–128.

Jeanrenaud, C., & Késenne, S. (2006). *The Economics of Sport and the Media*. London: Edward Elgar Publishing.

Jobber, D. (2004). *Principles and Practice of Marketing* (4th edn). London: McGraw Hill.

John Harkern, Michael, & Egan, John (2006). 'The Past, Present and Future of Relationship Marketing. *Journal of Marketing Management 2006, 22*, 215–242.

Kiedaisch, I. (1997). *Internationale Kunden-Lieferanten-Beziehungen: Determinanten – Steuerungsmechanismen -Beziehungsqualität*. Wiesbaden: Gabler.

Lee, D.-J., & Wong, J. H. P. (2001). 'A model of close business relationships in China (guanxi)'. *European Journal of Marketing, 35*(1/2), 51–69.

Lee, M. J. (1985). 'Self-esteem and social identity in basketball fans: a closer look at basking in reflected glory'. *Journal of Sport Behavior, 8*, 210–224.

Lenhard, M. (2002). *Vereinsfußball und Identifikation in Deutschland – Phänomen zwischen Tradition und Postmoderne*. Hamburg: Dr. Kovac.

Lovelock, C. (1991). *Services Marketing*. New Jersey: Prentice Hall.

Lovelock, C., & Wirtz, J. (2007). *Services Marketing. People, Technology, Strategy* (6th edn). Upper Saddle River: Prentice Hall.

Mack, R. W. (1999). 'Event sponsorship: an exploratory study of small business objectives, practices, and perceptions'. *Journal of Small Business Management, 37*(3), 25–30.

Malcolm, D., Jones, I., & Waddington, I. (2000). 'The People's Game? Football Spectatorship and Demographic Change'. In J. Garland et al. (Eds.), *The Future of Football* (pp. 129–143). London: Frank Cass Publishers.

Manchester United. (2004). *Fan Satisfaction Survey 2004 Feedback Report*. Manchester: Manchester United PLC.

Mediaedge:cia. (2003). *Inside-edge sensor*. London: Mediaedge.cia.

Meir, R., & Arthur, D. (2007). 'Pricing Sports and Sports Pricing Strategies'. In J. Beech, & S. Chadwick (Eds.), *The Marketing of Sport* (pp. 321–341). Harlow: Prentice Hall.

Morgan, R. M., Crutchfield, T. N., & Lacey, R. (2000). 'Patronage and Loyalty Strategies. Understanding the Behavioural and Attitudinal Outcomes of Customer Retention Programs'. In T. Hennig-Thurau, & U. Hansen (Eds.), *Relationship Marketing. Gaining Competitive Advantage Through Customer Satisfaction and Customer Retention* (pp. 71–87). Berlin: Springer.

Morrow, S. (1999). *The New Business of Football – Accountability and Finance in Football*. London: MacMillan Press.

Mullin, B. (1985). 'Internal Marketing - A more effective way to sell sport'. In G. Lewis, & H. Appenzeller (Eds.), *Successful sport management* (pp. 157–176). Charlottesville: Michie Company.

Mullin, B. J., Hardy, S., & Sutton, W. A. (2007). *Sport Marketing* (3rd edn). Champaign: Human Kinetics.

Nicholson, M. (2006). *Sport and the Media: Managing the Nexus*. London: Butterworth-Heinemann.

Nufer, G. (2002). 'Sports and Culture - Lessons for Strategy'. In H. Simon (Ed.), *Strategy International* (pp. 57). Frankfurt: Frankfurter Allgemeine Zeitung, 7 September.

Nufer, G. (2002). *Wirkungen von Sportsponsoring. Empirische Analyse am Beispiel der Fußball-Weltmeisterschaft 1998 in Frankreich unter besonderer Berücksichtigung von Erinnerungswirkungen bei jugendlichen Rezipienten*. Berlin: Mensch & Buch.

Nufer, G. (2006). 'Event-Marketing und Kundenbindung – Fallstudie adidas'. In C. Rennhak (Ed.), *Herausforderung Kundenbindung* (pp. 221–247). Wiesbaden: DUV.

Nufer, G. (2007). *Event-Marketing und -Management. Theorie und Praxis unter besonderer Berücksichtigung von Imagewirkungen* (3rd edn). Wiesbaden: DUV.

Nufer, G. (2008). 'Wirkungen von Sport-Event-Sponsoring bei Fußball-Weltmeisterschaften'. *Sportwissenschaft – The German Journal of Sports Science, 38*(3), 303–322.

Nufer, G., & Bühler, A. (2006). 'Lessons from Sports: What Corporate Management can learn from Sports Management'. *Reutlingen Working Paper on Marketing & Management 2006–07*. Reutlingen University.

Nufer, G., & Bühler, A. (2008). *Management und Marketing im Sport. Betriebswirtschaftliche Grundlagen und Anwendungen der Sportökonomie*. Berlin: ESV.

Nwakanma, H., Singelton Jackson, A., & Burkhalter, N. J. (2007). 'Relationship Marketing: An Important Tool For Success in The Marketplace'. *Journal of Business & Economics Research*, 5(2), 55–64.

Payne, A., & Rapp, R. (2003). *Handbuch Relationship Marketing. Konzeption und erfolgreiche Umsetzung* (2nd edn). München: Vahlen.

Pelton, L. E., Strutton, D., & Lumpkin, J. R. (1997). *Marketing Channels. A Relationship Management Approach*. Chicago: Irwin.

Pepels, W. (2001). *Kommunikations-Management: Marketing-Kommunikation vom Briefing bis zur Realisation*. Stuttgart: Schäffer-Poeschel.

Pierpoint, B. (2000). 'Heads above Water: Business Strategies for a New Football Economy'. In Garland et al. (Eds.), *The Future of Football – Challenges for the Twenty-First Century* (pp. 29–38). London: Frank Cass Publishers.

Pope, N. (1998). 'Overview of Current Sponsorship Thought'. *The Cyber-Journal of Sport Marketing.*

Posten, M. (1998). Basking in Glory and Cutting of Failure, in Psybersite, obtained from http://www.units.muohio.edu/psybersite/fans/bc.shtml

Ramkumar, D. and Saravanan, S. (2007). 'The Dark Side of Relationship Marketing', *International Marketing Conference on Marketing & Society, April 2007.*

Ramme, I. (2004). *Marketing. Einführung mit Fallbeispielen, Aufgaben und Lösungen* (2nd edn). Stuttgart: Schäffer Poeschel.

Reichheld, F., & Sasser, W. (1990). 'Zero Defects Quality Comes to Service. *Harvard Business Review*, 68(5), 105–111.

Rein, I., Kotler, P., & Shields, B. (2006). *The Elusive Fan: Reinventing Sports in a Crowded Marketplace*. New York: McGraw-Hill.

Roth, P. (1990). *Sportsponsoring – Grundlagen, Strategien, Fallbeispiele* (2nd edn). Landsberg/Lech: Moderne Industrie.

Sandhusen, R. L. (2008). *Marketing* (4th edn). New York: Barrońs.

Sarma, M. K. (2001). *Relationship Marketing*. Tezpur University. working paper.

Seydel, M. (2005). 'Sportsponsoring in der Praxis: am Beispiel T-COM und FC Bayern München'. In G. Schewe, & P. Rohlmann (Eds.), *Sportmarketing* (pp. 53–66). Schorndorf: Hofmann.

Shank, M. D. (1999). *Sports Marketing – A Strategic Perspective*. New Jersey: Prentice Hall.

Shank, M. D. (2008). *Sports Marketing: A Strategic Perspective* (4th edn). New Jersey: Prentice Hall.

Shilbury, D., Quick, S., & Westerbeek, H. (1998). *Strategic Sport Marketing*. Crow Nest: Allen & Unwin.

Shilbury, D., Quick, S., & Westerbeek, H. (2003). *Strategic sport marketing* (2nd edn). Crow Nest: Allen & Unwin.

Sir Norman Chester Centre for Football Research. (2002). *Fact Sheet 10–The 'New' Football Economics*. Sir Norman Chester Centre for Football Research.

Sir Norman Chester Centre for Football Research. (2003). *Fact Sheet 11 – Branding Sponsorship and Commerce in Football*. Sir Norman Chester Centre for Football Research.

Sleight, S. (1989). *Sponsorship: what it is and how to use it*. Maidenhead: McGraw Hill.

Sloane, P. (1997). 'The economics of sport: an overview'. *Economic Affairs, Vol. 17*(No 3), 2–6, September 1997.

Smith, A. (2008). *Introduction to sport marketing*. Oxford: Elsevier.

Smith, P. R., & Taylor, J. (2004). *Marketing communications: an integrated approach* (4th edn). London: Kogan Page.

Sparks, L. (2007). 'Distribution Channels and Sports Logistics'. In J. Beech, & S. Chadwick (Eds.), *The Marketing of Sport* (pp. 342–364). Harlow: Prentice Hall.

Sportfive. (2008). *Affinitäten_3*. Hamburg: Sportfive GmbH & Co KG.

Sports Marketing Surveys. (2009). *The World Sponsorship Monitor Annual Sponsorship Review 2008*. Wisley: Sports Marketing Surveys.

Stavros, C. (2005). *Relationship Marketing in Australian Professional Sport: An Organisational Perspective, Dissertation*. Melbourne: Griffith University.

Stavros, C., Pope, N., & Winzar, H. (2008). 'Relationship Marketing in Australian Professional Sport: An Extension of the Shani Framework'. *Sport Marketing Quarterly, 17*(3), 135–145.

Stiegenroth, H. (2007). Wie technische Innovationen den medialen Konsum von Sport verändern.Speech delivered at the Sponsors-Medienforum, 24. September 2007.

Szymanski, S., & Kuypers, T. (1999). *Winners and Losers*. London: Penguin Group.

Taylor, T., Doherty, A., & McGraw, P. (2008). *Managing People in Sport Organizations – A Strategic Human Resource Management Perspective*. Oxford: Elsevier.

Teles, N. (2007). *Kundenbindung durch CRM. Konzeption und Optimierung für eine erfolgreiche Implementierung*. Saarbrücken: VDM.

The English Football Association. (2007). *The FA's Customer Charter 2007*. London: The FA.

The LA Lakers. (2007). *Invest in a Winner*. Los Angeles: LA Lakers.

Träber, T. (2008). 'Ich bin kein Klein-Abramowitsch ', in *manager-magazin*.de, 19 May 2008.

Turner, P. (2007). 'Direct, database and online marketing in sport'. In J. Beech, & S. Chadwick (Eds.), *The Marketing of Sport* (pp. 239–266). Harlow: Prentice Hall.

van Heerden, C.H. (2001). Factors affecting decision-making in South African sport sponsorships, doctoral thesis, University of Pretoria.

Walliser, B. (2003). 'An international review of sponsorship research: extension and update'. *International Journal of Advertising, 22*(1), 5–40.

Werner, H. (1997). *Relationales Beschaffungsverhalten. Ausprägungen und Determinanten*. Wiesbaden: Gabler.

Zeithaml, V., Bitner, M., & Gremler, D. (2006). *Services Marketing – Integrated Customer Focus Across the Firm* (4th edn). New York: McGraw Hill.

Zeltinger, J. (2004). *Customer Relationship Management in Fußballunternehmen. Erfolgreiche Kundenbeziehungen gestalten*. Berlin: ESV.

Index